D1531987

STANDUP
GUY

STANDUP GUY

MANHOOD AFTER FEMINISM

Michael Segell

VILLARD NEW YORK

All rights reserved under International and Pan-American Copyright Conventions. Published in the United States by Villard Books, a division of Random House, Inc., New York, and simultaneously in Canada by Random House of Canada Limited, Toronto.

VILLARD BOOKS is a registered trademark of Random House, Inc. Colophon is a trademark of Random House, Inc.

This work was originally published in hardcover by Villard Books, a division of Random House, Inc.

Grateful acknowledgment is made to the Copyright Company for permission to reprint an excerpt from "If the Lord Has Not Been on Our Side" by Rob Mathes. Copyright © 1996 by Doulos Publishing (administered by the Copyright Company, Nashville, Tennessee). All rights reserved. International copyright secured. Used by permission.

Library of Congress Cataloging-in-Publication Data
Segell, Michael
    Standup guy: manhood after feminism / Michael
Segell.
        p.   cm.
    Includes bibliographical references (p. 215).
    ISBN 0-679-78360-1
    1. Men's movement—United States. 2. Masculinity. 3. Sex
role—United States. 4. Man-woman relationships—United States.
I. Title.
    HQ1090.3.S44   1999
    305.31'0973—dc21   98-50269

Villard Books website address: www.villard.com

Printed in the United States of America on acid-free paper

2 4 6 8 9 7 5 3

First Paperback Edition

Book design by Barbara M. Bachman

FOR DAD

CONTENTS

...

INTRODUCTION   XI

THE BITCHFEST   3

SIFTING THE ASHES   28

COCKTALK   52

I'M A *WHAT*?   77

PROMISES, PROMISES   94

WHAT WOMEN REALLY WANT   118

SEXUAL MANNERS   137

DADDY'S BOYS   154

DAD   174

BIG MAN   197

EPILOGUE   213

SOURCES   215

INDEX   223

INTRODUCTION

■ ■ ■

I FIRST BECAME interested in writing a book about the trials of modern masculinity and the collective male response to thirty years of feminism after listening to tales of woe and frustration from young people I know. (I have five kids, including three young adults.) I was writing a monthly column for *Esquire* called "The Male Mind," which explored, through the prism of sociobiology and evolutionary biology, what I believe are pretty fundamental behavioral differences between the sexes. As I interviewed groups of young adults around the country, it became clear to me that, put simply, their ideology is in conflict with biological drives and matchmaking paradigms that have been worked out and encoded over the last few hundred thousand years. The result is an epidemic of romantic malaise and confusion—a silent epidemic that's well disguised by the new and politically correct intergender "friendship." Women have been unable to moderate the prickly and often unrealistic opinions about gender roles they develop in college, while men, pressured to proclaim their ideological sophistication, are secretly too angry and resentful to woo women they view as competitors. Oddly, there's plenty of sex but no accompanying relationship of any consequence.

If you believe the young women in the following pages, the men in their dating-and-mating pool are profoundly allergic to personal commitment. If you believe the men, the women are so confused about what they expect of themselves and their mates that dating, such as it is, is futile. The numbers do describe a disturbing trend. Nearly 40 percent of women between age twenty-five and twenty-nine and more than a fifth of those between thirty and thirty-four have never married—triple the proportion in 1970. There are nearly forty-two million single women in this country, up by three million since the beginning of the nineties and still growing. Half of all men between twenty-five and twenty-nine and nearly a third of those between thirty and thirty-four have chosen to forgo plighting their troth. Lamest of all: almost a tenth of the men between thirty and thirty-four are still living with their parents.

But this book is not just about, or for, young men and women. Older men, too, are anxious about proving and maintaining their worth to a newly assertive and capable partner—an anxiety that, paralleling young men's romantic lassitude, shows up as a lack of sexual desire, the most common sexual complaint in America today (libidinous president and legislators notwithstanding). Nor is this apparent withdrawal limited to the realms of sex and romance. Cynically exploiting women's demands for equal power, many men have decided to let them take care of themselves—and their babies.

The mating arena is not the whole world, but it houses a stage on which the issues that plague all men in this contentious postfeminist era are clearly dramatized. Some of the characters in these real-life productions tell particularly disturbing stories. A couple of months ago, on a reporting trip to Chicago, I met an investment-banking trainee named Adam who laid out for me his version of a gender-war strategy I'd been hearing a lot about: payback.

With a salary of $40,000 as a first-year commodities analyst, Adam figures he's on track to acquiring the security that will allow him to begin thinking about long-term goals—like a wife, kids, house, golden retriever, "the whole family thing." Half of the trainees in his class were women, many of them smart, classy, sassy, and attractive. But Adam, a pleasant-looking cum laude graduate who played soccer in college, has had little luck with any of them. "We all have the same job with the same pay," he says. "But none of the men in my class are dating any of the women, because the women are going out with either thirty-two-year-old guys making three times as much or Marky Mark types whom they use as boy toys. These women are happy to be my 'friend' but when it comes to romance, forget about it. I date graduate students and au pairs." What looks like male retreat, he says, is a reaction to rejection.

Why aren't his female colleagues interested in him? According to Adam, there's an ideological rift among ambitious young women that divides along issues of male power and status. Many career-oriented young women still look for qualities in men that women have always sought, most particularly the ability to stake out a secure and dominant position in the world. But the female world-beater's drive mirrors the traditional male desire for and appreciation of power—and because hers is great, his must be even greater. Women, with unfortunate exceptions, simply do not marry down. The investment-banking trainee just doesn't cut it.

Then, says Adam, there are the professional women who are turned off by ambitious men, see the male status-seeker as their historic oppressor and still an obstacle in their path, and direct their romantic gaze toward physically attractive slackers with whom they can have uncomplicated relationships, at least for now. "Those women want to be in control of both their seduction and any relationship that may result," Adam says. They avoid men from the same socioeconomic niche—extending them the cool hand of "friendship"—because the sticky issues of "liberationist theology" are contested with them on a too level, and thus intensely competitive, playing field.

The same kind of female ambivalence plays out around sex, says Adam—at least with those women with whom he can have it. "There's all this pressure on women from the feminist culture to be sexually active and experimental. They can say whatever they want and act however they like—be sexually demure one minute, like a tiger the next—but still have this total protective cocoon where there are no consequences to their actions. And men have to accept that because it's feminism and legitimate.

"What that means is that the line you're not supposed to cross is like the tide. You can try to cop a good-night kiss and have her accuse you of making an unwanted sexual advance. But if you take it real slow, and wait for her to initiate physical contact, you hear from all her friends that you're not assertive enough, that you're probably gay. Women say that a lot these days: all the men are gay.

"So, depending on the situation, you face personal rejection and humiliation, the accusation that you're a rapist, or the slur, broadcast on the wideband women's gossip network, that because you haven't properly imposed yourself upon a woman, you're borderline gay. And if you're just so frustrated that you've completely lost your initiative, you're dyed-in-the-wool gay. It's ironic that women complain about men's behavior when it comes to relationships, because men act in ways that women prompt them to act. It's like we're the performers, and they're the critics.

"I'm so sick of it now that the only thing that's more enjoyable than having sex is making a girl want it and not giving it to her. That's what it has come to. Payback."

■ ■ ■

INEVITABLY, AS I MOVED around the country talking to men of all ages about the conundrums of modern masculinity and our society's ongoing gender experiment, my investigations took a personal turn. For one thing, I decided that whether I was attending an all-male retreat in which the focus was on sex or whether I was tagging along with some evangelical Christians seeking forgiveness for their bad behavior at a Promise Keepers rally, I would try to participate as enthusiastically as I could. More importantly, I began to see that formative events in my life that had shaped my own view of what it meant to be a man—events I thought were unique to me—were far more common than I thought. The interviews I did with Jim Zumwalt convinced me to include myself in the mix of voices and stories that follow.

The son of the late Admiral Elmo "Bud" Zumwalt II, the U.S. chief of naval operations during the Vietnam war, Jim also served in Vietnam with the Marines. Like a lot of buttoned-up soldier types, Jim was a master at containing his emotions, but had found that, over the past few years, he was letting his long-simmering resentment of the Vietnamese interfere with his ability to conduct business there as an international consultant. How he managed to break the hold his anger had on him makes for instructive reading.

On his business trips to Southeast Asia, Jim had also been conducting interviews with Vietnamese military officials to learn more about the strategies that had helped them prevail in the war. On one of those trips in 1996, Jim arranged to meet Major General Tran Hai Phung to learn more about the Cu Chi tunnels, an extensive 150-mile-long underground system just outside Saigon that enabled the Viet Cong to maintain an offensive position at the Americans' doorstep and, with maddening effectiveness, inflict severe casualties upon U.S. troops. Toward the end of the interview, General Phung mentioned that he was also responsible for planning and carrying out many attacks against

American targets in and around Saigon, including the Navy headquarters. "Would that have been in 1969?" Jim asked. Phung smiled and said yes. "And would it have involved a satchel charge lofted over the Navy compound wall?" Again, yes. "I realized," Jim told me, "that I was sitting across from the man who had masterminded an assassination attempt—an unsuccessful one, fortunately—on my father."

A curious thing then happened, Jim said. "Until then, I had held on to my animosity, but when we made this connection around my father, it was like suddenly all the barriers were gone." Jim saw the general on subsequent trips, spent time with his family, and Phung introduced him to other Vietnamese veterans, whom he sees regularly on his many visits to Vietnam. During a recent stay, Jim learned the elderly general was ailing, destitute, and in the hospital with heart problems. He dropped by the general's house to give his wife some money, then visited Phung in the hospital.

"He got a big smile on his face," Jim said. "He sat up; we shook hands and hugged. At that moment," he told me, his voice cracking, "I realized that, by being able to forgive him, I had finally, some thirty years later, allowed the wounds of the war to heal."

I was intrigued by Jim's story, for it dovetailed with what I was learning on other reporting trips: men are ending their isolation from each other and, through deep friendship even with former enemies, or simply by turning to strangers at all-male retreats or in one of the ten thousand men's talk groups that now meet regularly, are developing the fresh emotional insight necessary to function effectively in a gender-equal world. But during subsequent discussions on the phone, Jim's story resonated even more powerfully. It turned out his anger had been largely a substitute for grief he would not allow himself to express. His beloved older brother, Elmo III, had also served in Vietnam as a Swift Boat commander under his father's command in the Delta region of South Vietnam. There he was heavily exposed to the defoliant Agent Orange, which caused the cancers that killed him in 1988. The man who gave the order to use Agent Orange was his father, Admiral Zumwalt.

A murderous father, a rivalrous brother, a son who befriends his father's assassin—after piecing together Jim's story it was hard for me to suppress bloody and terrifying images of archetypal rivalry, the specters of King Laius and his son, Oedipus, and of Abraham and Isaac, the ghosts that, in some ways, stalk all men and drift across the following pages. I, too, have lost a brother. His death forever altered my relationship with my father—a relationship that, unlike Jim's and Elmo's with the father they adored, had been troubled in spectacularly achetypal ways since I was a young boy. Both of those events—my brother's death and my father's reaction to it vis-à-vis me—are described in some detail in this book, along with their repercussions and the lessons they provide to all men who are raising sons. Like Jim, I learned that there was much sorrow I had yet to process, and that if I didn't, I would continue to project my anger and grief into the world, which is what men do with nasty emotions. Unfortunately, the target of this projected bad feeling is often a woman—an independent woman who no longer has to put up with it, and usually the one we least want to hurt.

• • •

FINALLY, THIS BOOK IS about how men can find an acceptable way to *be* in a demanding gender-neutral world, how they can retain the aggressive and heroic alpha-male side of the traditional masculine model without contaminating its standup-guy gentle side—its capacity for love and compassion. I bring a couple of strong biases to this topic: I believe that a man is often transformed into a standup guy simply by finding the right woman, and that a robust sexual life—a powerful personal chemistry—is the foundation for that relationship. I believe that marriage and procreation are at the heart of a flourishing human life—and that they remain two of the most important accomplishments of standup manhood. And I believe that what a man manages to achieve in his love life sets the bar for what he can and will accomplish professionally. I speak from experience. There was a time in my life when I was slipping, foundering, tempted to withdraw. I fell in love, my responsibilities quadrupled, and I eagerly rejoined the fray. I was, and am, incredibly lucky.

As men, particularly young men in retreat, pick their way through the minefields of ideological correctness, they need to remember this ideologically incorrect fact: women choose mates, as they always have, who are willing to compete for them—prove their love again and again—by flailing around in life's achievement contests.

How many times they win or lose matters less than whether they stay in the game.

STANDUP
GUY

THE BITCHFEST

...

SARAH, KATE, AND ALISON—"downtown babes," they call themselves—share an overpriced two-bedroom apartment in a five-story
Greenwich Village walk-up. A few years removed from the comforts
and unreality of expensive campus life, they're all laboring at low-
paying but much-coveted and challenging jobs. Sarah is a junior editor at a young women's magazine, Alison an assistant account
manager at an ad agency, and Kate screens slush-pile manuscripts
and composes dust-jacket copy for a major publishing house. On a
recent balmy spring evening, they invited me to come by their apartment to gas about men—"a bitchfest," Kate promised.

Kate is the daughter of an old professor of mine. Over the years I've
watched her mature from quiet bookworm to glamorous high school
athlete, and now into a sensible, accomplished young woman. I didn't
see her much during her four years at Stanford, but since she graduated she's been over to cadge dinner several times. Like my own children, Kate, an honorary member of our family since her parents
divorced and moved out of New York, often tells my wife and me more
than we really want to know about her personal life. This is the awkward truth about boomer parents and their kids and the kids of their
close friends: they confide in you as they do in their best buddies, perhaps more. Nothing is off-limits. Sometimes your ears burn.

For a couple of years now, I've been hearing a troubling litany from
Kate: men her age don't have a clue. Are they all gay or what? The only

way she can get a date with someone who *might* be interesting is to ask him out, but then right away she's put him in a position of weakness—the last thing today's reticent guy needs. The only men who do have the courage to ask her out are hypermasculine throwbacks with Beatle boots, ape-drape haircuts, and an equally antediluvian attitude toward women. Kate's complaints echoed those I heard repeatedly at a women's magazine where I recently worked. The fecklessness of all men under thirty was attributed to a lack of "commitment"—just a fancy way, I suspect, of describing male fear and insecurity. Along with recent census figures that show startling increases in the number of women—and men—who remain single well beyond their usual reproductive years, the testimonials of all these women suggest that romance has fallen upon hard times. A lot of men, it seems, just aren't interested in getting the girl, or even pursuing her, which has always been an important challenge and defining accomplishment of manhood. I was hoping the downtown babes might have an explanation for the dearth of standup guys in training. I was also hoping to confirm a particularly troubling bit of information I'd picked up during interviews I'd done with other young women. After deploying their wiliest seductive powers over the course of an evening, some men, I'd heard, would at the crucial moment withhold sex, knowing their refusal delivered a more humiliating blow to their partner's ego than anything else they could do. If this were true, I figured, the ongoing gender war had reached a new low.

．．．

KATE AND HER ROOMIES are supremely attractive, bright, engaging, funny, and—dare I say without sounding lecherously middle-aged— sexy young women, not that any men who possess the "résumé" they'd be interested in reviewing would necessarily agree. And since the résumé men are all in hiding, how would they know? The résumé men they *have* managed to meet, the downtown babes say, are hopelessly passive, squirrelly, in perpetual retreat, like the one my wife and I set Kate up with a couple of months ago. We suggested she arrange to meet the son of another friend of ours, who was on summer break from his job as a private-school teacher at a boarding school. She called him, of course, because that's what girls do these days—they make the call. For the next three nights the two gabbed for hours on the phone. Naturally, we received daily updates (Kate was between jobs and stopping by for more than her usual number of meals): they'd read and reread all the same books, liked the same movies, food, and sports. When they finally met at the Time Cafe, they again talked for hours, gazing into each other's eyes, forging a "real connection," marveling at what seemed like incredible kismet, giddily in love. Kate couldn't believe it. They held hands as they walked to her apartment, and kissed at the door. "It was corny," she says, "like a thirties movie." She told us a few weeks later that it didn't work out. Despite calling him repeatedly, she didn't hear from him for a week. Finally, he left a message on her machine explaining that he just wasn't ready for a relationship right then. "I can understand that," says Kate, "but I wish he'd told me before I fell in love with him. Or before he encouraged me to fall in love with him."

"Men were like that in college, too," Alison says after we all crack open beers and settle in their living room around a tape recorder, but at least there was sex—"hooking up," in contemporary parlance. Surveys of campus life indicate that students are having more sex than any prior generation did, but doing nothing beyond groping each other in the dark on a drunken Saturday night to advance any kind of lasting relationship. At the first hint of anything deeper than mutual physical satisfaction—they know nothing about love, but they're pretty sophisticated sexually, it seems—the men would vanish. I ask them to explain the phenomenon.

"Well, there was always the question of who would call whom the next day, or the next week," says Alison, sitting upright and cross-legged on a threadbare couch. She's tall, fair, athletic—gorgeous. "Actually, there was no question at all. The guy would never call, even if you sensed he was dying to. Guys were just totally afraid of appearing one whit more interested than you. There was like a massive epidemic fear of rejection among men, at least at Cornell. So if I liked a guy, I'd call him just to make it easy on him. But I resented it. It made me mad. And right from the start, I'd have this idea that he was a passive wimp, a dick."

"There were times," Sarah offers, "when you were just looking for companionship, and you'd call up a guy you'd been with the weekend before and he'd diss you by pretending not to remember who you were. This is a guy you slept with! And you'd be pissed because you didn't even like him that much in the first place. It's a power play. He'd wuss out because he was afraid of it more."

"Afraid of what?" I ask.

"Everything," says Sarah, a lanky brunette with almond eyes. "Afraid of anything that might possibly lead to his being a boyfriend to your girlfriend. I mean, it's not like you're desperate! But every once in a while I'd meet a guy and go, 'Wow, this is somebody I could get to know better.' And you'd sense the same feeling from him. But it was like, when he had that feeling he had an allergic reaction."

"The men were just very wary of coming on too strong," says Kate, settling into an overstuffed loveseat after changing from her power suit into jeans and sleeveless top. "A lot of guys thought that if they took the initiative, women would think they're assholes. So they went way in the other direction. They acted like dicks—passive and quietly hostile. There's nothing in between. They were totally afraid of intimacy, so if you hooked up, intimacy was not an issue. Although you could have sex."

So as both parties circled each other, afraid to make the first move, how did so much hooking up ever come about? "There are a lot of things you learn at college so you don't cross the line into being too aggressive," says Alison. "You arrange it so the guy makes the move, but it's because you've set it up. It's subtle. It's called 'waiting it out.' Like, if the party is emptying out, you say to yourself, 'If I go to the bathroom and he's still there when I come out, then I know he's waiting to go home with me.' Then, like at Cornell, where a lot of people live off campus, you share a cab home. You kiss on the way there. The result is sex, but no one has actually had to say, 'I'd like to go home with you.' "

After graduating, Kate and her friends expected this all to change. As dynamic young career women, they'd be mingling with other budding world-beaters, forward, confident, accomplished young men with résumés—and the sense that a relationship can offer more than a night of boozy wrestling with the lights off. None of these women says she's looking to get married—immediately, anyway. They all speak passionately about wanting to be established in a career before shuffling toward the altar, of being independent and capable of taking care of themselves in case the marriage doesn't work out. Of course, in the next breath they also talk about how, if after seeing a guy two or three times and they can't imagine marrying him, he's toast. "Even though you're not consciously looking for a special partner," says Alison, "it is, ultimately, what dating is all about."

If there were such a thing as dating. Meeting men is not the problem, according to the downtown babes. Alison receives regular invitations to parties sponsored by media buyers; Kate shows up at three or four book parties every week, and Sarah is a regular at magazine glamfests. They pool their invitations and travel in a pack to the same functions. But most of the guys they meet there, guys with the "résumé" whom they could bring home to meet Mom and Dad—men they expect one day, despite their current nonadventures, to marry— are even less interested in them than those they experimented with sexually in college. Excuses for male disinterest are tendered: everyone is working obsessively on his career, striving to gain some purchase in an unreliable workplace. Still, they find the passivity of the boys mystifying. As we work on our second beers Kate confirms for me what I'd heard elsewhere: more than just a few of today's young men appear to be using sex—withholding sex, that is—as a weapon.

"I don't even know how to talk about this, it's so humiliating," says Kate. "In the last two years, I've met three men I liked a lot. Unless I'm just totally delusional, the feeling in each case was mutual. Without putting too fine a point on it, we got to where it was like, the penultimate moment. I mean, we were naked. And why are you naked unless, you know, you're going to do it? He's naked, too, and ready. But then he says no." She sips her beer, catches her breath, her face flushing at the memory, blue eyes flashing. "What is that? I'd like to know. When in history has that ever happened before? And with me it's been three times."

Alison leans forward. "God, I thought I was the only woman on the face of the earth to whom that had ever happened."

"Well, there are at least three of us," says Sarah.

"God, why haven't we talked about this before?"

"Is there, like, some conspiracy among them? Maybe they all chat on the Internet and go, 'Okay, for those of you who have never done this before, listen up: Wait until you get her dress off, then say, *No way, José.* The effect will be devastating. But don't say it until she's naked.' "

"My mom said when I got to college men were just going to want to sleep with me," says Alison. "And when I was a young career woman, that would be even more the case. But they don't. They reject you. I know this guy who has started relationships with three different women, but they break up with him because, after they get close, he won't have sex. He's on like some kind of mission."

"A mission to be a dick," says Sarah.

"Maybe he has an old-fashioned sense of honor," I suggest. "Maybe he's very maturely pulling back, saying, 'Hey, I like this girl, and it's moving too fast.' Maybe amid all this meaningless and frenzied copulation, he's holding out for something better."

"I don't think so," says Kate dismissively. "Why would he take it so far? I think he fears women are going to get attached to him. But today, women don't do that. Women our age have gotten past that idea, and they can have sex without all the baggage."

Ultimately a problem for a guy, I can't help but think. At least for this guy.

"It's just a mindfuck when someone does that," says Alison. "It's the most manipulative thing. It's a power trip. Men are withholding sex to maintain power. In this supposedly new world, where men and women are equal, it's all they've got. Maybe they feel that, with sexual equality, it's the only power they have. But it's major: there are so many issues a woman goes through to get to the point where she wants sex, but when the guy says no, it's a huge slap in the face."

"Well, if you think about it," says Sarah, "for centuries it was women's only power—to say no. And now we sit here and say, 'Oh god, that's so mean.' But that's what men have been saying for centuries."

"Yeah," says Kate. "But at least men are taught they're going to want to have sex and that women will reject them. We never learned that, so the rejection hurts more. It's a total shock. So you go, 'What the hell's going on? Am I hideous? Am I fat? Did I do something?' "

"It's just amazing how men can dictate our own sense of sexuality and beauty. Still."

"That's it," says Alison. "Historically, women have been attracted to powerful men—Daddy Warbucks—because we had no opportunities to acquire our own power. And men were attracted to, I don't know, youthful goddess-virgins. But now men are feeling diminished because what they've always had, money and power, women can acquire, too. So this is payback: we erode their power base, they attack our self-esteem."

"Payback. God, Alison, that's brilliant."

"And depressing."

"It's not really my idea," Alison admits. "It's like, you know, Backlash 101. I had this really cool professor at Cornell . . ."

"Well, I've got the solution," says Sarah with a little shrug of embarrassment. "I'm dating a surfer now, a guy who still lives with his parents. I don't know if he's even graduated from high school. But he's sweet and big and handsome and treats me so much nicer than any other guy I've been with. He calls when he should—I don't have to call him and ask him out. And he likes sex."

The other downtown babes roll their eyes.

"I really admire that he has this passion, surfing, that he loves something that much and is totally psyched about it. When a guy really loves something and goes for it, that's really attractive, because he's so strong when he's doing what he really wants to do."

"I could swear I hear purring in the room," says Kate. "Is that coming from you, Sarah?"

"I know my surfer guy is a rebellion, that my parents are horrified, and that the reason I couldn't see him tonight was that he had to pay off his dealer. I still feel the pressure to marry the guy with the education, the job, the résumé, the genes. So I keep setting up my surfer boy to fail. Like, last year Kate and I made rules about the kind of man we'd marry. He'd have to be able to answer certain questions. He had to know who John Donne was. He had to know the difference between Chinese and Vietnamese food. He had to be able to distinguish Beethoven from Mozart."

"So he has a passion for the metaphysical poets, too?" Kate asks, a little derisively.

"Well, now I'm rethinking all that. I've tried the guy with the résumé, the guy who can answer those questions, and he fucked me over. He left me naked and cold and humiliated on my own bed. The fact is, my surfer is a really great guy. And he's not afraid to show it."

"But, Jesus, Sarah, he lives with his parents."

"I know, I know . . ."

The women are silent, wistful for a moment, and then, laughing, Kate and Alison say in unison, "Does he have any friends?"

■ ■ ■

WITHHOLDING? MEN? Is this what thirty years of feminism and gender equality have wrought—men's right to sexually spurn women and give them a case of what used to be called blue balls? Aren't all young men willing and eager, at every opportunity, to come into her, as the Bible refers to sexual intercourse? I remember sitting at a dinner party a couple of years ago next to a recently divorced fortyish psychologist discussing, perhaps a little unwisely given the amount of wine I'd drunk, libidinal differences between men and women. Averting her eyes coyly, my attractive companion suggested that at the right moment the cleverest and most seductive swordsmen occasionally choose to play it cool. Modernizing a male sexual code, the byword for which has always been "urgency," they suppress their own ardor to get their partner a little bewitched and bothered—in a pleasant sort of way. Why? "Women enjoy heating up slowly, even over a couple of days," she said. "If your lover is always at you, as most men I've known have been, you never get to savor your own desire. You can say 'Yes,' 'No,' or 'I'm not interested but I'll do you a favor,' but you never get a chance to recall what it's really like to want sex."

Having pondered this for a couple of days, perhaps for all the wrong reasons—my dinner companion had given me her business card in case I was interested in "consulting" her for "research"—I took a little poll among the guys I play music with each week to see whether they ever held out on their wife. "Yeah, like after a fight," said our band's guitarist. "When she locks the bedroom door, I yell through the keyhole, 'That's it! You're cut off for a week!' " Our saxophone player mused, "Or you phone her from the car phone as you're setting up your cot in the garage: 'You're really going to have to beg me for it now!' " Our pianist, recently remarried to a younger woman, shook his head sadly, as though wondering whether I was a candidate for Viagra or a penile implant.

Historically, of course, withholding has been an important strategic dodge within the female mating guidebook. By refusing sex, women effectively jacked up the price men were willing to pay, as measured by their promises of not only heirloom jewelry but also food and shelter to the future family. If the only way a suitor could come into a desirable female was by investing heavily, he'd reach deeply into his portfolio and do it.

It would be difficult to believe, however, that by suddenly reversing a mating paradigm fine-tuned over eons of evolutionary history, young men who withhold sex are demanding evidence of their girlfriend's resources. Or that, like the patient and clever lovers admired by my flirtatious dinner companion, they're deploying a sophisticated seduction technique. Something else must be going on in this first generation of men and women to grow up with feminism. And it sounds like hostility to me.

· · ·

SO, TRAVERSING THE SAME demographic terrain, a few days after I interview Kate and her friends, I gather a group of young lions to explore the same topics—a "dickfest," I suppose Kate would call it. All are recent graduates, or at least not more than five years out of college, who work in media, banking, education, or law. Four of the guys inhabit a loft overlooking the Hudson River and the burgeoning New Jersey condoscape not far from the Greenwich Village apartment the downtown babes share. I fantasize for a moment about bringing all of these smart, attractive people together: if they're all having such trouble meeting potential soul mates, why not resort to a little matchmaking?

The topic is sex, I tell them. They all seem eager to boast about what they know, or should know. I'm particularly interested in their views on why there's so much furtive mating with so little follow-up. Isn't it polite at least to call in the morning? Say, "Thank you, that was great," even if it wasn't? And of course, I want to know about this withholding business, though not just yet.

Defensively, with a little swagger as they crack open beers and light cigarettes, each claims he could walk down the street to the Lemon Bar or the Jet Lounge—local hookup scenes—get laid that night, crash at his own place, and be at work on time in the morning. But that stuff is for college kids; they'd all outgrown that. They were now looking for something more *meaningful*—a buzzword of the evening. Follow-up is polite, sure, but you have to be careful. Why follow up with a call if you don't intend to, you know, ever see her again?

I take a poll on how many are currently "involved" with a woman. "I just broke up with my girlfriend," says one. The others are silent, gloomy, and shake their heads. I imagine Kate's response: *What a waste!*

When I tell them that Kate and her roommates characterize guys like them, "résumé" guys with impressive degrees and promising careers, as passive wusses, they laugh nervously. A couple shoot dagger eyes at me. *Whose side are you on?!* The others stare at their beers—all but Dave, a muscular Wall Street bond-sales trainee with a head of thick, curly black hair. "I know the kind of women you're talking about," he says. "They call us dicks. I see them every day. We don't have to be aggressive, because they are so fucking aggressive. To the extent, that is, that they're interested in us at all."

The lid pried off, resentment flows freely. "I don't think you can underestimate the power of political correctness and the effect it's had on us," says Paul, a Harvard graduate who works in publishing. "The sad thing is that most guys don't realize how emasculated they are by this crap. It's pounded into us first in college and now at work: men are bad, inferior versions of females and need to be fixed. I was an art history major, and I couldn't take a single course without hearing and having to talk about how women were degraded by being the subject of male artists, the object of the male gaze. I'm surprised there isn't a course titled 'The Male Gaze.' The only course in which we didn't talk about how men look at and paint women was 'The Use of Geometry in Renaissance Architecture.' "

"I don't know about you guys," says Dave, "but most of my first day at my job was spent in a seminar instructing me how to properly address women. The second was spent learning how not to address women. You'd think we were talking about visiting dignitaries, royalty or something. You get so that if a pretty or sexy colleague walks by—and keep in mind she's the one who put herself together that way when she got dressed that morning—you have to avert your eyes, or put on sunglasses. So yeah, maybe I am afraid to be forward with women. I don't want to get arrested—or lose my job."

"But of course, they can come on to us," says Jeff, an ad agency account executive. "It's a really warped double standard. But if they do, and you're in a work environment, you can't help but think that maybe you're being set up. Ask her on a date, and she'll call the human resources mobile response unit."

"I don't know," says Dave. "I think I'm less afraid of being forward and more turned off by female aggression. Women aren't afraid to take the initiative, and sometimes you find that an ego boost—even a nice break. But men are into the thrill of the chase, and women are supposed to be demure. When you reverse that, and women say, 'Let's go home, big fella,' you go, 'Hmm, I'm not sure I like that.' You want to be in control, be the man."

"Another thing is," says Jeff, "today you have to be a little careful. Sex can kill you, or if it doesn't kill you it'll give you warts or a chronic infection. So when a woman is coming on to you within fifteen minutes of meeting her, you have to wonder: Where has this girl been? And how many times?"

"If we're a little shy," Paul suggests, "maybe it's because sex is under the microscope more. Every magazine, every newspaper talks about it. That's ultimately how you are judged. When you're younger, it's about hitting baseballs or draining hoops. Now, suddenly, it's whether you're good in bed. That's the common denominator. And there's no transition: you go from hoping you're the guy who can sink the trey in overtime to hoping you're the guy who can get it up three times before the *Seinfeld* reruns come on at eleven. So when a woman comes on to you, you feel a certain pressure."

"It's like the only thing that counts. I mean, we all work the same jobs. So a woman doesn't need you to support her. If there's something wrong in her apartment her super will fix it. If she gets attacked on the street by some homeys and you try to defend her, they'll kick your ass, too. Your entire male job description relates to your dick and how well you can use it."

We work through our beers, and I decide to float the burning question: Has any of them ever withheld sex as a power play? Is it true that when they're rounding third at a full sprint they pull up short before they get home?

"It does happen," says Dave. "But I think it's still more common for women to say no. Women still have this huge power to ridicule and reject men, and they use it."

"You can't have too much sex that's meaningless for women," Paul offers. "They very quickly want something more. So if I say no, it's because I'm trying to be respectful."

"Yeah, there have been times I've pulled back," Jeff volunteers. "When I feel things are going too fast, when it's not what I want now. I'm not afraid to walk away. It's not a popular move, though."

"I want meaning as well," says Chandler, a teacher. "It's not just for the woman's sake that I say no. Especially if I like a girl. If we have sex, it means I probably won't see her again."

The nub of the problem, I suggest. Why is that? Sex is supposed to be binding. Good sex, anyway.

"Dave Matthews has this song with the lyric, 'Tonight let's be lovers, tomorrow go back to being friends,' " says Jeff. "But I don't think that happens that often. If you have sex, it either has to go to another level, or end. I'm not ready for another level."

So it has nothing to do with payback, with a subtle, even unconscious attack on female self-esteem, as Alison theorized? The men crack open more beers, light more cigarettes, and shake their heads. "Sounds like a good theory," says Chandler, "but I don't think so."

"If it does, it must be unconscious," says Jeff. "That's not what I feel like I'm doing."

Then he gets up and begins to pace the room. I sense a shift in the barometric pressure. I've witnessed a lot of sensitive, sophisticated posturing, but now I feel defensive ramparts crumbling, as when the bitchfesters confessed their utter humiliation at being sexually rejected. And I'm right. Jeff says, "But you know, I don't think we're being totally honest here. These women we're talking about, the ones we're supposed to be dating, aren't interested in us. They say they are, but they're not. Sometimes I feel like I did in high school: when I was a freshman, all the girls in my class were dating sophomores. And when I was a sophomore, they were dating juniors and seniors. And when I was a senior, they were falling all over the football and hockey captains, or road-tripping to visit their boyfriends in college. All the women I've met want the Marlboro man."

Or a surfer, I suggest. Why is that?

"I saw this play recently that was about that very thing," says Dave. "The woman has this romantic guy with a good job who loves her, but she doesn't love him. She's in love with this tough guy, but he doesn't want her. That's how women are today: they want what they can't have. They want commitment from some long-haired cowboy with a huge dick and big muscles."

"Whoaa," says Chandler. "That explains your celibate streak. You're waiting to grow an extra inch!"

"But it's true," says Dave. "Women can afford to have the Marlboro man now, the surfer, because they don't need to be taken care of. They can support him. To the women, those guys are an adventure—risky, dangerous, fun. And for the guys, the boy toys, the construction laborers in tight jeans and the badass impoverished downtown artists, it's like they died and went to heaven."

"I think maybe something else is going on," Chandler says. "Women want friendships with us—guys who are interesting, appropriate, men of their age. But they go after guys who are the biggest losers because they know they won't be rejected. Between us and the losers they can create a complete male—the friend who's ultimately the best choice down the line, and the boy toy they can boss around and have a physical relationship with."

"The other day I had a conversation with an older woman friend of mine," says Paul. "She's thirty-two, married, with a kid. I told her I couldn't figure out why the women I'm attracted to, like women I meet at work, aren't attracted to me. I told her women think I'm too nice. And it's true, they do. She said, 'Yeah, they think that now, but they'll want the nice guy in a few years. You'll win in the end. Those macho guys will be doing that shtick forever.' "

"It's true," says Chandler. "It's gotta be true. Women will grow out of that. They'll realize that that guy, the Marlboro man, is how he lives, and he'll never be any different."

"The idealization of ourselves is that we're the high-IQ guys whom women will eventually want."

"Yeah, but when? I feel that I've been raised to be egalitarian, to have friendships with girls, be sensitive—the whole nice-guy thing. For years I've been watching the women I like grovel before the captain of the football team. Suddenly there's going to be a sea change? I feel like I've been faked out. I'm supposed to develop this special sensitivity women will like, but they turn around and go for some aggressive shaved ape."

"I think they'll change. A girl's going to want a different guy when she's thirty than when she's twenty. I'm expecting all these girls who haven't been interested in me are suddenly going to start coming around."

"When they want kids."

"Or someone they can have a conversation with."

"That's why guys aren't thinking long-term now. They know it's pointless. We've just got to wait them out."

The guys shift in their seats, pull on their beers. "I think you guys are too optimistic," Dave says sullenly. "There's an imbalance in how attractive we are. Women our age are in their physical prime, this is their greatest moment. But financially, we have nowhere to go but up. As promising as that is, they couldn't care less. They're interested in older guys with the salary or boy toys. Anyone but us.

"I'll tell you something: I can't wait until I'm forty-five and bald and fat and driving a Porsche, and all those women who wouldn't date me when I was twenty-five will be desperate to go out with a guy like me. They'll be bitching about my relationship with a twenty-eight-year-old aerobics instructor. *What does he see in her?* I look forward to that. I can't think of a more satisfying payback."

■ ■ ■

ARE RELATIONS BETWEEN young men and women really more distant and hostile than those of previous generations? The sexual insecurity of young men—along with their anxiety about ever being able to demonstrate their value to the world—is hardly new. Exploring this psychic terrain with groups of young men, I recognized a familiar, though thankfully ancient, dread. When I was their age—younger, actually—I was also taking my first tentative steps onto a career path, doubtful I'd make it to the first turn without screwing up or being sabotaged by a jealous overseer. Broke, socially retarded, poorly clothed, with no life skills or experience and little confidence, I felt thoroughly unattractive to women. Insecure and lonely, I married my college girlfriend. Predictably, the marriage failed, although it produced a terrific daughter.

Feeling weak, I sought refuge in marriage, while today's young men run from it. I jumped in at twenty-one, as did my wife, with the same result. Had we not made these early, impulsive choices, we never would have met, never would have fallen in love a decade later, never would have put together our dynamic and large family, home, careers—our "corporation," as we call it. The wrong choice, for us, led to our eventual happiness.

Does that mean getting married when we were still kids was the right thing to do? Certainly our children didn't think so when we divorced their other parents. Nor, it's safe to say, were all the other children of marriages that imploded during the divorce boom of the seventies and eighties happy to see their parents split. GenXers avoid personal commitment not just because they want to get marriage right, *unlike* their parents, but because they're afraid of getting it wrong—just *like* their parents.

Still, their romantic aspirations seem unusually fraught. As the average age at which men marry continues to climb steadily (it's now above twenty-seven), a fifth of all men between ages twenty-five and thirty-four still live with their parents, and 11 percent between ages twenty-five and forty-four live alone. Despite this apparent flight from kinship, a higher proportion of today's college students and recent graduates say they want to get married and have a family than that of any previous generation. So why are half the men and 40 percent of the women under thirty still single? According to Arthur Levine, the president of Teachers College in New York and director of a recent survey of college students, "Their short-term behavior doesn't coincide in any fashion with their long-term goals."

Based on nine thousand interviews, focus groups on thirty campuses, and surveys of three hundred chief student affairs officers, Levine's study found that young men and women are hooking up more, but making fewer forward-looking commitments to see each other—what was once quaintly referred to as dating—than any previous generation. "They have extremely high hopes and aspirations for a successful, happy marriage," Levine says, "but they're doing nothing to work toward that goal."

The contradictions and shifts in young adults' attitudes about sex and romance have been documented elsewhere as well. A National Opinion Research Center poll found that people in their twenties are now the most sexually conservative group in America—regarding their views of adultery, that is. As defined by the youngest-copulating and oldest-marrying generation ever recorded, though, adultery is less a sin of the flesh—a hookup doesn't count—than an affair of the mind and heart. The sacred, inviolable component of the new marriage is no longer sexual fidelity but intimacy: as the bitchfesters testify, it's a rare and precious thing indeed, within or without marriage. That may explain another of the poll's findings: unlike their mothers, who are much less likely to have had an affair than men of the same age, married women in their twenties are more likely to stray than their husbands. If they can't find intimacy in their marriage, they'll look for it elsewhere.

Many of the students in Levine's survey said their parents' divorce was the most shattering event in their life—and the most life-shaping. Viewing all relationships as undependable, they instead mate hyperactively, rejecting socially prescribed activities—once called "courtship"—that might result in a more lasting union. Ferrety predators, young men seem to see all women in the short term as equally good, and so are at once casual and carefree, pessimistic and humorless about getting along with them. The young men I talked to found the concept of an "ideal mate" laughable—a fairy-tale notion that no GenXer worth his cynicism believes in. That skepticism has managed to creep into some unlikely venues—like the wedding announcement pages of *The New York Times.* Every Sunday the paper provides details of a zany local wedding in a section titled "Vows," which itself suggests something ironic, tenuous, and slightly less than serious about the marriage covenant.

Understandably, the children of divorce say they plan to delay marriage because it's vital that they choose well. They're loathe to have their own children repeat their painful experience. But how long are they willing to wait? What you can't know at twenty-five but learn, unhappily, by thirty-five is that, like the brief but critical period during which a mother and infant can form a deep, mammalian attachment, the life stage during which it's possible to adjust to the foibles and weird habits of someone who may want to sleep in your bed for the rest of her life may not last long, either. At thirty-five, according to some oft-cited research, a woman has a 5 percent chance of marrying; a man who is still a bachelor at forty should be avoided at any cost. Desperate, lonely, under pressure to produce some grandchildren for the folks but perhaps a little too set in their ways, couples who marry late may be setting themselves up for failure—just like those of us who married too young.

■ ■ ■

SEVERAL OTHER FACTORS contribute to this widespread avoidance of attachment. The main mode of communication among college students today is electronic. As convenient as it is, on-line bantering doesn't exactly encourage meaningful human interaction. At Dartmouth, for instance, 250,000 Blitzmail messages a day travel among the five thousand students and three thousand faculty and staff members, or about thirty messages apiece. A recent Vassar graduate told me, "People spend easily three hours a day sending and receiving messages. It's the number one way that romances go on at college. It's like *The Dating Game* on-line."

At Brown University, students are apparently so romantically inept that one of them formed HUGS (Helping Undergraduates Socialize), a computer dating service to match students based on their answers to a survey. Nearly a third of Brown students, 1,500 in all, filled out the questionnaires. At other colleges around the country, students voice a similar lament: there's no real dating scene and people socialize in unpartnered packs, which give students a sense of self-assurance and identity but keep them from forming deeper, more committed relationships.

For a variety of complex reasons, many young men are also simply taking longer to grow up, languishing in what has been called "postmodern postadolescence." (I know many parents of young men who say, somewhat balefully, that adulthood doesn't begin until at least thirty.) At one end of the spectrum are those who leave college with huge loans to pay off and are forced to move back in with their parents, their opportunities for rapid career advancement stifled by the huge cohort of baby boomers warming managerial chairs farther up the ladder—and not about to vacate them any time soon. While seeking a life partner who might help hoist some of these burdens or at least provide joyful diversion would seem a good plan, most young men have decided to go it alone.

At the other end are the superambitious GenX cowboys who seek personal affirmation in Xtreme sports like sky surfing, or in high-risk business affairs—twenty-five- to thirty-four-year-olds are starting companies at three times the rate of thirty-five- to fifty-five-year-olds. Eighty-two percent of GenXers polled in a recent Yankelovich survey believe "competition encourages excellence" and "I have to take what I can get in the world because no one is going to give me anything." Despite these bold displays of self-confidence, however, the poll also found this same group to be deeply wary of serious, committed relationships. Nearly half of them had spent time in a single-parent home by the time they were sixteen. For many, their mantra, "No Fear," seems to apply to all of life's challenges except the biggest one—finding a soul mate. Meanwhile, women spend their entire twenties, prime childbearing years, and beyond rooming with their girlfriends or living alone and contemplating single motherhood. As the beautiful bitchfester Alison told me, "I think it's more likely that I'll have kids in the next five years than get married."

At the risk of raising an issue that invites immediate attack—when in doubt, blame your Mom—I can't help but wonder how many young men are intimidated by their own mothers, who are now often as powerful and accomplished as their fathers, or even more so, and in many cases were the ones who raised their kids after divorce. I hear from many mothers of young adults that their sons have stopped talking to them or are rude and insulting when they do. A young man's twenties, typically, are a time when he puts some distance between himself and his father in his attempts to supersede him. Is this developmental task now twice as difficult?

■ ■ ■

AS THE DICKFESTER Paul testified, it's also virtually impossible to overestimate the influential forces of political correctness upon young and impressionable male minds. Not long ago, in the bosky confines of Lewis and Clark College in Portland, Oregon (now famous for graduating a student who had a decidedly politically incorrect relationship with a president), I attended a meeting of the National Organization of Men Against Sexism. NOMAS is made up of a group of sociologists, psychologists, and academics whose values are "profeminist, gay affirmative, antiracist, and enhancing men's lives." That "enhancement," however, didn't appear to extend to men who embodied traditional manly virtues. Nor did the profeminists' "values" affirm the notion that men's tendencies to be aggressive, confrontational, risk taking, emotionally contained, independent, achievement-oriented, and often heroic seekers of status may have an innate or biological basis—or any value at all, for that matter. Instead, NOMAS collectively embraces the social constructionists' view of sex roles—that is, that who we become, whether a sweathog or seamstress, is an infinitely malleable function of social and political forces, the influence of parents and peers, and experience. (Evolutionary biologists dismiss social-constructionist theory with the joke, "If it walks like a duck, quacks like a duck, and looks like a duck, it's a social construction of a duck.") Anything, the thesis goes, is possible for any of us—the premise of the group's pet concept, "queer theory." The goal of queer theory is to dispense with the "rigid, monolithic association of male bodies with male gender," with the association of "female bodies with female gender," and with the idea that the "male/female model," which they refer to as "heteronormativity," is natural. Its theorists have planted roots at even our finest institutions of higher learning: At Harvard, the $29,000 tuition entitles students to the counseling services of "designated sexual orientation tutors," who dutifully introduce malleable young minds to the varieties of gender-bent experience.

Admittedly, NOMAS occupies the extreme outpost of the gender correctness spectrum. Unfortunately, many of their members are also tenured lecturers in one of the fifteen thousand women's studies courses offered in colleges and universities around the country. (At last count, there were seventy-one courses in the nation that examine men and masculinity.) The ubiquitous message: men are screwed up, and the opposite of a screwed-up man is a woman. As one Big Ten university professor told me, "The academy today is an incredibly toxic and hostile environment for young men."

That may be one reason a growing number of them are choosing to forgo college altogether. Women now make up, on average, 60 percent of the students in every category of higher education, including public, private, religiously affiliated, four-year, and two-year institutions. The trend not only results in more men with limited life choices but has troublesome romantic consequences for the bitchfesters and their friends. According to Arthur Levine, some colleges are trying to achieve gender balance by softening the admissions standards for boys. But, he says, "if you take men who are not of the same caliber as the women, the highest-performing women leave, because the men aren't as interesting." It's an old story.

· · ·

WHEN I ENTERED kindergarten in a small Midwestern town forty years ago, I thought I was in heaven. Not only did I get to spend all day with my neighborhood pals, I was surrounded by strange, lovely creatures in party shoes, white anklets, and frilly dresses. I fell madly in love with the parade of Miss Dairy Maid and Miss Winter Carnival title winners who regularly alighted upon our school amid, I almost remember, clouds of fairy dust. Forever changed by the vision of these love goddesses, for the rest of the year I'd unroll my mat behind the upright piano at the rear of the classroom and spend the half hour of mandatory quiet time winking at whomever among my kittenish classmates I could lure into my winking chamber. Occasionally, I'd steal a kiss. At night, I'd trudge up to the hockey rink, mostly to play, but also to spy on the mating rehearsals of the neighborhood postadolescents. Most of what life was about, my little brain theorized, was one's relation to girls. My views have changed somewhat since, but not much.

Compared to today's indifferent, communal teen dating scene, the playground was like estrus season at a bonobo colony. At night, the warming house, a wooden boxcar with a potbellied coal stove, swayed with doo-wop and jump blues from an old tube radio donated by my parents. Every evening, my puny friends and I would eagerly await the arrival of older neighborhood girls. Scantily clad despite the subzero temperatures outside, the young glamour-pusses would tease their hair, daub their pretty mouths with white lipstick, fluff the pompons on their skating boots, and arrange their tidy bottoms on the benches lining the boxcar, waiting for Kit Larson to show up.

Kit was a neighborhood prince, a lanky, muscular boy who captained his high school hockey team and drove a '56 Ford pickup he'd customized with chrome air intakes, Hollywood mufflers, mag wheels—kind of a motorized testicle. An alpha male in progress, he embodied for me a protoversion of masculinity that complemented the übermodel of my father—a tough, ambitious, but deskbound federal prosecutor. Though I was several years younger, Kit and my older brother, Dean, who were buddies, let me tag along on their adventures; when I was six, they showed me how to enter a sewer spillway along the Mississippi riverbank, navigate with a flashlight through a maze of scary underground culverts and tunnels, and surface through a manhole onto the street just fifty yards from my house. A few years later Dean died, and Kit, an only child, continued to teach me things he felt boys should be taught by their older brother, like how to hop a slow-moving train or race across the narrow catwalk of the railroad bridge that spanned the river's roiling waters while dodging salt pellets shot by sadistic tugboat captains below.

But the most important thing he taught me, though he probably didn't know it, was that a boy's sense of adventure extends to the opposite sex, too. On particularly frigid evenings, when it was almost too cold to skate, someone would inevitably begin playing with the lights in the warming house. The girls would giggle in the dark, and when the switch was flipped back on, Kit was usually lip-locked with a lucky coed. A few minutes later, the lights went off and on again, and he had his arm around someone else. Cocooned in hockey gear and cold-weather clothing that probably matched my naked body weight, I got to observe what I knew was big, big medicine.

Today, such forward behavior can land a kid, whether he's six or sixteen, in real trouble. In 1998, a first-grade boy was kicked out of school in North Carolina after kissing a girl, and readmitted only after extensive psychological counseling. Another boy in New York was accused of harassing a girl by asking to hold her hand on the way to school every day for a week. For him, a one-week suspension. At a summer sleep-away camp that both my older and younger children attend, directors instituted a new policy requiring campers to obtain permission if they wanted to "touch" one another. Today, even puppy love has to be kept on a leash.

Over the past few years, I've admired how my teenage children and those of my friends have formed what appear to be genuine friendships with members of the opposite sex. They talk on the phone, hang out together, confide in each other, often refer to each other as "best friends." This never happened when I was a kid. If I told a girl a secret or went with her to a movie it was because I wanted to kiss her—or, in my extreme youth, at least wink at her. But today's teens don't date; they hang out in packs. For the vigilant parent who tries to talk straight with his kid about sex, this presents a problem. In counseling our teen girls on their inevitable first time, my wife suggests waiting to "do it" with their best friend.

It's hard to see these romantically neutral friendships as a bad thing, but as my sixteen-year-old daughter, Eliza, recently informed me, girls have only reluctantly accommodated to pack-dating. Boys are so reticent, it's the only way girls can get to be with them. Arthur Levine's study of college students illuminates the rougher edges of these relationships as they mature. Many young men commonly say their closest friend is a woman, but in the next breath admit they have no idea how to talk to "women." There's woman the friend, and woman the potential romantic object, and for some reason many men, like Jerry on *Seinfeld* or the confused romantics on *Friends,* are unable to join the two together. Jerry and Elaine were once lovers and are clearly meant for each other but decided their friendship was too strong to permit romance or marriage. It would ruin everything. Go figure.

Levine's tally of campus crimes and misdemeanors reveals an uglier subtext to this conundrum of intergender friendship. The worst graffiti on campus is entirely sexual and depicts women as sadistic, man-hating, devouring, or homosexual, Levine found. The greatest number of acts of vandalism—of dorms, locker rooms, art exhibits, and publications—are no longer motivated by racial or religious hatred, but by gender bias.

In other words, men say there are women they like, but they don't really like "women."

■ ■ ■

SEX, ATTRACTION, THE MATING games of the young—the bitch-festers' favorite topics—form a reliable prism, then, through which to assay the current state of gender relations among all age groups. How did we come to this pass? Is this the collective male response to thirty years of feminism? Or is something else going on? Sure, the bitch-festers and dickfesters, if you will, are a special crowd: highly educated, privileged, self-obsessed, and of course, New Yorkers— inhabitants of the Xtreme City. But they are the hetero world's van-guard, and the future they represent looks like this: women are the pursuers, have more affairs than men, but dislike having to be sexually aggressive. So they date male "babes" who are unafraid to come on to them but will never, as my grandmother used to say, amount to much. Desirable young men, the ones with "résumés," are reticent, soft, and withholding—naysayers when it comes to meaningful sex, and turned off by forward women. The dickfesters are, however, willing to have anonymous, commitment-free sex, almost as if they're trying out the primitive reproductive strategy practiced by many older men who have abandoned their roles as fathers. Like chimps, those men are willing to propel their genes into the next generation but are uninter-ested in whether their progeny actually survive.

No wonder The Rules—remember the silly best-seller of the same name a couple of years back?—are so appealing. They at least suggest a code of courtship otherwise absent in this era of static romantic sig-

naling, impersonal sex, and gender-role upheaval. Among the sugges-
tions guaranteed to bag a man for good: Don't call him and rarely
return his calls. Don't talk to a man first. Don't rush into sex. Judging
by what the men and women whom I've interviewed say about the current dating scene, it appears that men have reversed all the pronouns
in the book and adopted The Rules for themselves.

If anything is distressingly apparent to a veteran gender-war corre-
spondent, it's that young men and women are still responding to
deeply encoded mating cues, but that their prickly opinions and inse-
curities are short-circuiting their romantic connections. In experi-
menting with the surfers and the Marlboro men, the bitchfesters are
deploying what anthropologists refer to as a short-term mating strategy—they're selecting one-night bedmates based only on the men's
"babe" quotient. And in holding out for Résumé Man, if he ever gets his
act together, they're expressing a time-honored preference—although
they appear not to know it—for what women have always looked for in
a life partner.

And therein lies the rub for Résumé Man. Just a generation ago, all
the Ivy League colleges, with the exception of the University of Pennsylvania, were all-male, and men were the overwhelming majority in
law, medical, and business schools. In that simpler, one-paycheck era,
older résumé men needed only to compare themselves to women, who
had subordinated their own sense of accomplishment to their husbands', to feel manly, successful—like a good catch. It wasn't very long
ago that women's magazines advised their readers to act dumber than
their date or their husband. As lady editors of a certain age knew,
many men could experience a sexual frisson only if their wives or girlfriends handicapped themselves. But today men are a minority in college, and have relinquished half or more of the spots once reserved for
them in graduate schools. Not only have market forces shrunk the
opportunities for Résumé Man to get ahead, he's vying for a paycheck
with the dynamic, no longer handicapped young women he'd like to
woo. And in the gender-strained, amarital, and unromantic 1990s, he's
getting his signals crossed: his ascendant girlfriend arouses in him
feelings of competitiveness, a desire to dominate that is normally
directed toward other men, and she becomes classified in some primitive sense as being like another male. Not exactly a prescription for
love—for either of them.

So it's no coincidence that the male flight from marriage has exactly paralleled women's increasing presence and parity in the workplace. In the sixties, women wore buttons reading "59 percent" to point up the inequities between men's and women's pay. By the nineties, the difference had narrowed to 76 percent, and a recent federal study found that the earnings of childless women between the ages of twenty-seven and thirty-three had reached a level 98 percent that of men's. Meanwhile the average age at which men marry has climbed dramatically. *If* they marry, that is: the proportion of young singles has tripled in three decades, and it looks particularly hopeless for that huge number of thirty-somethings living in Mom and Dad's basement. Despite their extensive training in gender correctness and sensitivity, single young men have retreated from the mating game (starting, in some cases, with their decision to skip college) because they don't consider themselves capable of attracting and keeping an accomplished career woman in the old manner—by competing—and aren't willing to risk humiliating themselves by trying.

■ ■ ■

So how do young men get back on track? Should they look to the generation in front of them, their boomer parents, for models of righteous masculinity? *Hell-ooo!* We're the ones who introduced an epidemic of divorce to America. The paternal irresponsibility of my generation prompted a flood of new legislation governing the deadbeat dad. I know of many marriages in which the level of hostility exceeds anything experienced by Kate and her friends—the couples are just better at disguising it. But the issues that divide them are as intensely political as those wedged between the dickfesters and bitchfesters. Many of our peers, whom we've elected to Congress and the White House, are still haunted by the free-love sixties and end up paralyzing government because they can't keep their flies zipped. Much of what the dickfesters know about a man's relationship to a woman and his responsibility to his family they learned from us, their fathers, who are still reeling from the dramatic changes wrought by America's great gender experiment.

Somewhere, though, there's a new model for us all, a guy good at work and love, devoted to family and a protector of his community, a man who combines the best of the old masculine codes with the fresh personal insight necessary to win the love of the New Woman. He's competitive, naturally aggressive, a risk-taker, and pursues wealth and status not just to attract a desirable mate but so he can give back to his community as well. His emotional sophistication releases his wife from her historical role as his emotional gatekeeper, laying the foundation for a more equal partnership. His empathic powers make him a devoted and considerate lover. He's a coach, mentor, adviser, and protector—a lover and a fighter. He's a real standup guy.

I figure I owe it to the bitchfesters and dickfesters to find him.

SIFTING THE ASHES

...

THE ROOM IS STIFLING and still, rank with the effluvia of twenty-seven anxious, sleep-deprived men who haven't showered in three days and have eaten nothing but apple chips, a wedge or two of banana, and a few mouthfuls of grains. We've all descended from various regions of the Northeast upon a church camp outside Wilmington, Delaware, to do New Warrior training, which at this particular moment on this airless June afternoon means stepping onto a "sacred" carpet surrounded by our confrères and weekend leaders to confront our "shadows." Later, I'll hear that two men have died over the years on this carpet, a hideous swatch of orange-and-yellow shag that resembles something that might have been rescued from a motel dumpster. It's not hard to imagine other brothers shrugging off the mortal coil here: most of the men ringing the orange-and-yellow square shift their weight uncomfortably, faces blotchy and twitching in fear, blood pressure climbing dangerously, hearts flipping about madly—somatic wrecks. It seems a lousy place to die, if that's what it comes to.

Could these "shadows" really be so scary? I'm about to find out, for it's my turn to step onto the carpet. There is no assigned order for this stage of the process, which is called "guts work"; the leaders have told us each man will know when it's his time. Unfortunately, two other men have also heeded the inner summons, and we have a minute to stare wordlessly at one another to determine who will remain. A burly young man with long blond hair and an eagle tattoo on his shoulder quickly decides he can wait to expose his frailties and failures before the gathered strangers and steps off the carpet. The other fellow and I lock eyes. There is power in stepping down, the leaders tell us, but if neither of us yields, neither of us will go on this round. Well, there's power in digging in your heels, too. The night before, as we divided up into groups of four and five and silently selected team captains, I yielded to a rheumy-eyed older man who clearly wanted affirmation as a leaderly sort, as if to make up for all the times in his life he's been denied it. I felt momentarily proud of my generosity, of my ability to stifle the rabid competitiveness that seems to govern even my casual social encounters. But enough's enough. I bore into the eyes of the man opposite me who, after half a minute or so, begins to blink and avert his eyes to the sidelines. I know I've won. As the leaders count down the final seconds of our standoff, he steps aside.

I'd expected a lot of this to be silly, and much of it was that and more: humorless. This, the retooling of our manhood, we were reminded repeatedly, was deadly serious stuff. During the previous thirty-six hours of this three-day psychic boot camp, the leaders had led us through a series of quasiphysical confrontations and guided visualizations designed to "open us up." We had sat across from one another and, locking eyes, candidly described what we saw: *As a man among men, I see a mature fellow with acne scars, troubled teeth, and a healthy appetite.* We'd stumbled in teams of four through dense, brambly woods illuminated only by shafts of solstice moonlight, transporting heavy six-foot logs that were supposed to represent fallen comrades. We'd stood for hours with eyes closed, listening to stories of innocent young boys embarking upon dangerous journeys, and were encouraged to conjure up and confront monsters of our own unique psychic chemistry, to imagine ourselves as brave and glorious heroes taking on evil elders and wrathful enemies. At several points during the stories, we were asked to write in our notebooks and gradually assembled a diary of wishes, goals, self-appraisals, and regrets, which we then formulated into what became our personal affirmations and "mission" statements. We spent most of the three days in a single room, catching a few hours of sleep each night on mattresses laid side by side on the floor, arising to cold showers and black coffee served out of a bucket, a scoop of porridge in a styrofoam cup, occasionally sprung for a few minutes from the psychic excavations to venture outside, where we stumbled about blindly and tried to guess the time by the angle of the sun or the brilliance of the moon.

What was I doing here? During the first few hours, while trying to think of a way to quietly escape, I tried to remind myself: a year before, I had heard Robert Bly praise the New Warriors during a debate with a group of feminists who maintained that all-male retreats like the one I eventually found myself at widen the divide between the sexes and encourage greater oppression of women. I had thought that the New Warrior group, like the rest of the mythopoetic avatars, was passé—dead, in fact, and buried by cynical male editors like myself who had lampooned all the New Men who fled to the woods a few years ago to drum on coffee cans and screech like hooty owls. But interestingly, several women in the audience rose to testify that their husbands had been wonderfully transformed by recent New Warrior training, had emerged from the weekend both more assertive and emotionally accessible, more involved husbands and fathers, and that the changes had seemed to stick. Would I find the standup guy here? I decided to revisit this early men's-movement claque, but despite repeated inquiries, I could find out little about what actually happened during a retreat. No one would talk in any detail about how the group had evolved over the years—those initiated into the brotherhood actually sign a covenant pledging not to—but I gathered that the primary focus was on intense psychological work especially well suited to male instrumentality: if you've got a problem you'd like to deal with, why not work on it all weekend with a bunch of other guys until it's fixed?

I'd arrived at the Delaware church camp with my cynicism perfectly intact, but by the end of the evening I'd given myself up to a feeling I hadn't had since my early days in college when, as a naïve Midwesterner transplanted to the louche surroundings of an elite Eastern college, I'd often walk into a freshman dorm room in which everyone appeared to be acting a little odd and realize I was in a completely novel social situation: *Everyone here is on LSD!* I could remain on the outside, a prissy observer, or look at the world through the same prism as my new friends.

In a nostalgic reverie, surrounded by a bunch of sweaty men pursuing an altered state, I'd decided to go with the flow.

· · ·

STANDING NOW IN THE center of the orange shag, I sense my adrenals dumping cortisol into my bloodstream. The leaders gather round, look me over, and ask me for my affirmation. I had come up with a good one, I thought, reflecting my independence, self-sufficiency, and resilience. I tell them: "As a man among men, I repair myself."

"And is that true?" someone asks.

Having watched the guts work of three men before me, I've already figured out that all the writing we had been asked to do, concluding with the one trenchant affirmation statement, was cleverly designed to reveal a self-deception of great magnitude. But I figured mine was resistant to attack. "I think so."

"You *think* so? Do you *know* so?"

"I try to repair myself, but, like everyone else, sometimes I'm more successful than others."

"Tell us about that."

I can feel myself dissolving, tiny fissures opening up in the edifice I had long ago erected around a sadness I've never been able to shed, tearing along fault lines that I patch and fill regularly. "When I was a young boy, my world blew apart," I tell the men. "My older brother, the firstborn, died when he was thirteen, and my family changed forever. My father started to drink, refused to have much to do with me—resented me, I think, because I was now the oldest boy in the family, and every time he looked at me, he thought of Dean and how I wasn't him. So I've worked really hard to make a good life for myself, I've done it by myself with no one else's affirmation—certainly not my father's." It's true, and I'm proud of it.

"But something still bothers you about that, right?"

"Well, yes. I worry . . ."

The leaders lean in close, encircle me, poke at my chest. A code verb. "*Worry* about what?" one says angrily. "What do you *worry* about?"

And now, totally unexpectedly, I'm starting to lose it. In front of twelve strange men, no less—all the men in my guts group. "I feel if Dean hadn't died I wouldn't be who I am. And I worry"—I can barely say it—"that one of my own children will die."

The leaders spring into action, signaling other men hovering about. A man named McCoy grabs my arm and pulls me aside. McCoy's sinewy arms are covered with florid tattoos of big-busted half-woman/half-animal creatures; a long, gray ponytail dangles down his back. His pale blue eyes shine and quiver with manic intensity. Like the other leaders, there's not a bit of softness about him; he's a walking testicle. Counselor McCoy is missing a couple of teeth, and his long, thin nose doglegs to the left, proudly unrepaired following its brutal rearrangement during some nasty dustup. McCoy places both hands on my shoulders and squeezes, not consolingly but painfully, almost menacingly, making sure he has my attention. His lips are stretched thin; he seems pissed off to see another man distressed. "Listen to me," he says, squeezing tighter. "This is a magical place. And you can perform real magic here. Just let go, do the work, and let the magic repair you. But you've got to do the fucking work."

■ ■ ■

THE NIGHT BEFORE, I had driven from New York to the Delaware retreat with Jonathan, the executive chef at one of New York's fancier restaurants, and Manuel, an assistant Broadway producer. New Warrior organizers had encouraged attendees to carpool to the gathering to get a head start on generating salubrious male vibes. Their advice had its desired effect for, even before we hit the New Jersey Turnpike, Jonathan, in his mid-forties, was talking about his very strained relationship with his mother, her loveless marriage, and how they continued to affect his feelings about women he wanted to get close to—showing up, he believed, in an extremely worrisome bout of impotence with a woman he was now wildly attracted to. It had happened before, he said, but only with women he really liked, women with long-term potential, and he wanted to get to the bottom of it. Manuel, the son of a Hispanic Pentecostal minister, entertained us with stories—at once horrible and hilarious—about being thrown out of his house at fifteen after his mother found out he was gay. On his way out the door, she handed him a packet of family photographs; his face had been neatly excised from each picture. *Vaya con Dios!* Manuel didn't know much about New Warrior training, but a friend had told him he'd get a lot out of it.

After arriving at the retreat, we were forced to turn over all personal possessions—even wedding rings—and were assigned a number, scribbled on a name tag that we wore on our shirts. We were elaborately depersonalized, but by the end of the first evening we were allowed to climb back onto the phylogenetic scale—onto the lower rungs, at least. We abandoned our numbers and assumed an animal name, one of several steps on our return to personhood—or manhood—throughout the weekend. I was first known as Number Eight, then named myself Wolf, figuring I could at least be in a dominant predatory position, if it came to that. Between activities, I managed to get a reading on just who was in the group—a pretty equal mix of blue collar and professional men. There was a carpenter, landscape architect, casino manager, plumbing contractor, lawyer, venture capitalist, ex-priest, owners of small businesses, a recent college dropout. The men's ages ranged from twenty to sixty. Most were married with kids, or recently divorced with kids. Jonathan was the only chef, Manuel the only gay man, and I the only writer.

Toward the end of the first evening, we were asked to tell the others why we had come. Most of us, unaware of what was in store the rest of the weekend, made oblique references to the issue that, the next day, would be the focus of our guts work. Several men echoed each other: "My father died recently." "I'd like to be less fixated on sex." "I feel sad about growing older." "There's some old stuff I need to work out." "I've never really been able to take care of myself." "I alienate every woman I come in contact with." "I've been a lousy father." Having read the New Warrior brochures, we all knew there would be some sort of corny ceremony initiating us into manhood after we'd completed certain tasks, which Warrior elders promised would be physically grueling. But some of us were beginning to sense that the real challenge of the weekend was to discover and flex a different kind of strength: we were to tunnel a vent to our highly pressurized emotional centers, and, scorched and blinded by the escaping effluvia, trust other men to help us find our way back out.

■ ■ ■

DENNIS SHACKLEY, SKINNY, HANDSOME, on the cusp of middle age, about six foot four and wearing a T-shirt that boasts of his having completed a fifty-mile run, pulls me over to a corner of the orange-yellow shag. He's flown here from Indianapolis, along with three other "facilitators," to direct the guts work. This is his fortieth New Warrior weekend, meaning he's helped about 1,200 men take a look at their fears, sorrows, and hatreds—for thirty or forty minutes, anyway. I've watched gestalt therapists at human potential outposts like the Esalen Institute and am surprised to see how efficient and skillful Shackley is. As he led three men before me through the process, I was awed by his ability to cut to the heart of each man's anger and sorrow and firmly but compassionately lead him through catharsis and to some sort of resolution.

Shackley, a mental health administrator who works with troubled young men, is partial to big challenges. In 1990, he took a five-month leave of absence from his job, and, starting at Springer Mountain, Georgia, hiked alone through fourteen states along the Appalachian Trail to Mt. Katahdin, Maine. He did his first New Warrior training in 1992, and has done regular "shadow" work, an intense, more heavily Jungian training for New Warrior initiates, ever since. He describes his own explorations as "going down into the ashes, looking at stuff there, seeing where the wounds have been and looking at the shadows that exist, then coming back out and playing with the awarenesses I've received."

Shackley asks me to look around and select a man who will role-play my brother. I know immediately who he is: Hughes, a leader in training who projects the self-confidence and strength I imagine my older brother would have. Hughes is tall, fair, mustachioed, with piercing, otherworldly blue eyes. This is the first image I've ever had of my brother as a grown man. My cousin, a retired psychiatrist in his seventies who also lost a brother in his youth, and I once talked about how odd it is that our dead siblings never get older in our mind's eyes, despite the undeniable ways in which we've changed, matured, and aged. We're adults; they're eternally children, yet we still think of them as our senior siblings. To me, Dean is still thirteen, which may be one reason so many of my feelings about him are only as mature as an eight-year-old's—my age when he died.

Hughes is honored to be my brother. McCoy props up a grave-marker-sized chunk of foam rubber on the floor with R.I.P. scrawled on it. Hughes lies down in front of it and pulls a black shroud over his body. Shackley kneels on the floor next to me, talking softly into my ear. "This is your brother," he says, "and you can speak to him now. Pull the shroud from his face and tell him what you want him to know."

The idea of actually communicating with Dean in the grave I never got to see is shattering—and confusing. I want to tell him everything that's happened since he left, but at the same time feel he already knows. Or do I? Does he? After he died, I used to speak to him at night, believing that he was still on the bunk bed above me, despite the absence of the telltale sag in the mattress. As a teen, I would lay beneath the stars, mesmerized by vastness, in a godly swoon, and think of my brother, a particle up there somewhere, an angel. But as an adult, I rejected religion, often preferring a chemically induced feeling of expanded connectedness. As a father, I knew I should offer some sort of spiritual model to my children, if only so that they could later reject it, but I could bring myself to neither church nor synagogue. What kind of God would kill a young boy and wreck a family? Not one I could believe in. Yet I also dreaded that I had made a mistake, was petrified that this wrathful God would take one of my own children. For that was my experience.

I pull the shroud from Hughes's face. His eyes, burning, intense, surreal, lock on mine. "Tell him now," Shackley says, "tell him what you've wanted to say for so long."

■ ■ ■

STIFLED GRIEF, I'VE LEARNED, is caustic, a cauldron for what Jungian scholars call dark moods, which I've typically projected onto the women in my life. Overloaded by feelings I've never learned to process, I've often disengaged from others (particularly when I was younger), gotten caught up in webs of negativity. Or I've simply vented—my father always said I was "filled with rage." The "magic" of New Warrior guts work, Shackley says, is that by "owning" our sorrow and anger—a valuable resource that many men discover to be a powerful source of energy—we liberate ourselves from dark moods and clear the way for a more viable and honest connection to our family, friends, and community. We can be standup guys.

How? "Guts work offers the safety of what I call a ritual container," he will tell me later during one of several interviews following my New Warrior weekend. "It's a place I can safely step into and look at my perpetrator side—that side of me that isn't nice. If I can bring that part of myself from suppression and denial right out in front of me in a safe place, then it isn't so likely to come out in some other way. I have a lot more control over it. And I can actually use that energy, that very powerful energy, in a positive way."

The ritual container is also a safe place for men to experience sorrow. For years—decades, really—I've felt sadness well up inside me inexplicably, often at times when I had much to celebrate. I always knew it had something to do with Dean, who died in 1959. It also had a lot to do with my father, who taught me how to suppress that sorrow.

Dean was one of those lanky, athletic, all-American boys of the fifties with a butch haircut, big ears, and a guileless smile. Of the four children, he was the only one who had inherited my father's swarthiness; the rest of us resembled my fair-haired English mother. Though my memories of Dean have been subconsciously edited to preserve his mythic stature, I can't recall his ever being jealous, hostile, or rivalrous with me. Unlike his cronies, he always seemed proud to have his little brother tagging along. On Sunday mornings, he'd wake me up at five A.M. so that I could accompany him on his paper route, and we'd lie down in the early morning gloaming in the middle of Pelham Avenue, thrilling to the possibility that a car just might come along, although none ever did. He was the most gifted athlete in our neighborhood, and made sure that when sides were chosen up for baseball, football, and hockey games, I was on his team. We shared a bedroom and bunk beds, and though my mother insisted I sleep on the bottom, he always let me have the top after the lights went out—although that ended after I rolled over in my sleep one night, fell out of bed, and broke my nose.

Dean had spent the last two weeks of his life at home in an oxygen tent, wasted and withered from leukemia. I hadn't been allowed to see him during his months in the hospital, nor at home, and only on the day before he died did my mother tell me he would not live. I can't remember anything about that time, can't remember ever questioning why he wasn't around, why I couldn't see him, why his sickness was dragging on so long—nothing. Two days after my mother told me he would die, he was lowered into the ground in a cemetery along the banks of the Mississippi River, but I wasn't allowed to attend his funeral or burial. Later, at the wake, my older sister and mother sat on a couch crying, and asked me repeatedly why I was not. I was too angry at being left out to cry—too "filled with rage." I do remember that.

Within a week after he died, there were no pictures of him in the house, no hockey trophies, awards, report cards, Boy Scout projects, clothes, stamp collection—no clue that he had ever existed. My father was simply unable to utter his name, and threw himself into his work.

But his fiery career as a federal prosecutor and then as a trial attorney gradually cooled: he had a heart attack at forty-two, then decided to take a cut in pay to become a local judge, trading his glamorous job as an independent lawyer for the generous pension benefits my mother would receive after his death, which he expected—hoped, it seemed—would be mercifully premature. He retired early with full disability, suffering from back pain, obesity, alcoholism, and the early stages of emphysema.

A few months after Dean's death, I lost my voice for about six weeks. My parents, panicked, took me to a doctor who decided that I'd had a mild case of polio, even though I'd been vaccinated, and that my vocal cords were partially paralyzed. I would never be able to sing again, he said, and I'd have to curb my yelling on the hockey rink. It seemed like one more bad deal, since these were the two activities I enjoyed most. Many years later, I saw an otolaryngologist, who was about to repair the nearly collapsed septum of my oft-broken nose. I told him about my childhood diagnosis, but after examining my throat, he could find nothing wrong with my vocal cords. I was also seeing a psychiatrist at the time. My first marriage had collapsed, and I was living in Harlem, sharing custody of my one-year-old daughter, trying to resurrect a writing career I'd lost interest in after a precocious start, and hoping to figure out why I worked so hard to alienate anyone who took an interest in me. The shrink and I figured out that my vocal paralysis was the delayed psychosomatic response of an active, noisy eight-year-old who had repeatedly been told to be quiet and not disturb his brother who, unbeknownst to the boy, was dying in another room. Men somatize their emotions, I've since learned, install them in their muscles, veins, and bones, where they spasm, congeal, and fracture. My father's early heart attack was just grief strangling his heart, I believe. It's a process that can begin even in little boys.

Seven years after Dean died, I awoke one night in tears. Grief had finally arrived, broken through. I sat up, startled, instantly recognizing the face of this ancient sorrow. It was too late for me to work backward with all this, I decided. I had worked so hard to step into Dean's shoes—become the hockey player and student he never got to be. I even began playing the trombone, as he had. I became him to honor him, even though every accomplishment seemed to further distance me from my father, who seemed unwilling to acknowledge my unearned status as number-one son. So I stuffed those tears back into some dark corner of my psyche, hoping my sorrow would be satisfied with that one adolescent, late-night expression. It wasn't, of course, and every June, the month Dean died, I fight a descent into depression, trying to combat an immature, primitive, insidious sadness that I've allowed to set up a permanent residency.

■ ■ ■

SO, KNEELING ON the carpet on this feverish June afternoon so many years later, seasonally primed with sadness, incarcerated in some isolated all-male theater of the surreal, what would I like to tell Dean? That I felt my father always resented me because I succeeded his beloved firstborn? I start down this path, but it feels fake and self-aggrandizing. For the first time, I'm not sure I believe that. Staring at my surrogate sibling, I can feel other falsehoods, other carefully guarded self-deceptions crumbling. I would like to be over this thing. I would like to process this old sorrow, own it, as Shackley would say. I feel a compelling need not to screw this up with a lot of slick talk and defensive posturing. For once.

"Dean," I say, "I want you to know how much I love you. I want to thank you for teaching me how to lift a puck. And for protecting me, like the time you came home, found out a neighborhood boy your age had punched me, and went out and beat the guy up. I never thanked you for any of that. I was so surprised that you died, everything changed after, and I felt so bad that I'd never got to say good-bye. I didn't even know you were dying, in fact. I didn't cry when you died, and everyone thought I was a monster. I cried about you once when I was fifteen, and then I decided never again—everyone thought I was selfish, unfeeling, cold, so I'd let them feel that way. I've always been afraid to release those tears, terrified that, after gathering for so long, they would never stop. And now look at me."

Hughes reaches for my hand, clutches it. Rivulets of tears track from the corners of his eyes to his temples. I'm not easily spooked, but this is so real, this gestalt stuff. I'm vaguely aware through my own blurred, anarchic vision that the other dozen men in my guts group are sobbing, too. Shackley squeezes my shoulder. "Tell Dean about the guilt you feel," he says.

And now, the terror I've felt so long seizes all of me like some deadly biological agent. "I feel a terrible, corrosive guilt," I say to

Dean/Hughes, "because, paradoxically, I feel blessed in so many ways. I was really lost for a while, when I was a young adult, but I pulled myself out of it. I repair myself. I've had good luck, I've got a beautiful, smart wife; we have terrific children, a good home. But I feel it's because you died. It's hard to explain. Had I not succeeded you, I wouldn't have this good fortune. Do you understand that? I feel blessed because of the hard time I had earlier. That's how I see it. And all of that was at your expense. You died; I got to live. There's some deep stuff I know about life that other people don't know. And I feel grateful for knowing that. But I'm always waiting for the other shoe to drop. I'm terrified that one of my own children will die, because that's what happens to fathers, and sons, and brothers—to you and me and our dad."

Shackley leans toward me again. He has a long, black cloth in his hands. "You've always felt guilty about Dean," he says in a soft voice. "You feel guilty if you feel good, guilty if you feel bad. What does the guilt feel like?"

"It feels like it's suffocating me," I say.

"Exactly. It strangles you, doesn't it? It makes it difficult to breathe. It causes your chest to become tight, and the deeper breaths you draw, the less air you get." Shackley's tone is strident now. He takes the long scarf and begins wrapping it around my neck. "The guilt is suffocating, isn't it?" He knots the cloth tightly. I feel like I'm choking. I tug at the scarf. "Does it feel like this?"

■ ■ ■

A FACILITATOR IS ONLY as good as the personal work that he's done, says Shackley. "The most important ingredient is his having done his own work first. He has to be able to own things he's been afraid to look at, transform things in himself that have been keeping him at a lower level of energy and potential—mentally, physically, and emotionally. If a man is willing to risk that, then when he steps into that cauldron to work with other men, it's like there's a safety cord between him and the others. There's a connection, an identification, a sense of, *I'm going to walk with this man as far as he wants to go.* And that man will let me know how far that is. These men are entrusting their souls to us, and we need to be very sensitive to how we step into that place with them."

■ ■ ■

SHACKLEY MOTIONS HUGHES, my brother, to arise from the grave and tells me to climb into it. I am now Dean, with his little brother's guilt wrapped round his neck, and Hughes is me. "Tell Mike what he needs to hear," Shackley instructs me.

I settle myself into the grave. As I lie down, I see that all the other men in the group have dropped to their knees, closely circling our little theater. Oddly, the grave is soothing, peaceful. It's cooler down here beneath all the heavy panting of the pallbearers and mourners. Hughes reaches for my hand, and we look into each other's eyes. My boundaries are wonderfully fluid. I am at once a little boy and my brother, but possessing the wisdom of a father. I'm unconfused about what I, Dean, need to tell myself as a young boy and as a man. "Tell him," Shackley says again.

"It's not right that you feel guilty," I say to Hughes, "because you had nothing to do with my dying. You are blessed, not because I died, but because of what is inside you, who you are, what you've done on your own, not because of me. I'm so proud of you, and I do watch over you, just as you thought in those first years after I died. But you've mythified me. I was just a boy, your brother, who died. Just a boy."

Then, I'm struck by a blinding insight, embarrassingly simple and doubtless obvious to everyone else. "You have to realize," I tell my surrogate, "that the guilt you feel is just a childhood touchstone, a talisman, just an eight-year-old's primitive, immature guilt. It's magical thinking to feel responsible for my death. You don't have that power. It's an eight-year-old's view of the way the world works that produces the fear that your own children will die. But maybe, in a perverse way, you actually like to feel the pain and guilt. Because it's a way of getting in touch with me, of keeping me alive."

Now I'm crying and laughing, flushing tears of immense relief. I feel possessed of an uncanny wisdom, although it's no greater than the insights I have into my own children's behavior. "You should know," I say, "that you don't have to feel guilty in order to get in touch with me. You can talk to me whenever you want."

Shackley nods, pleased. I'm a good carpet worker; I laid my guts out on the floor, and now I get to reel them back in. He moves a little impatiently. He's "walked" with me as far as he can, and there are nine other guys behind me nervously waiting to dump their poisonous entrails onto the carpet. He helps me rise from the grave, and Hughes and I again switch roles. "It's time to say good-bye," Shackley says.

Hughes and I again join hands. His tears now spill out onto his cheeks, and he speaks for the first time. "I'm so proud of you," he says. "I always watch over you. And you can keep me inside you and talk to me whenever you like."

I rest my head on Hughes's chest, in my brother's grave, and listen to the pounding of his heart. This is the burial I never attended, the good-bye I never got to say. We're role playing, but I'm reluctant to give up the part. I know nothing about this man, but am enormously grateful for what he's done for me. He is my brother.

Finally, Shackley helps me up and the other men rise with me. With an edge of the black cloth, I wipe my face. "Do you still feel you need to carry around this guilt?" Shackley asks, tugging on the scarf.

"No," I say. "I'd like to get rid of it."

He unwraps the scarf. "What do you think we should do with it?"

"Bury it," I say.

He hands the cloth to another man. "Now," he says. "What was your original affirmation?"

" 'As a man among men, I repair myself.' "

"Do you still think that's true?"

"No."

"Can you think of a better one?"

I look at Shackley, Hughes, McCoy, the assistant leaders, the dozen men ringing the carpet, some working hard to pull themselves back together, preparing for the next wrenching round of guts work. I stretch my arms wide, visually embracing all the men before me. "As a man among men," I say, "I am not alone."

. . .

A FRIEND, A SHRINK, once said to me, "There is only one separation." At first I was puzzled by what she meant, and then the wisdom of her observation hit me. At some point, all of us are blindsided by loss. For the lucky ones, it's nothing more than a developmental milestone—the routine but still painful early withdrawal from a parent. Others, like me, experience a loss that trumps the earlier one. Our reaction to the separation forms a template for our responses to all the other separations in life—whether from a job after being fired or from a lover after an argument. In my case, the consequences of shutting down when I was a young boy have plagued me for a long time. Numbness comes easily.

Dennis Shackley has seen a lot of this. "A lot of men fear that if they climb down into their grief or sadness, they may never come back out," he says. "And most men never get the support and encouragement to do it to begin with."

Thirty-eight years after experiencing the one separation upon which so many of my emotional responses were modeled, I finally worked through its end stage in a steamy activity center supported and emboldened by a dozen men I had never met before. For a few minutes afterward, as the next man squirmed on the orange-and-yellow shag mouthing his pathetic self-deceptions, I sat in a corner sipping water, blissed on endorphins, feeling as though I had just run a marathon, grateful for all Shackley and Hughes had done for me, remodeled by the firm hand of male compassion. But I was only the fourth man to be processed. It was time to step back onto the hideous orange-yellow— maybe even "sacred"—carpet.

■ ■ ■

"TAKE YOUR BALLS BACK!" Shackley screams. He's holding two oranges, standing at the end of a line of twelve men who have locked arms to form a gauntlet. A thin, sandy-haired man with glasses thrusts his chest against the web of locked arms, reaching for the oranges. We strain to maintain the human chain. "Don't make it easy for him," leaders whisper in our ears as we tighten our sweaty grips on each other. If he's going to break through, he's going to have to summon a lot more strength than he's shown so far. "Come on, Raven," Shackley yells, referring to the animal name the man has taken. "These are your balls, and your mother's got them. You want them back, or not?"

After stepping onto the orange-and-yellow shag, Raven had told the leaders that since his father had died a few months ago, he had felt confused, childlike, anxious, and had trouble sleeping. He missed his father, he said. That was the only thing he could figure was wrong.

After some prodding from Shackley, though, the man admitted that his mother was making increasing demands on his time, calling at all hours of the day, asking that he come over to fix this, bring her that. "She wants to turn me into her little husband," Raven said.

Shackley rested a finger on his lips, then said, "And that feels familiar to you, doesn't it?"

"What do you mean?" Raven asked. He shifted his weight, looked at the ceiling, then suddenly his face flushed and contorted. He wrapped his arms about himself. "Well, I guess so. When I was boy she'd take me into her bed after my father went to work. I remember I was about four or five. She'd whisper in my ear, 'You'll be a much bigger man than Daddy some day.' It felt cozy, but it never stopped. When I was seven, ten, even twelve, she'd try to pull me in. She'd whine, 'Just for a minute. Your dad never cuddles with me. And you're my little man.' If I didn't get in bed, she'd sulk, refuse to talk to me or give me snacks. So I'd get in, with my back to her, and she'd pull me close, whispering, 'There's my little man.' I'd lie there, bound up tight, thinking, 'No, this is wrong. I'm not your husband.' There was no actual physical sex; she never touched my cock or anything. It was just emotional incest."

Over the next ten minutes, Shackley skillfully pulled more details from Raven. For years, he was a compulsive womanizer, Raven admitted, though he's never been married. He was never content with just one girlfriend, he had to have three or four at a time. He could only be satisfied if he had sex with at least two of them on the same day. For a while, with the help of a therapist, he managed to remain celibate. But since his father died, he was again trolling compulsively.

Now, with Shackley's prodding, Raven gradually stokes his anger, and the leader encourages him to hold an image of his mother in his mind as he does. Then we reinforce our twelve-man gauntlet, and yell and goad Raven to bust through our slimy phalanx as Shackley, holding his surrogate testicles, taunts him at the end of the line. Raven pushes, scrapes, and claws his way through us, breaking each armlock with a loud grunt as we try both to force him back and egg him on. With one final guttural scream, Raven breaks through the last armlock and seizes the oranges. With a demonic look, he squeezes the orange globes, which explode into a harmless geyser of pulp, juice, and oedipal rage.

∎ ∎ ∎

"OFTEN YOU ASK what you would like to have happen, and the person doesn't know," says Shackley. "So I go on intuition, and follow my heart. What is my heart connecting with this man? His pain around a grief issue, his anger, his never being able to celebrate just being alive?

I don't know of any man I've met on the carpet whose guts work I haven't been able to identify with, at least partly. Sometimes it's just a matter of asking a few questions and opening myself up and being a vessel for this man to come through, to let me understand how he lives now so I can walk with him for just a little while.

"Some men step onto the carpet with predator energy, killer energy. There's a part of him that defies authority; he's looking to kill a king, or someone in authority. They're usually passive-aggressive and look like nice, sweet men, but underneath they're murderous; they harbor a vampire energy that needs to come up and be owned. They seethe inside, but they're unwilling to show their anger, so they put it in shadow. Then it's much more likely to come out by accident than on purpose.

"That's why it's important to set up a ritual space and invite them to do on purpose what they could do by accident. Then they can use the energy to protect themselves instead of perpetrating. You ask the man what it is he doesn't want to be and invite him to model that. He thinks he's acting, showing you what this looks like in somebody else, not him. But once he touches that, feels that juice, you ask him what the energy wants to do. He's probably fantasized about this. And it turns out the energy wants to tear, stab, shoot, maim. And you invite him to go into that energy, and tear, stab, shoot, and maim.

"Sometimes it takes forty minutes before it's over. Then you ask him just to feel the energy as energy. You ask him what the energy really wants. And it turns out that the energy really just wants to be loved."

■ ■ ■

OVER THE NEXT FOUR hours or so, the remaining men step onto the carpet as the rest of us gather round in a supportive circle. Other men also have seductive mothers who have to be ritually killed off. Several men viciously slam a tennis racket into a mattress until they can no longer lift their arms, murdering fathers who had told them repeatedly they would never amount to anything, that they were stupid, weak, uncoachable, without talent or potential. Some men role-play their father so they can feel what it's like to raise their arms and fists in rage and bring it down upon themselves. Two men, fathers themselves, become weak in the knees, their forearms literally numb, and fall onto the orange-yellow shag sobbing, mortified by the ease with which they morph into their abusive dads, by how natural it feels to clench a fist and shake it upside a young boy's head, perhaps stunned by how often they've felt the same boiling rage with their own sons, and hating themselves for it. One man steps onto the shag carpeting but can find nothing to talk about; after fifteen minutes of fruitless probing, the leaders angrily wrap him inside three mattresses, tie it tight with rope, and leave him in a corner. An hour later, the man finally wriggles free and crawls onto the orange-yellow shag, his clothes soaked, literally frothing at the mouth, and announces that he's thought of something to talk about: how, twenty-five years earlier, he had been raped by a senior officer at military school.

Some men ram themselves against the human gauntlet, others pummel pillows, some are asked to strip and crawl through a tightly bound tunnel of plastic mattresses to be reborn, emerging scraped and bloody from their journey through the crude birth canal. One young man who has tracked down his biological mother to find out why she'd given him up for adoption climbs atop a table and, with eyes covered, falls back into the outstretched arms of twelve men, who then hoist him high, carry him outside into the blinding sunlight, and present him to the universe, a beautiful manly gift. Some men, says Shackley, just need to "open up and be truly blessed for who they are, for their sovereign energy—not for what they do, but just for being there, being the man they are."

At the end of each process, we exhale a collective sigh of relief, ritually banish the negative vibes from the room, and sip from water bottles. As the guts work continues—we've been at it now for five hours—I wonder how much more of this I can take, because as each man steps onto the orange-yellow shag to unload his story, I find myself riveted, addicted to the novelty of watching raw, violent, male emotion being unleashed harmlessly, dumbfounded by the sadness so many of us carry around inside.

The day before, we'd all arrived in one piece, most of us accomplished and successful, many of us husbands and fathers. Now we were being broken down and reassembled. Some of us find some of the pieces no longer fit, and we let the other men—strangers with whom we'd forged a powerful trust—grind them into the hideous orange-yellow shag.

...

ONE OF THE LAST men to step onto the carpet is a young college dropout named Eagle. Pale and pimply, Eagle wears a white, sleeveless T-shirt and has the slouchy, avoidant, and amotivational look of a stoner. Eagle shifts his weight nervously, his hands clasped behind his back, head slightly bowed, as though awaiting sentencing from a judge. Shackley and the other leaders pick at him for details until, in a timid voice, Eagle reveals that he has no job, no goals, no ambition, and an inability to stick with anything he starts. He's lost.

Eagle's mother had died when he was twelve, he finally reveals—suffered a stroke and fell to the floor at his feet. After she died, his father and older brother retreated into their own worlds and never paid much attention to his.

Shackley and his crew again spring into action. They prop up the venerable foam-rubber gravestone and unfold the shroud. Shackley tells Eagle to look around and select a man who will play his mother. The young man raises his eyes from the floor and, after scanning the surrounding faces just long enough to find mine, nods at me. Just as I knew Hughes was my brother, Eagle has been imprinted with some vision of me as his mother. McCoy, the tattooed warrior, directs me to lie down at the foot of the grave marker and covers me with the black cloth. Shackley and Eagle kneel beside me. "This is your mother's grave," Shackley tells Eagle. "You can speak to her. Just pull the shroud from her face."

Eagle's eyes bear down on me, bright and moist. He finds my hand beneath the shroud and grasps it. Shackley whispers into his ear. "Tell her," he says. "Tell her how you really feel."

"I just wish you hadn't died, Mom," says Eagle.

I look into this young boy's face—he could be one of my children—and my chest swells with a familiar sorrow. Only it's larger—not just mine, but ours. He and I know something about the one separation that is truly wrenching. We have a bond. I'm overcome by a desire to help this desperate young man, take him into my family and help him straighten out. "I wish I hadn't, too," I say, but Shackley, kneeling behind Eagle, shakes his head with a finger across his lips, motioning me to be silent.

Shackley talks softly to Eagle, who now clasps my hand with both of his and flashes back to the morning his mother died. He tells me how he stared into her frozen eyes as she lay on the dining room floor, life draining from her face as it settled into an anguished rictus. For ten minutes this sad young man with the gaping hole in his heart, so shy and distant during earlier activities, tells me about his life in high school, his girlfriend, his brother's job, his father's stony silence after her death. "I want you to know everything, Mom," he says. "I've had no one to talk to."

Then we switch places, and as Eagle, now playing his mom, lays in the ersatz casket, I give voice to Shackley's promptings in my ear. "I want to know that you still love me, Mom," I say, "that you're proud of me, and that no matter what I do, you'll always be my mother and be proud of me. I need to know this." And Eagle, his body wracked with sobs, tells me that he is, and always will be.

We switch roles again, I lay beneath the gravestone, and, mouthing Shackley's whispered importunings, reassure Eagle that I will always be his mother, that all the things he loved about me are still alive within him. Shackley urges Eagle to say good-bye, and the boy lowers his head to my chest. I stare up at a ceiling fan as it directs our emotional exhaust back down upon us, stroking the boy's hair, his now peaceful, moist exhalations dampening my shirt.

■ ■ ■

THE NEXT DAY, my fellow initiates and I gather in a silent circle outside the meeting hall in which all of us—most of us, anyway; a few were absolutely resistant to the process—dumped our guts onto the orange-and-yellow shag. By then, we had returned quarts of perspiration to the earth in a sweat-lodge, showered (finally), gorged ourselves at a celebratory outdoor feast, and smoked cigars as we prepared to leave the safety of our ritual container and return to our real lives. Shackley warns us not to overwhelm our families with the personal insights we've received or talk at great length about the ways in which we might feel changed. "Too much change too fast can seem threatening to those who love you," he says.

Later, Shackley elaborates on his warning. Some women aren't happy with their reconditioned warrior when he returns from the weekend training, which many men augment for years with weekly talk groups. "Women who feel a need to control the relationship don't like what they see," he says. "But most are very positive about the changes. I hear over and over from women that they no longer have to carry their husband emotionally, that he can carry himself. And that there's a great release in that. It's very freeing. In terms of laying a foundation for an equal partnership, it's about the most effective thing a man can do."

This is the lesson for the aspiring standup guy. By developing emotional autonomy and independence, he makes himself more attractive to the modern woman, who no longer has the time or inclination, as her mother did, to crisis-manage her partner's inner life. His psychological sophistication not only confers greater personal power, but is an important component of a truly egalitarian relationship.

Now, one by one, each of us moves along the ring of men and locks eyes for a few seconds with the man in front of him before moving on to the next. Some of the men are weepy, the few hard cases who successfully resisted the counselors' intensive probings still cannot make eye contact. Eagle, whose real name is John, steps before me, pulls himself up straight, and takes a deep breath, his face breaking into a broad unabashed grin. Though we're not supposed to talk, I say to him, "You're going to be fine."

We then move to the twenty-odd weekend staffers who stand in a line near the parking lot. I look into the eyes of each one. With a half dozen of the men, I know I've experienced what psychiatrists call "transference." I've identified my high school hockey coach, my best friend's father (my "good" dad), a professional mentor, my sixth-grade teacher. I stand before Hughes, who mouths the word "brother," and, brimming with gratitude, I mouth the word back. Shackley whispers that I did "really good work," and McCoy grins at me fiercely, looking like he'd like to bite my ear off. Some of the leaders' faces are streaked with tears, despite their having been through this dozens of times.

I find my carpool mates, Jonathan and Manuel, and we strap ourselves in for the long ride back to Manhattan. As we exit the camp, Jonathan exhales and says, "I don't think I'll ever look at men the same way again."

▪ ▪ ▪

NOR WILL I. An important criterion of standup manhood, I realize, is the psychological independence Shackley considers to be the goal of carpet work. Most men handicap their psychic autonomy by ceding their emotional lives to women—often in the name of the new "sensitivity." But as guts work makes clear, men are meant to have an affective dimension that's developed with other men, not just women and shrinks. As I discovered, it's uniquely liberating to shed decades of weighty emotional baggage in the presence of other guys. For one thing, knowing that all the other hostile forces of nature are just as bruised and bloodied helps level the playing field. More important, by taking responsibility for managing our own feelings, we free the women we love from a job they never wanted in the first place.

Encouraged by the "work" I saw being done at the Delaware camp and thinking I must be hard on the trail of the standup guy, I immediately decide to sign up for another men's retreat, this one with a radically different focus. After posting my application, though, I begin to have second thoughts. How lasting is the little bit of self-knowledge you gain after emoting with a couple of dozen other smelly guys? Can you really put an abusive father behind you after bashing his imaginary head with a tennis racquet for fifteen high-gestalt minutes? What does a man do with his little slivers of insight into, say, his adult-child reaction to his brother's long-ago death?

It occurs to me that before I head off to another "ritual container" I've got more to do before I can process, or "own," what I learned on the carpet. After my guts work, one of the leaders had torn off a piece of the black shroud Shackley had wrapped around my neck and given it to me as I recovered in a corner. "Do whatever you think you should with this," he'd said. I remembered telling Shackley that I wanted to bury it, this symbol of my childhood guilt, and decide that's what I'll do.

The next weekend, my family and I head to our summer house near the headwaters of the Delaware River in upstate New York. Almost a hundred years old, our converted one-room schoolhouse is surrounded by burbling streams on two sides and backs up to an old-growth hardwood forest strewn with glacial boulders and carpeted with clusters of ferns. As I untangle my son Tom's fishing line one morning, I tell him and his twin sister, Molly, and my oldest daughter, Eliza, a little bit about what I'd experienced during my weekend retreat. I'd never been allowed to bury my brother, I tell them, and I'd like them to help me do it now. I ask them to pick out a special place in the woods where we can install Dean's spirit so that we can keep him near us and visit him whenever we like. Then we'll have a little ceremony.

The next morning we clamber onto one of the rocks at the highest point in the woods. Dean's new resting spot, selected by the kids, sits amid a thatch of evergreen ferns and has a sentry's view of the little yellow schoolhouse. My wife, who loves liturgy, has brought a scented candle, Molly a posy of wildflowers. The children are silent, grim-faced, and stare straight ahead as they wait for me to begin.

I explain that a long time ago, when I was just a little boy—Tom and Molly's age, in fact—my brother died of a very unusual sickness when he was about Eliza's age. I didn't see him for a long time before he died, and after he passed away I wasn't allowed to go to his funeral. I wasn't sure what happened when a person died, but I decided I'd try to talk to him, as though he were an angel, and I did—every night before falling asleep. But after a couple of years, I stopped. I didn't know where he was, and had decided that he probably couldn't hear me. But as I grew older, I was still often very sad, particularly in the summer, which was when he died. I want to learn how to talk to him again, I tell my kids, and I think that if we hold a special ceremony, maybe we can bring their uncle near to us, and he can watch over us like a guardian angel. "Though he died a long, long time ago, I still miss him a lot," I say.

I tell them about the happy times with Dean. And I tell them how, even though I'm a grown man, I still feel a childish guilt about his death because I have so many good things in my life—like my children and my wife. I show them the little piece of black cloth and explain that the men I'd been with recently had given it to me as a symbol of this silly guilt, and that now I plan to bury it, right here between these rocks, as a way of remembering Dean.

I ask the kids to read the messages they've written. Tom pulls a crumpled piece of paper from his pocket and reads, "Dear Uncle Dean, I'm sad to hear you died of cancer. If you didn't die of cancer, you would be a good uncle. Love, Tom." Then he bursts into tears.

Molly, holding her message tightly in her fist, reads, "Uncle Dean, I'm Molly. I think that there is some of you in all of us. We're all happy to learn from you." Tough little Molly, her father's daughter, stares straight ahead with a pinched face.

Eliza reads, "Dear Uncle Dean, this is Eliza Dean. I have thought of you and wondered about you many times while growing up. I have always felt like a part of you was living through me every time I wrote my name or said it. I only wish I could have known you to have a better understanding how to honor your memory through who I am. Please ease my dad's pain if you can. Love, Eliza."

Dumbstruck by the wisdom and compassion of my children, I collect their scraps of paper, wrap them in the bit of black shroud, and slip it beneath some leaves between the rocks. We all sit silently for a moment, then my wife says, "I believe Dean is with God. One day, not long after Daddy and I fell in love, I was riding home on the F train and I saw him. He was smiling at me through a window with his little boy's face, and I knew then that ever since he died he's been looking out for Daddy. And now he's here looking after all of us."

She then reassures the children that although Dean died when he was young, this would never happen to them. And she tells them that it's important for them to understand that even their dad, whom they think of as a big strong man whose job is to protect them, can be upset and cry sometimes. "But now Daddy has a place where he can come visit Dean when he's sad," she says, "and it will make him feel better."

Molly and Eliza rise and sing "White Choral Bells," a song they'd been practicing for the talent show at the camp they'll be attending next week. Then, feeling at least for a moment like the luckiest man on earth—"blessed" indeed—I suggest we all head to the river for a swim.

COCKTALK

. . .

"WE CALL THIS PART of the program cocktalk," announces Griff, a roly-poly black man who's one of the organizers of Man Week ("explorations of manhood"), as he unhitches his belt. "We spend a lot of time thinking about sex, we obsess a lot about our cocks, but we rarely talk to other men about it, or them. So for the next ninety minutes or so, or for as long as it takes, anybody who wants to can say anything they like. You can tell the group about your great moments, great numbers, sexual misdemeanors, or you can just listen. This is a safe environment for anyone who wants to participate. Personally, I feel more comfortable in these sessions naked, and if you don't have a problem with that, I invite you to get that way, too."

Uh-oh. I'd been waiting for something like this. How could I expect to plumb the anguished soul and beleaguered spirit of contemporary American manliness without at some point dropping trou' with my brothers and engaging in a little confessional gutter talk? I'm halfway through another men's retreat, this one at a lakeside camp in northern Minnesota and the first in which much of the focus is on the collective penis and its currently tormented relationship to women—the mysterious and fascinating other. I'm not sure I want or need to share with a group of strange, naked Midwesterners my own hang-ups about sex, kinky erotic fantasies, or details about my physical relationship with my wife. But of course, I wouldn't mind hearing other men talk about theirs.

Women, along with many shrinks (who happen to be, increasingly, women), like to say that sex is often about something else. Men, as I know and am about to reconfirm, can grasp the general validity of this assertion, even if they're often ignorant of the emotional particulars, for we say the same thing about sports. Sometimes, when the stars are generously conjoined, we get to link the two and have sex *as* sport— unlike women, who for all their liberated tough talk are rarely interested in enjoying sex with the casual detachment men can. It's why the new withholding strategy is so effective: if sex were just about sex, the bitchfesters wouldn't be so devastated when the guy reels in and walks out.

But as anyone who is capable of seeing through the new withholding strategy has figured out, sex has become increasingly fraught for men, too. The male sexual brain, once thought of as a single-celled organ obeying a simple biological imperative, is actually far more nuanced, fragile, and impressionable—and, as it turns out, insecure— than its female counterpart. And after guiding men's behavior in predictable ways for so long, blithely spurring them on to achievement and mating contests, it's experiencing a crisis of confidence. Reeling from a barrage of postfeminist-age assaults, it's suffering some anxiety thoroughly unbecoming to a standup guy, as some of the cocktalkers are about to testify.

"Getting naked puts us all on sort of an equal plane," says Griff, pulling his T-shirt over his head. "If there's body language to read, it will be writ large. We're all just a bunch of naked apes here with the same primitive drives. And those of us who choose to testify will be able to hide nothing."

My mind riffs for a moment. Body language was actually a lot easier to decode when we had furry coats, and a rival's fear or anger was signaled by the horipilating hedgerow at the nape of his neck. Maybe we started shaving and grooming to camouflage our emotions and press an advantage over a rival. Someday, a women's studies course will undoubtedly cite shaving as the first deliberate attempt by men to hide their feelings. Or maybe we decided to scrape all our hair off as part of a reaction to the intimate physical language we were required to speak in our human past—during Old Testament Man Weeks, say. Biblical figures, for instance, swore oaths by placing their hands under one another's "loins" or "thigh"—euphemisms for the scrotum or penis. Hence the common Latin root of the words "testament," "testify," and "testicle." Feudal lords mercifully reduced the familiarity of this act by demanding that a vassal swear his fealty upon the landowner's "sword." I'm hoping Griff's idea of testifying is a thoroughly modern and sanitary one.

And do we really want to communicate like our less-evolved simian bro's? Rivalrous monkeys often threaten each other by flashing their erect penises. Even when extending friendly greetings, male baboons jostle and mount each other to establish dominance. Older male baboons, who have been greeting each other like this for years, eventually settle upon a particularly elaborate form of salutation. They perform a series of intimate, carefully balanced greetings intended to convey their mutual solidarity and preempt any rivalrous feeling. One animal will approach his pal and present his rump. The other will smack his lips, then tickle the other's scrotum and pull on his penis. Primatologists call this "diddling," and it's thought to signal mutual trust. The monkeys then reverse roles to keep their relationship in perfect harmony.

Maybe, Griff is suggesting, the younger participants among us should pair off and wrestle, while the older ones sneak off to the corner for some mutual diddling. Me, I'm thinking about just sneaking off, period.

■ ■ ■

THE OTHER EIGHTEEN CONFRÈRES rise from the floor of the old recreation center and begin shedding their clothes. As we undress and then gingerly settle our naked butts onto the cool, splintery floor, our chubby "facilitator" briefs us on cocktalk protocol: No cheap analysis or criticism of another man's comments are allowed; however, we may affirm the personal resonance of his words with a simple low wave of the hand. And we can speak only when in possession of the ten-inch rubber phallus Griff is unsheathing from a long white tube sock and about to pass around. Finally, it's considered polite to share with the other participants the nickname we've given our penis. *Mojo, meet Mr. Python.* I sense the simultaneous retraction of nineteen nearby puds with secret monikers into the protective warmth of the scrotal chamber. "Since I'm holding the magic wand now," he says, "I'll start." He holds up the flesh-colored rubber shlong for all to see. "Oh, I forgot another rule: No abusing the phallus. Treat it with respect."

Griff grips the phallus with one meaty paw and announces, "Caesar." Growing up on Minneapolis's tough north side, Griff begins, he learned early on to equate his sense of adequacy with how many girls he was screwing. "That was how you took the measure of yourself in the 'hood. The key thing wasn't what was happening with me and the girl, but how many of my friends knew about it." As he got older, he could never quite ditch the notion that sex had to do more with who knew he was having it than with his lover. "It took me a long time to work through that," says Griff, who looks to be about thirty, "but I think I've finally learned what it means to make love, to focus on the woman I'm with right then and there, and not be thinking about who I'm going to receive my affirmation from later."

Recently, he says, he recognized himself in a joke he heard. It's about a guy who's shipwrecked, an only survivor, who washes up on a tropical island. The island, magically, is teeming with resources, there's plenty of food, and the man constructs an elaborate, comfortable shelter for himself. He's got a good life, but of course he's lonely. Which in cocktalk also means horny.

One day, the body of a beautiful young woman floats ashore. She's barely alive, and the man slowly revives her. He realizes that the young woman is Cindy Crawford. He can't believe his good luck, even if she is married. As he nurses her back to health, they fall in love.

All is bliss. He and Cindy are madly, happily in love. But something nags at the man, and one day he decides to do something about it. He takes her aside. "Cindy, do you love me?" he asks.

"Of course."

"There's a favor I have to ask of you then," he says.

"Sure, anything."

"Will you wear my shirt?"

"Sure," she says.

"And my pants?"

"If that's what you want."

"And will you take this bit of charcoal and draw a little mustache on your upper lip?"

"If it's really that important to you." She puts on his clothes and etches a mustache on her lip. "Okay?" she says.

"There's just one more thing," he says. "Will you let me call you Frank?"

She gives him an odd look, but says, "Well, all right."

"Great," he says. "Now, let's go for a walk."

They shuffle off down the beach, hand in hand. Suddenly, he stops and faces her. "So, Frank," he says. "Did you hear I'm fucking Cindy Crawford?"

■ ■ ■

WE ALL LAUGH, some of us in relief. Maybe this won't be so bad, I think, delicately adjusting my testicles on the rough-hewn timbers. I know a couple of good jokes, too. Maybe we can limit cocktalk to locker-room humor and discourage wussy confessions of sexual confusion and insecurity. Boasting, weird fantasies, anecdotes about embarrassing public boners—I can get behind that kind of cocktalk.

We should be so lucky. Pleased with the laugh he gets, Griff passes the phallic scepter to the man next to him, Frank, who quickly snuffs out the advancing high spirits. "I don't think about my penis much because there's not much to think about," says Frank. "I wish I had a joke that could make me feel better about what a joke *it* is. I wish I could give it a proud and glorious nickname, but the only thing I can think of is 'Runt.' Particularly compared to this thing." He hands the towering rubber shlong to the next man.

Like everyone else in the room, I sneak a look at the object of Frank's concern and judge it to be of perfectly normal size. So it's not destined for the Smithsonian; it could make some woman perfectly happy—assuming he knows what to do with it.

What is it, lately, with all the emphasis on penis size? Even the staid American Medical Association, which you'd think would have far more critical issues to report on (like, say, the average number of erections produced by one Viagra pill among college-educated widowers with an income above $50,000), recently declared this male neurosis to be "nearly universal." Even David Cassidy ("Donk" to his brothers) and mighty Milton Berle are doubtless concerned that somewhere there's a guy packing a bigger wad than them. (Only LBJ, who used to swim nude in the White House pool and swore aides to secrecy about his longhorn appendage, was pretty sure he was big enough.)

At least part of this anxiety is clearly in response to the "Bigger Is Better" and "It's the Meat *and* the Motion" stories that have been appearing with regular frequency in women's magazines and to the worshipful references to stallionesque boy toys on hip TV shows like

Ally McBeal. The advertising community, never one to shrink from tastelessness, has co-opted the mantras too, devising "Size Counts" campaigns for everything from candy bars to sport utility vehicles. For their part, women used to be fairly circumspect, even kind, on the subject, but after decades of being told by men that there is no such thing as a breast that's too large, it's payback time.

Or, maybe *koro,* an exclusively male psychiatric disorder that, until now, has been confined to Asian men overly worried about their ability to meet the demands of manhood, has spread to America. Symptoms include acute anxiety, palpitations, and a variety of other nervous reactions, but *koro*'s distinguishing characteristic is the belief among the afflicted that the penis is shriveling or retracting into the body. *Koro* sufferers believe that their manhood is literally disappearing. The syndrome is widespread throughout China and most of Southeast Asia, and has affected men in far-flung provinces of Thailand and India. According to Asian psychiatrists who have studied the disorder, the affliction typically appears in young men of "immature, dependent personality who lack confidence in their own virility."

America's version of *koro* causes men to obsess not about a penis that has shrunk but about one that was never majestic enough to begin with. The sequelae of rampant phallomania have resulted in some men trying to attenuate their penises with weights and pulleys hidden in their pants, or stretching them out with vacuum pumps. The obsession has landed thousands of others in the offices of doctors who promise to lengthen it or plump it up with injections of silicone or cellulite—customize it into an organ of towering splendor, albeit one often desensitized by nerve damage. The elongating operation, which involves altering suspensory ligaments and shifting part of the base outside the body, costs about $6,000. In addition to being left with a penis that often pivots at its base, men who undergo the procedure end up with pubic hair growing on the newly exposed part (problems that cancel each other out, the docs say half seriously: if the penis does a one-eighty when erect, the hairy patch would be on the underside, ha, ha). Most of the extra length gained is in the flaccid state; in fact, many men say they just want to look more potent in the locker-room shower. Erect, the surgically enhanced penis boasts an extra inch at best.

The real root, so to speak, of this anxiety reaches deep into evolutionary history. And there is something to it. To evolutionary biologists, a male animal's genitalia work as a courtship device. The penis's distinctive shape, size, or filigree is designed to induce a female not only to mate with him (or not) but to use his sperm instead of his rivals' (or not). If he can somehow encourage contractions or other movements of his partner's reproductive tract, there's a good chance his sperm are going to be moved along toward their target before any others. The females of some species also have glands that need to be activated in order to keep sperm alive once they've been deposited. Of course, that's where a particularly artful penis comes in handy.

In the males of many species—particularly those that reproduce by internal fertilization—the genitalia are the body's most complex structures. Some feature a fantastic array of barbs, spikes, flanges, and nobs. Snails, for instance, are endowed with genitalic darts that they thrust into the female during copulation; the penises of male cats have backwardly directed spines designed to stimulate the female upon withdrawal. Primate penises tend to be the most ornately filigreed in species like the rhesus, the females of which are particularly promiscuous, and less complex in species like the gibbon, in which competition for females is less intense.

What all these fancy penises mean is that a male's reproductive success is not based solely on the number of females he copulates with but whether he can get one of them jazzed up enough with his wonder wand to select his sperm. In using his gametes but not others', she exercises what scientists call "cryptic female choice"—a decision that may be largely influenced by the unique adornments of his genitalia. According to natural selection theory, if enough females favor these proficient swordsmen, their little world will become populated by sons every bit as talented as Dad. William Eberhard, an expert on animal genitalia and a member of the Smithsonian Tropical Research Institute, says this ongoing penis popularity contest can, in theory, "give rise to a runaway process in which males develop increasingly elaborate apparatus and females become increasingly discriminating."

So female choice may explain why men ended up with the largest penis in the primate kingdom: women, perhaps even more than their animal forebears, favor sexually exciting partners. And the men of many of the world's primitive cultures take this competition seriously. In twenty cultures of Southeast Asia, men ritually insert objects like bells, balls, pins, rings, or marbles under the skin of the penis to enhance their sex appeal. In Australia and New Guinea, a number of traditional peoples subincise the penis—cut its underside to make it look wider. The Dyak men of Borneo transect the head of the phallus with a *palang,* a smooth bar with rounded ends made of bone or metal. The To Saloe-maoge women of Sulawesi often demand to know the number of penile marbles a man possesses before they will consider a proposal of marriage. The connubial compact is designed to insure both pleasure and propagation: the better the sex, the greater likelihood of orgasm, which causes contractions that launch sperm toward the fallopian tubes.

It's an old story. Somewhere along the ancestral line, though, women decided six inches or so looked like enough to accomplish this important task. How do we know, despite all the payback in women's magazines, that they really feel this way? Because that's the dimension of most men. If all our mothers preferred men with big hammers, all of us would have one.

So how do we explain the sudden cultural fixation on big penises? And why are many men so unnerved by it? I don't recall that pop idols of my father's generation tucked a sock in their Fruit of the Looms to lure fans backstage (although some, at least, didn't have to: Ava Gardner once commented that of Frank Sinatra's 140 pounds of body weight, 130 pounds were cock). Do women really expect men to resort to surgery in response to their taunts about size—as they did with breast implants?

Probably. By definition, payback is not pretty (think of Lorena Bobbitt). But the withering of the American penis can also be traced to a specific event: the publication in 1969 of an essay by Anne Koedt titled "The Myth of the Vaginal Orgasm." Koedt articulated the feminist implications of the then recent findings of William Masters and Virginia Johnson, the sex researchers who broke with Freudian theory and declared that the clitoris, not the vagina, was the female orgasm's hot button. Koedt, and her feminist sister Susan Lydon ("The Politics of Orgasm"), claimed men—Freud was the chief offender, as always— had long trumped up the "more mature" vaginal orgasm to keep women dependent upon them. Recognition of the clitoral orgasm, Koedt declared in queerly theoretical terms, threatened everything about heterosexuality, for the same sexual pleasure was in fact obtainable from men or women or oneself. Suddenly in competition with the tongue, slow hand, or battery-operated device, the penis, unless it was deployed as a clitoral massage tool or called upon every few years or so to catapult a battalion of sperm into the reproductive tract, might then be considered superfluous, a lowly alternative that was occasionally allowed its pleasure only after all other business had been taken care of.

Ironically, there are signs that the same sexual ideologues who undermined penis power may be encouraging its resurrection. A burgeoning interest in tantric sex, evident in select pockets of gender correctness around the country and on campuses, offers the possibility of closure to this sorry chapter in the history of sexual relations. Authentic tantra emphasizes masturbation techniques and prohibits intercourse, allowing men to be sexual in a nonthreatening way—hence the interest among ideological pointy heads and academics. To give his partner pleasure, a man delivers a two-fingered massage to her *yoni*, a sensitive bundle of enervated tissue halfway between the back of the pubic bone and the cervix, until she collapses into a thirty-minute paroxysm of ecstasy—or so they say.

So what does this have to do with the rehabilitation of the penis? Well, many tantra devotees cheat. Few actually observe the proscription against vaginal penetration, but deploy the techniques to broaden their sexual repertoire. The focus on *yoni*, also known as the elusive and controversial G-spot, means the vagina, after a thirty-year time-out, is back in play, and the penis is again wanted—essential to G-spot stimulation among couples who consider sex a mutual act and, thus, to the thunderous female orgasm. All men need to know this.

Hail to the chief. Welcome back, old friend. Stand up and receive your applause.

You're back in the game.

■ ■ ■

FRANK HANDS OFF to Nate, who, I learned during introductions the day before, owns a small restaurant in Philadelphia. Lean and lanky and goateed, Nate twirls the doingy dick in his fingers like a billy club until Griff quietly reprimands him about phallus abuse. "Johnson," he says. "I call it Johnson. Mr. Johnson, sometimes, when I'm in a respectful mood. I know it's not original or anything, but that's its name."

Nate sits quietly for a moment, staring at the rubber phallus, and then, with a little shrug, begins. "My wife and I have always had a pretty good sex life, nothing too exciting, but all right. A couple years ago, though, she developed endometriosis, which made sex painful for her. So now I consider myself lucky if we have sex, say, once a month. I've tried to get her interested in doing things that don't involve intercourse, but she's just not into it. It's really a drag because what I see is that she really doesn't miss sex with me at all. I wonder if she ever liked it, in fact.

"Where does that leave me? I'm forty, and unwilling to just give it up. I mean, I love sex! I guess if I weren't sitting here surrounded by a bunch of naked men I've never met before and probably will never see after this is over and holding this ridiculous thing, I'd be embarrassed to say this. I've wanted to tell my friends, but . . ." The phallus does a little dance in his hands. "Well, I pay for it. I don't know if anyone else has ever gone to a prostitute, but—" Half the men nod as they give a low wave of the hand, and Nate smiles. "Wow. More than I thought. Well, I just decided not to feel guilty about it. On some level, I think my wife knows and she's okay with it. What's she going to do? What does she expect me to do?"

He shakes his head, his eyes now riveted on the floor. "This is such a relief," Nate says, "just to talk about this. I used to think I felt guilty, but I think I misinterpreted my feelings. I was sorry about my relationship with my wife and happy about what I'd chosen to do. I pay a lot of money to get laid, I use only high-end call girls, and I have to say . . ." He laughs. "It's great! Every encounter is a fantasy come true. I mean, Griff tells the joke about the guy and Cindy Crawford . . . well, I live that life, at least as far as the sex goes. Twice a week, a drop-dead gorgeous woman who will do anything I ask. You all should try it.

"I guess if there's a downside to my sex life, it's that, you know, there's no lid on where it can go. I'm like a kid in the proverbial candy store. But that's a downside I can live with! Like, I've always had this fantasy about being with two women at once. So if you pay for sex like I do, it's easy to live the fantasy. All you have to do is pay twice as much. So I did. And it was weird, but, again, interesting! A little voice inside me says I should feel guilty, but I don't. It was fucking great!"

Nate, again twirling the phallic billy club, looks up from the floor. All eyes, wild with jealousy, are fixed on him. "But here's something I can't get out of my mind," he goes on. "Now I want the two girls to have sex with each other, while they're having it with me. I've tried to figure out what this means. Am I gay? I don't think so. Perverted? Definitely, but aren't we all? If anyone has any insights into this when it's their turn to talk, I'd appreciate hearing them."

I wonder if there are any proprietors of "adult" video stores here, because they could easily assuage Nate's fears—not that he seems terribly tormented by them. All men—straight ones, anyway—are aroused by the idea of two women diddling each other, hence the ubiquity of lesbian entanglements in porn films. According to the people who study such things, men engage with the fantasy at levels that range from active to voyeuristic. Some, like Nate, arrange an actual ménage à trois—the activity, second to oral sex, most frequently requested of prostitutes, in fact. Others consciously boot up the fantasy to aid arousal—while masturbating, say. Even buttoned-up types who have never spontaneously run the scenario across the back of their eyes turn out, during psychological experiments, to be stirred by pictures of two gals *in flagrante*. Male fascination with female coupling is so universal, in fact, that some researchers consider an erotic response to lesbian sex a reliable diagnosis of heterosexuality.

Although Nate's favorite lesbian vignette may have some personal nuances, its script probably adheres to a universal formula. Most lesbian-sex fantasies proceed sequentially: at first, the encounter is exclusively between the women, with a man (the proprietor of the fantasy) looking on. Later, the lucky girls are joined by a male participant—the fantasizer, perhaps. The mood in the boudoir is blissful and generous: no one expresses jealousy or possessiveness, there's a lot of sexual sharing, and no one feels excluded. The beauty of the lesbian-sex triangle is that it's actually a twofer: it encompasses the second most common male fantasy, that of the ever available, instantly lubricious woman who has no sexual needs of her own. In this vignette there are, happily, two of them.

Like most fantasies, this one offers an end run around inhibitions and fears and reverses reality. In psychoanalytic terms, it's known as a classic "Adam" fantasy: it's a way of being the only man in the world. The fantasy enables "Adam" to defeat and eliminate all other competitive men, and provides him with his own harem. He's the only game in town.

Not surprisingly, this preoccupation with triadic sex originates with an underlying anxiety about potency, and the fantasy, in the wonderful way fantasies work, resolves it. Observing the entangled women, a man first fears that he's redundant—the gals seem perfectly capable of getting all hot and bothered without him. But, asked to join in the fun, he finds that only his manly powers can truly satisfy them. The women not only thrill to his magical ministrations but protect him from any lingering sense of inadequacy by doing some of the heavy lifting for him—pleasing each other—and easing his performance burden.

The fantasy provides gratification at just about every level of the mind (one reason it's high on the Top Ten list). Probe deeper, and you find that one of the women is often significantly older than the other. No mystery here: the scenario also offers a safe way to experience the forbidden delights of incest, even though in some scenarios the maternal figure is represented as (horrors!) a mother-in-law. And among all those rivals you've vanquished to ascend to this very special love nest is a certain other powerful parental figure. Finally, the fantasy enables men to tweak a couple of other taboos: their own unconscious feminine identification and homosexual desires. Again, the fact that the sex partners are lesbians offers a reassuringly safe remove from these threatening psychic conundrums.

That's the deal, Nate. Like every other man's, so much of your brain is devoted to converting sexual signals into arousal that you're getting more for your money than you thought.

■ ■ ■

THE FAT PHALLUS quickly passes through the hands of three men, all of whom decline to speak, before settling in the clutches of Steve, a tanned, fit, thirty-five-ish lawyer from Chicago. "The Mayor," says Steve. "I call it the Mayor, because it seems so authoritarian."

Steve's eyes focus on the middle distance, somewhere between the floor and the naked gonads of the men sitting on the other side of the circle. "What do I mean by that?" he says in a sharp, nasal tenor, self-dialoguing like a trial attorney. "I mean that my dick rules, it's got a mind of its own, and it's hard to satisfy. It's a real taskmaster."

Steve examines the meaty, artificial wad in his hands. "Let me just throw this out," he says. "Does anyone here masturbate?" Most of the men wave affirmatively. "I do. I'm married, and during some periods I jerk off every day. Sometimes twice a day. Sometimes after having sex with my wife. Sometimes after crawling into bed late at night, with my wife sound asleep beside me. Has anyone else ever done that?" A few hands flutter. "I always wondered whether it meant I was nuts or normal. I mean, there I am in bed with my wife, with whom I have a good sex life, fantasizing about having sex with her."

The data would say that Steve is pretty close to normal. More than three quarters of men in happy, sexually gratifying marriages regularly go solo. Even sexual icons like rock stars and professional athletes, who get to live out the real-life fantasy of being surrounded by ever-available sex kittens, opt for solipsistic sex every now and then. Dennis Rodman, who claims women are as sexually available to him as oxygen, admits to an ongoing relationship with Judy (his right hand) and Monique (his left). (Not that Worm would fit anybody's definition of close to normal . . .) There are three oft-touted excuses for men's penchant for narcissistic pleasure. First, our pressure-cooked sex drive requires constant ventilation. Second, masturbation ensures future potency: in its compact traveling state, a penis is oxygen-starved; erect, it's transfused with nutrient-rich blood, its tissues fortified to rise to future challenges. And third, handling yourself when it's inconveniently late is an act of supreme solicitude. As Norman Mailer once pointed out, one of a man's most important contributions to a successful marriage is making sure his wife is well rested.

Steve's concern isn't surprising, given masturbation's notorious past. For many of us, the guilt inculcated by centuries of prohibition and taboo is rooted as deeply as a racial memory. In 1758, in *Onania, or a Treatise upon the Disorders Produced by Masturbation,* the Swiss physician S. A. Tissot lofted the idea that solo sex leads to insanity. Benjamin Rush, the father of American psychiatry, corroborated this zany notion by observing that "self-pollution" caused poor vision, memory loss, dizziness, epilepsy, and a host of other ills. By the 1800s, doctors discerned a link between masturbation and rich and spicy foods, which "increase the excitability and sensibility of the genital organs." Sensing a huge marketing opportunity, John Harvey Kellogg, who remained chaste during his marriage but spawned the world's cereal industry, developed cornflakes to inhibit the base desires that tempt men when they're alone. Well into the Dr. Spock era, the AMA was still roundly denouncing solo sex—when it wasn't editorializing about penis-size anxiety.

For most boys, a little self-diddling comes as second nature. Babies often pull on their penises while nursing or when they need to soothe themselves. Later, in anxious adolescence, masturbation provides passage to a psychic realm boys feel safe in—their own. Most adult men continue to revisit this private Idaho.

Shrinks say that for some men, solo sex is a way of asserting independence. To the extent that a man loses himself in a woman during sex, masturbation allows him to define his body, etch it in relief, and reassure himself that he's still intact. More prosaically, self-love sometimes offers an affirmation that no one else can. If a man has suffered a financial blow or a hit at work, he may seek comfort by taking himself as a kind of love object.

In these love-strained times, someone's got to do it.

■ ■ ■

WE'RE ROLLING NOW. The phallus has moved only halfway around the circle of men, and already we've covered lesbian fantasies, masturbation, the vaginal orgasm, and whoring. The attention level is high, Griff looks pleased, the lid is off. Cocktalk is fun. Who says women have a richer erotic life?

The scepter arrives in the hands of Jack, a thirty-eight-year-old programmer. His pleasant, round face slowly compresses into a pained, pinched expression as his fingers fret over the rubber organ. He seems unable to decide whether to pass it on. "I relate to everything that's been said here," he says finally, stammering a little. "Actually, it's kind of reassuring to learn that other men have this stuff going on too, these ways of looking at sex. This is good for me, you know, because I too have often wondered: Am I normal?"

We wait patiently. Something interesting is coming at us. Jack's conflict is visible; he clearly wants to unload, but he struggles. "I don't know which category this falls into, so I'll just say it, confess it, and someone else can talk about it more if they like. Sometimes I wear women's underwear—usually my wife's, though she doesn't know it. It's just something I do." He looks up, trolling for affirmative waves, his face reddening as the men stare blankly, and passes the phallic baton to the man next to him. Then he retrieves it. "I don't know why, or have any insights into it, I just do. It makes me feel good."

He hands the phallus along again, but quickly grabs it back. "The only thing I can say is that women's underwear makes me feel special. In case you were wondering, you know, why. I'm not gay or anything."

Hmm. Is Jack exhibiting the male equivalent of penis envy? Is there such a thing? It's tempting to look to transvestites for clues. The great majority of cross-dressers are high-achieving married men with children—and dedicated heterosexuals (RuPaul and a certain former FBI chief being notable exceptions). Shrinks say the cross-dresser's core fantasy is of a world made up of women, some of whom, like himself, have a penis. In this exclusive realm, liberated from oedipal threats and competitive males, he's allowed to achieve an intimacy with women denied most men. But like women who fantasize about possessing a dick for a day, the cross-dresser's fantasy is all about potency: disguised in his pumps and decolletage, secretly harboring an engine of male power in his silky undies, he feels even more mighty than he does in his loaded Power Wagon with the cab-mounted gun rack.

So when Jack stuffs his bag lunch into the side pocket of his laptop carrying case, loads his pens into his pocket protector, and heads off to his cubicle with his love stick surreptitiously packed into his wife's La Perla, he feels like a special boy, a very powerful special boy.

Women's underwear excites some already hypersensitive neurons in the male sexual arousal grid. I can relate to Jack, to his fondness for female undergarments (although wearing them would do nothing for me, I *think*), which is why I respond to his comments with a sympathetic wave. (Let the others think what they may.) When it's my turn, to make him feel better I might tell him that when I feel a little low I cruise the intimate apparel departments, too. Lost amid a surfeit of sexy thingies, each one destined to trace a lovely rondure of breast, thigh, or buttock, I feel my spirits soar like the selvage of a skimpy silk chemise. Holding one up, a size ten, I admire its filigreed trimmings and clever infrastructure, smile at the special-boy status it confers, and picture its fit. *Just so.*

A friend of mine buys his wife's shoes. This requires far more courage—or confidence—than that needed to procure a Saturday-night teddy at Saks. His spouse prefers sensible walking shoes and those hideous brown-soled, black canvas Petunia Pig pods imported from Korea. He sees her in sandals with straps that climb halfway up her calf, snakeskin flats, pumps. Decorum prohibits our discussing when it is that she wears the spiky heels, though we both know. He's willing to brook the snickers at the checkout counter to have his way with their erotic life.

My friend and I are a little fetishistic—and proudly so. We're aroused by dressing up our mates and—like most men, whose partialism makes them, in the parlance of a cruder era, ass, leg, or tit men—would admit to a fondness for a particular zone of their bodies. We're lower on the fetish spectrum than someone who snatches women's undies off a clothesline or steals a single shoe out of a sidewalk bin to covet in private—or from Marla Maples's former publicist, who was caught on videotape sniffing and licking his boss's high heels. (The police later found thirty pairs of her shoes and seventeen pairs of her boots—so who really had the obsession with footwear?—in his apartment, along with a copy of *Spike*, a foot-fetish porn magazine.) But, on an elemental level, we can identify.

Fetishes are one entry in a class of sexual behaviors called paraphilias. Paraphiliacs are dependent upon unusual, narrowly focused, or forbidden stimuli to achieve arousal. There are many paraphilias, ranging from frotteurism (compulsively rubbing up against strangers) to acrotomophilia (an attraction to amputees). Most are characterized by an obsession with a particular visual stimulus, but their most striking feature is that they are an almost exclusively male phenomenon. The rare paraphilia in women almost always involves subjugation and bondage, reflecting the female dependency on a sense of touch, even a rough touch, to achieve genital arousal and orgasm.

Fetish culture opens a revealing window upon the sad state of contemporary male sexual psychology. Classic objects of obsession, such as rubber, shoes, or even President Clinton's alleged thing for "big hair," are now considered artless by New Wave fetishists. Trendy paraphiliacs include "crush fetishists," who thrill to the sight of women stomping everything from food to cigarettes and insects; "microphiliacs," who imagine their sex partner reduced to the size of a Lilliputian; and "infantilists," who beg to be diapered and experience the liberating joy of total incontinence. The link among the new obsessions: a fear and awe of Superwoman and a desire to relinquish total power to her. That and, as one aficionado explains, "the opportunity to express sexuality without having sex." Even fetishists, obsessed with sex, withhold.

The origins of such behavior? Here's one theory: Tickling his erect penis, a toddler scans his environment, focuses upon rubber ducky, his sister's Barbie, Mom's big hair—or just Big Bad Mom. From his perspective, he also sees a lot of his mother's shoes and legs (sometimes deliciously pulverizing a bug). Lacking a mature concept of sexuality, his primitive noggin develops a bizarre association: *Whatever boosts my erection must have sexual significance.* (The lack of an equivalent hydraulic response in girls may account for their lack of such fetishistic learning.) Researchers have duplicated this response in the laboratory. In a classic experiment, they showed men pictures of boots followed by pictures of naked women. Using a plethysmograph, a device that measures blood flow in the penis, they found that the subjects soon became aroused when shown the boots alone. The incredibly plastic male brain can learn to associate sexual arousal with anything—even, it seems, a paralyzing dread of powerful women.

Physiology kicks in, too: brain researchers now know that oxytocin, a powerful peptide that seems to be around during moments of intense bonding, also floods the male brain during orgasm. The chemical not only stimulates sex drive but also produces feelings of attachment—to a mate, a baby . . . or a bug-crushing Joan and David snakeskin pump. Add a dose of anxiety and shyness, which most hard-cores tend toward, and you end up with some mixing of the signals that usually cause arousal.

Another key male talent is at work here: the spatial skills we evolved as hunters and builders probably contribute to our voyeurish dependency on visual stimuli for sexual arousal. For the fetishist, visual foreplay lengthens this natural remove. As psychiatrist Robert Stoller observed about the paraphiliac's levels of dissociation, "A fetish is a story masquerading as an object"—but it's a story with no surprises. Control over the highly nuanced plot is everything. To bring a satisfying end to the sexual experience, for instance, some fetishists have to pay their sexual partners—even their wives.

Fortunately, most of us aren't as perturbed by our wiring as hard-core fetishists. We have will, we can make choices—choose to integrate our narrow focus on the fragment, on the Saturday-night teddy, into a richer, more sophisticated erotic life. This was apparent to Georges Braque, who, along with his cubist buddy, Pablo Picasso, happened to possess extraordinary spatial skills. One afternoon the two artists saw a pair of black lace undies in a French lingerie shop, which

Braque promptly purchased. "Are they for your mistress?" asked Picasso, a tireless philanderer. "No, for my wife," said Braque. "That's what makes them interesting."

．．．

BEN, A THIRTY-TWO-YEAR-OLD patent attorney, examines the phallus. "I've really got nothing to contribute," he says, smiling unnaturally. "I've been divorced for six months, and haven't had sex for at least a year before that." He laughs skittishly. "I've just had a completely uneventful sex life—I was a virgin when I got married—and now I'm thinking, listening to the rest of you, that maybe that's why I'm single. I'm just boring. Maybe I should buy some panties."

Ben turns to Jeremy, a pale, freckled man sitting next to him, and holds the rubber phallus up to the man's mouth as though it's a microphone. "The man in the street," Ben says nervously. "Perhaps he knows sexual secrets that will change my life and turn me into Superstud." Shifting into the robotic tonality of a television broadcaster's voice, he adds, "Tonight, at six and eleven!"

A small wave of charitable laughter ripples through the room. "No abusing the phallus," Griff warns softly.

Apparently emboldened by Griff's admonition, Jeremy swipes the phallus from Ben and lowers it to his knee. A crimson flush spreads from his neck to his cheeks. "I don't appreciate your holding that thing up to my mouth," he says, his voice quavering. "What is there about me that made you do that?"

"Hey, come on, man, it was a joke," says Ben. "You know, a dick-shaped microphone. All reporters should have one."

"But what were you trying to tell me?"

"Trying to tell you? In a jokey way, that it's your turn."

"It didn't seem *jokey*. It was hostile."

"Oh, Jesus . . ."

"You held a fat cock up to my mouth and expected me to do something to it. Right?"

"I expected you to take it. And talk. Or pass it on."

"Or suck it. Right? You did it because you think I'm gay."

"What?"

"You think I'm gay."

Ben, now a little angry himself—he's got all that libidinal energy stored up, after all—leans away from his neighbor, and the two men, naked and uncomfortable on the splintery floor, lock eyes. "I hadn't really thought about it," he says. "But, hey, I don't mean to steal your thunder. If this was going to be your big coming out or something, your announcement to the world . . ."

We all look at Griff, hoping he'll put an end to this before Jeremy morphs into Jonathan Schmitz, the guy who, in 1996, was convicted of blasting two shotgun shells through the chest of a gay man who had admitted on television to harboring a secret crush on him. Following the murder trial, the killer's father announced his plans to sue the show's host, Jenny Jones, for creating what he called "this unnecessary, unreasonable, negligent risk." Just what risk was he talking about? That his son, like any "normal" man, would respond to the sensitive news, indelicately delivered on a tawdry talk show, with a burst of homophobic rage.

Griff picks up the vibe and responds. "We've had plenty of gay men here and they feel very comfortable," he says uneasily. This is the last thing, of course, Jeremy wants to hear. Fuming, he slaps the phallus in Ben's lap, gets up, grabs his clothes, and leaves.

I'm sure everyone in the room is thinking the same thing: repressed homosexual. Or maybe he's just homophobic. Which often means, according to a research paper I looked at recently, just about the same thing.

In that study, researchers tried to learn whether homophobic men are more sexually aroused by homosexual cues than nonhomophobic men. The researchers recruited sixty-four white male heterosexuals between eighteen and thirty-one years old and measured their aggressiveness and their scores on the seven-point Kinsey Heterosexual-Homosexual Rating Scale, which grades sexual preference and experience from exclusively heterosexual (1) to exclusively homosexual (7). The participants were also measured by the Index of Homophobia, which quantifies a person's "dread" when placed in close proximity to a gay man.

The cues consisted of four-minute segments of explicit erotic videotapes depicting heterosexual activity and both male and female homosexual acts. Arousal was measured by a mercury-in-rubber strain gauge attached to the base of the penis that detects erectile response and records it on a computer. The study's findings: three quarters of the participants characterized as homophobic showed moderate to definite tumescence while viewing the homosexual video, compared to only a third of nonhomophobic men. Curiously, the homophobes' subjective ratings of erection and arousal were low—they didn't think, or at least admit, that they had been aroused.

The findings confirm anecdotal evidence and conjecture that's circulated in clinical literature for years: homophobia is the result of repressed homosexual urges or a form of latent homosexuality. "Men who are upset by being around gay men probably have these tendencies themselves," the investigators concluded. "The thing you dislike most in yourself is the kind of thing you might jump on somebody else for."

■ ■ ■

GRIFF SUGGESTS WE all stand, shake our limbs out, and chase the vile energy from the room. The remaining nineteen of us, each with two nasty red blotches on his butt, pull ourselves to our feet and stretch out. "Sex can be a pretty loaded topic," he says, "and we just witnessed a good reason not to keep our fears and worries about it inside us. It can be very liberating to let them out. I hope Jeremy returns." I'm not sure the rest of us do, though.

After we again settle on the floor, Ben, still holding the phallus, politely hands it to a tall man with thick, white hair and handsome, chiseled features. "I'm Jayson," he says, "and I don't have a name for my penis, but I guess I could, with a lot of justification, call it Trouble."

He sighs. "I have to admit, I feel a little foolish here. My wife signed me up for this and threatened to make a federal case of it if I didn't go, so here I am. I didn't plan on saying anything but all you guys have been so honest it seems wrong not to. I run a multimillion-dollar company, which I started by myself, I work all the time, and I've never really had any hang-ups about sex."

He pauses. "But that, I suppose, is my problem. In my wife's eyes it surely is: I've slept with maybe a hundred women. My wife knows of a few, and each one has broken her heart. It makes no difference to her when I say that it's just meaningless sex, it's just, like, a release, it's recreation.

"I'd like to stop, but honest to God, it's a compulsion, like working. A psychiatrist I saw once told me plain: I'm a sex addict. Well, no kidding! Then he sent me a bill for his brilliant diagnosis. I really don't know what's behind this need. Do any of the rest of you feel this way?"

Well, sometimes I do, but not every day. How grueling must that be? I wonder what Jayson's hormonal profile looks like. In professional athletes, testosterone, the principal male hormone and the libido's nuclear plant, rises in anticipation of competition, and rises further following a victory. Experts theorize that professional athletes' hormone levels may rise as their careers unfold because of the constant surges of testosterone. A feedback loop takes over, accounting for phenomena like extended winning streaks: each win reinforces a high T level, which in turn promotes further competitiveness—and a sex drive that puts up numbers like those achieved by Wilt Chamberlain and Magic Johnson.

It doesn't take much imagination to see the parallels between pro athletes and the greenmailers, CEOs, and media moguls who slam-dunk mega-mergers through the Federal Trade Commission. Many of these men have what shrinks call a hyperthymic temperament. Men who fit the description are indefatigable, extroverted risk takers who tend to run the world. They need very little sleep and have extremely active, and often promiscuous, sex lives. (A certain leader of the free world comes to mind.) Contrary to what makes sense to the rest of us, the overachieving men's lack of sleep may be what contributes most to their hyperactive sex drive.

Scientists know that animals deprived of rapid-eye-movement sleep, which occurs four to six times a night in most people and is associated with dream sleep, show dramatic increases in drive-oriented behaviors. They develop a greater appetite and interest in pursuing prey, and become more aggressive and hypersexual. Very few human studies have been done, but one showed that men deprived of REM sleep display an obsessional interest in sexual imagery. (Depressives, whose symptoms include a loss of libido, can effectively restore sex drive by depriving themselves of sleep.) Most REM sleep occurs in the second half of the sleep cycle, long after most world-beaters, who pride themselves on getting three or four hours of sleep each night, have awakened.

Perhaps, though, Jayson is driven to succeed—and to mate promiscuously—because of a "narcissistic injury," a sense he developed in childhood that he's loved only when he overachieves. I'm mulling this over when, inevitably, the cock comes a'courting, and it's my turn to talk.

■ ■ ■

SO WHAT DO I SAY? I'm the last in the circle of men and feel an obligation to end on an uplifting note. For a moment, I consider offering a prayer of thanks to the god of love for making me a heterosexual, so that I can devote so much of my cerebral downtime to contemplating the mystery of female sexuality. Homosexual men often claim their sex lives are better than heteros' because they know exactly what to do to each other—which is why I would find the life boring. The challenge of cracking the female erotic code—"cryptic female choice"— which, even in a long-familiar mate is subject to constant rejiggering, can goose a man's libido for a lifetime.

I wonder how many of the cocktalkers think women, as the mythical Greek seer Tiresias declared after spending a few years as a female, really get more from love? Many of us who have done our personal research happily bow to and honor women's superiority in the sustained-ecstasy competition. I count myself among them. The volunteer in my boudoir laboratory describes sex as something that just happens to her. "It's like the ocean," she says, "and it just rolls over you." I can see, during those liquid erotic moments, that something very transformative is going on, but I also have to take her word for it: when it comes to oceanic experience of the sexual variety, I spend most of my time on terra firma.

Which is not to say I'd swap my physiology for hers. I think I could successfully argue that Tiresias had it wrong: men have more sex and more orgasms than women, who generally don't climax during every sexual encounter (on average, about a third of the time). Personally, I'd take quantity over quality any day. But then, I don't really know what I'm missing. I'm curious about that oceanic sense of merging that sexually sophisticated women often describe as the peak erotic experience. I wonder what it would be like, just once, to be an aroused Lady Chatterley, who was "like the sea, nothing but dark waves rising and heaving, heaving with a great swell, so that slowly her whole darkness was in motion . . . till suddenly, in a soft, shuddering convulsion, the quick of her plasm was touched . . . and she was gone."

Like most men on the brink of ecstasy—whether in nature's cathedral, while channeling God, or in the swelter of the bedroom—I retreat to the safety of cozy and familiar psychic bunkers, while women plunge ahead toward transcendence and the unknown, willing to run the risk, as D. H. Lawrence said, of "shedding into oblivion." The mere thought of a roiling Chatterley-like voyage on the sea of love is enough to provoke in most men a severe bout of mal de mer. Why? Well, to be subsumed by the oceanic requires a certain receptiveness and passivity, qualities not routinely stockpiled in the masculine cargo hold (save, perhaps, among the new generation of withholders). We're also particularly sensitive to issues of control, as in we don't like to lose it. Perhaps the biggest reason, though, is that men respond to the oceanic, to naked contact with "the inorganic condition from which life arose," as female. Giving yourself up to it jeopardizes your essential manliness.

This reticence prevailed even among some of the early twentieth century's deeper thinkers, such as Lawrence, Carl Jung, and André Gide, who were infatuated with primitive culture, which they considered a gateway to the oceanic. Each of these men had journeyed to Africa or the South Pacific seeking renewal and relief from psychic distress and cultural alienation. Yet, at crucial moments, each man's desire to merge with "primordial beginnings" gave way to a fear of being swallowed up by "Mother" Nature. Gide, swooning from sensory overload as he felt the "delicious" power of the subcontinent "closing over me," nonetheless worked desperately to collect his wits amid "this strange excitement." Jung, who saw the African landscape as the embodiment of "maternal mystery"—even the geographical site of the unconscious—finally concluded that "the primitive was a danger to me" and that "my European personality must under all circumstances be preserved intact."

Of course, self-preservation in the presence of maternal power—or as psychoanalysts would say, the "devouring vagina"—is a familiar theme in male psychology. Faced with the opportunity to transcend their narrow and prissy European states of mind at least momentarily, Gide and Jung chose to short-circuit ecstasy with a kind of psychic premature ejaculation.

A lot of us do this, it seems, in the bedroom, too. Like these gentlemen's flirtations with the maternal mysteries, we find women's sexuality both fascinating and overwhelming. (I mean, they can have an

orgasm while giving birth! How mystifying, and cool, is that?) For
men, getting in touch with the primitive means a quick hump out-
doors, or slipping between the sheets while still sweaty after a run.
Truly great sex is in a way voyeuristic—it's all about pleasing her,
about urging her carefully toward the water's edge, so the quick of her
plasm can be touched, and, for a moment, as we revel in our ability to
unleash a power we can only marvel at, we can watch her disappear.

On one level, this makes us generous lovers. Observing and, if your
hands are in the right places, feeling your partner momentarily escape
her corporal boundaries is one of the truly great joys of sex. But part of
our motivation to get her off is selfish: one of the utilitarian aspects of
the female orgasm is the boost it gives men's egos. Another drive is at
work here as well: effective sexual technique is self-perpetuating. Her
cries of pleasure and release are a signal that you've done all you can
to propel your genome into the next generation.

The Jewish law of *onah* demands that a husband keep his wife sexually satisfied. But some of us insist on her satisfaction whether she
wants it or not and sometimes get angry when our special ministrations evoke only a fainthearted response. At such moments, the activity often becomes frantic and frictional, grinding to a halt only after
that most ignominious of deceptions is deployed: the faked orgasm.

What motivates the compulsive pleaser, who can't take "It's just not
happening tonight, dear" for an answer? A narcissistic anxiety that
he'll be considered unmanly if she doesn't come, for starters. But his
persistence is also a clever, sexually correct variation on a familiar but
ugly theme: the control of women's sexuality. He may be in awe of the
supernatural female orgasm, but he still wants to maintain the right to
release or contain it—whenever he likes.

Occasionally, I contemplate telling the naked men who surround
me, I'm guilty of pursuing sex as a power trip. And at peak moments, I
worry about how quickly I'll be able to have it again. And so what is
that? An overweening need for affirmation like Griff's? A compulsion
like Jayson's? A reaction against anhedonia? An emotional disconnect?
Or is it simply a base manly desire to control the female libido as men
have done for so many thousands of years?

My head hurts. For every cocktalker's obsession, for every sad-sack
confession, I've got a quirky and colorful and worldly wise explanation. But now, as I clutch the symbol of this instantly corruptible thing

I've come to identify as the male sex drive, I'm brought low by simple disgust. For one thing, can men really talk about sex only while gripping some outsize fantasy (for most of us) of an erect penis? And for another, isn't it better just not to talk about it at all? One of the inherent liabilities of the ancient resources-for-sex arrangement is that our arousal apparatus remains forever base and primitive, so no matter how clever a spin we put on it, we end up acting like jerks during the final negotiations. We'll do anything to get laid, so we develop easy associations—between sex and eating, sex and fighting, sex and shoes—so that we never have to worry about being understimulated. The possibility of sexual reward looms as the backdrop to almost everything we do, motivating our behavior toward not just women but each other—our fellow hostile forces of nature. Like size anxiety, it's an old story: the Greeks and Trojans managed to spin out their rivalry over Helen for nearly a decade, forever cementing their reputations as possessive, sex-mad fools in need of a few therapeutic hours of cocktalk. Clearly, they weren't any better at putting sex in perspective than those of us who feel compelled to confess our sexual weaknesses to a phallus.

Is there a standup guy in the house? Not in this one, it seems. I and my naked confrères are all too obsessed with our own variations on kink. So where is he? Certainly not among our supposed leaders in Washington, where gangs of elected philanderers, even those outed by *Hustler* (which reflects the most repulsive dimensions of the male sexual brain), have tried to bring down a president for covering up the sex they all have. They belong here with us, naked and twitchy on the splintery floor.

Meanwhile, what can I report to Kate and her pals, other than that sex—even sex withheld—obsesses men in much more complicated ways than they might think and that standup behavior, at least in bed, is not easy to define? I hate to endorse the bitchfesters' view that men fall into two categories—dicks or assholes. Are these really our only choices?

Before we decide, it helps to understand the distinction.

I'M A WHAT?

. . .

THE OTHER NIGHT, my wife and I attended a dinner party with the three men with whom I play squash every week and their spouses. My partners and I make an odd group, with little in common aside from our love of smashing a ball against a wall. Maybe we're typical of the kind of eclectic unions formed at big-city university gymnasiums by devoted alumni and professors. Pat, the youngest at twenty-six, is a shy (but on the court, rabidly competitive) research physicist whose wife, Gretchen, just completed her MBA. Joe, at fifty-two the oldest but fittest, is a pension-fund investment manager; his wife, Bonnie, is a financial analyst at a pharmaceutical company. Don and Julie are both art professors in their early thirties; my wife and I are journalists. We all have children. Over the past few years, the dinner party has become an annual event, rotating among the partners' homes, but this time the gathering had a dual purpose: we were also saying good-bye to Don and Julie, who were leaving New York to share a job at a college in rural North Carolina.

This was supposed to be a night of celebration, but instead I'd end up with new and depressing insights into how the toxic forces of correctness that have made the recent battles of the gender war particularly bloody also poison men's relations with each other—particularly those between men who are under pressure to conform to new and often unrealistic gender codes and men who resist them. After being identified as a card-carrying member of the resistance, I'd also come to understand why so many women—particularly younger women—quickly dismiss men as either bossy and selfish or dependent and weak, but in either case misogynist. Or, in the locution of the bitch-festers, as either assholes or dicks. Despite my loyalty to the manly camp, I'd also see that they have some legitimate gripes, and that the standup manqué, if he wants to be a player in the new world, should listen up. It would turn out to be a long night.

Although I see these men almost every week, I can't say I've gotten to know them terribly well over the seven or eight years we've been sparring with one another. Our interactions consist largely of trying to outmaneuver one another on the court, contest a "let" call, or apologize for whacking one another in the face after following through a little too strongly on a backhand. Yet I do know a lot about each man's character. I know who will fight to the last point even when deep in the hole, who will tank when far behind, who will play more fiercely when hurt, who will deploy squash "rope-a-dope"—feign fatigue or muscle strain to lure his partner into a sympathetic stupor, then roar back in the fifth game. The verbal exchanges are mostly confined to the five minutes of warm-up preceding the match and the postgame deferrals and analysis. In the beginning, chatting with Pat was particularly challenging: his massive brain seemed too crowded with equations governing the behavior of skittish leptons, quarks, and cosmic rays for social bantering, although he has since opened up. As the senior members of the group, Joe and I have an easy, genial relationship. We brag about our children, some of whom are the same ages, and discuss, increasingly, our various injuries and crackpot schemes for staying healthy.

Recently, though, Don has violated the unspoken pact that prohibits discussion of anything too personal or serious. He's frequently turned to me during those five-minute warm-ups for advice—about buying real estate, asking the chairman of his department for a raise and better housing, and, not long before he announced his move, about how to handle a particularly sensitive marriage issue. Our friendship has quietly evolved from a casual sporting acquaintance to something deeper and more intimate. Or, until the dinner party, so I'd thought.

I'm not sure why Don chose to confide in me about his marriage. Most men I know are extremely chary about talking about their spouse—much more so than women are. Men can unload upon a best friend, a mentor, or someone with a professional remove like a shrink, but male decorum prohibits revealing marital secrets to casual buddies. Naturally, I'd like to think Don chose me because of my extraordinary wisdom and experience: as a father of five, including two stepchildren, and a partner in a good marriage, how could I not know something? Perhaps my selection had to do with the fact that I lived outside the hypersensitive academic environment in which he labored. Whatever the reason, Don apparently felt comfortable revealing to me sentiments he dared not voice at home or to prickly campus colleagues, who often traffic in rhetoric rather than in plain truths.

Julie was unhappy, Don had told me during those warm-ups, often picking up the conversation as we stretched and showered after the match. She had a lousy job at a small state college in New Jersey, and a two-year search had turned up nothing better within commuting distance. Recently, she had widened her sights and found something for both of them at a small school in North Carolina. Figuring it would never pan out, or that even if it did they would ultimately decide not to leave the city, Don got involved with the interview process and let the whole fantasy spin out of control. Now, officials at the college, realizing they might be able to poach an academic star—Don—had offered them a deal that amounted to their sharing a department chairmanship with another half-job thrown in. Julie was ecstatic. She just assumed Don would resign his tenured position at New York University—one of the most prestigious jobs he could ever hope to have in the rarefied art world—give up his connection to the New York museums and his publishing contacts, and take a three-quarters position in a remote second-tier school. He loved his wife and, like most men, felt it was partly his responsibility to make her happy, but thought maybe she was asking too much of him. On the other hand, this was a dilemma a lot of married academics faced. He asked me what I would do.

Don's question was the equivalent of what hockey players call a screw-your-buddy pass. On your way into the offensive zone, your linemate sadistically or just stupidly passes the puck to you as you cut in front of an opposing defenseman, who plants his feet and tries to graft his shoulder onto your solar plexus as you lower your head to catch the puck. There was no way I could handle Don's screw-your-buddy question and remain on my feet. Lined up behind him was a squadron of ever vigilant sex-police referees ready to hit me with a life misconduct were I to suggest that Julie was making an unreasonable demand and they should find another solution to her discontent that didn't involve his having to sacrifice his very happening job so that she could have a better one. And I'm not sure I really believed that, anyway. What do I know about their life together, the difficulties of dual academic careers—about the intricate and intimate calculus of another man's marriage? So I said something about how every marriage requires a lot of give and take, that compromise cuts in both directions, and it's pretty hard for both partners always to get what each wants. And then I suggested we play squash.

Cut to the dinner party. Joe and I are talking about our teenage daughters, the specific topic curfews. It turns out Joe is more lenient by a half hour than I am. Don, who has been quiet all evening and appears, in fact, depressed, looks up from his plate of lasagne and says, "That's because Mike is an asshole and Joe isn't." My food catches in my throat. Uncomfortable laughter ripples through the dining room. "Don't hide your feelings, Don," Joe finally quips, trying to banish the nasty vibes from his dinner party. "Just let 'em rip." My wife leans back in her chair and throws me a look: *What was that all about?*

Good question. Did he insult me because I'd won our last three matches? (He was packing for his move and had a good excuse.) Because my wife was not only an independent modern woman but has described herself as "one of the last man-worshippers"? Because he had begun to see me as a confidante and mentor, and now, as he was leaving town, he had to ritually murder me? Because he was depressed? Or was it because he suspected I didn't approve of his decision to ditch a prestigious gig at a prestigious university so that his wife, who had a mediocre job, could have a better one? Because I thought he had made the wrong decision, one that might ultimately harm his marriage more than he could have predicted? Or because, finally, he agreed with me, and it was easier for him to project his anger onto me?

I'd bet this last surmise is closest to the truth. This is what men do with messy inner conflict, after all—they fling it out into the world and hope it sticks to someone else. And in some ways, he's right: I wouldn't have made the decision he did, and I know my wife wouldn't have asked me to. Perhaps, after calculating the pluses and minuses, he felt it made more sense to go. Many men, after all, are trying to put family before work. And he did say he would like to have more time to write; I don't know the result of the final arithmetic. But I do know that I didn't particularly enjoy being called an asshole before my friends—and by someone I thought a friend—because of a presumed difference in sexual politics.

Gender ideology has become so murky that women are no longer the only ones to attack men as assholes. Some men, particularly those under pressure to embody some hopelessly flexible paradigm of "reform" masculinity, are leading the charge.

■ ■ ■

SO WHAT MAKES a man an asshole? It bears some thought, for in the parlance of modern male bashspeak, "asshole" is second only to "dick" as the leading pejorative of choice. In some ways, the asshole/dick dichotomy mirrors the worst of men's conflicting attitudes toward women—our often unrequited need to press close and the urge to flee, our over-the-top reverence and nagging resentment, our wheedling dependency and desire to dominate, the whole Madonna/whore thing. As the dichotomy suggests, we can very quickly morph from asshole to dick and back again, often unconsciously. Before he can offer a more appealing alternative, the standup guy has to know which behaviors qualify him as one or the other.

An "asshole" is qualitatively different from a "dick" mostly by dint of the aggressive nature of his assholic behavior. An asshole exhibits his assholism vigorously and willfully, unafraid of, or perhaps just oblivious to, potential censure or rebuke. (A horn-leaning tailgater is an asshole. An Army sergeant who gropes female soldiers is an asshole.) If the word were cleared by the television standards police, there would undoubtedly be shows titled *Men Behaving Like Assholes* and *The Secret Lives of Assholes.*

A dick's behavior, on the other hand, is more passive, less confrontational, more ferrety and devious, but equally maddening. (A friend who borrows small sums of money with no intention of paying it back is a dick. So is a guy who acts as though he's fallen in love on the first date but never calls again.) Whatever the reason for it, Don's attack was low and chickenhearted, since it avoided the real issue between us, and unfair, offering me little opportunity for retaliation unless I wanted to ruin Joe's dinner party. If I'm an aggressive asshole, Don unquestionably revealed himself to be a dick.

Interesting, isn't it, how the nastiest name-calling enlists the precious sex organs to convey disdain? Men can be "pricks," "cocksuckers," "dicks," and (when they're not being pricks, cocksuckers, or dicks) "pussies." Most men consider oral sex one of the great erotic pleasures but invoke the intimate blowjob to demean a rival: *He sucks!* In another era, women could be "cunts," but today the term is considered so vile that not even the most ideologically obtuse person would dare use it (although a famous lady editor I once worked for often extolled the wonders and efficacy of "cunt power"). Judging by the frequency with which women increasingly refer to men as dicks, I guess I'd rather be a regular old asshole.

Why should the penis be so maligned? Perhaps it's an intuitive thing: when men become angry, they often become sexually aroused, a legacy of our simian ancestry, when fighting was often a preliminary to mating (one reason rape is so common in war). Women may have figured out that when a man starts acting like a prick, he's just an unrestrained impulse away from hauling it out and using it.

Are there more dicks in the world than there used to be? A lot of women, particularly single women, seem to think so. One reason has to do with very contemporary and decidedly impolitic conflicts in eons-old mating strategies. If women almost universally list a man's status at or near the top of her wish list, men rank a woman's physical attractiveness at the top of theirs. Surveys reveal this is especially true of ambitious and highly accomplished men—a fact not lost on highly attractive women, who use their comeliness to secure a signed and notarized prenuptial agreement from the most successful captains of industry. In fact, the more a man's social rank exceeds his wife's premarital status, the more likely she is to be especially beautiful.

These preferences, still so much in evidence today, are particularly galling to single professional women, whose numbers have increased enormously in the past two decades. Why? Like all women, they largely reject the idea of marrying down—they're simply unwilling to consider as potential husbands men whose education, job prestige, and income are lower than their own. They need only look to their iconoclastic sisters—powerful women who married a construction laborer, personal trainer, surfer, or the Marlboro Man—for proof of their slim chances of marital success with a lower-status guy. The female mating standard is as deeply encoded and religiously observed as men's. "Let's look at his record," many mothers still advise their smitten daughters.

Men, though, are relatively indifferent to women's socioeconomic status, except when it's far greater than their own, in which case they're not interested (unless they're professional gigolos). They're not necessarily turned off by women's confidence, assertiveness, and success. In fact, surveys show they do want to marry a woman with a good education and job. But the mate standard that seals the deal for men is beauty. That means that the ever-growing pool of high-status women have to compete with all other women for the high-status men who meet their lofty standards. Men's partiality to a pretty face and a good bod—as opposed to, say, brains, an impressive "record," or sheer earning power—means an attractive nurse, paralegal, or executive assistant has a larger cohort of men to choose from than a female doctor, lawyer, or CEO. The younger they are, the greater their advantage: single women over age thirty are considered demographically challenged, as opposed to men, who become increasingly desirable as they mature and acquire more "resources." This is bad news for the thirty-five-year-old women who have decided to postpone devising the Marriage Plot and concentrate on the Career Plot. Only one in twenty will ever marry.

So one reason women think there are more dicks populating the sexual landscape is that more of them have witnessed just how much a man relies on it—his dick, that is—to measure his attraction to a woman. Or much of the time, anyway. When the penis rises to the sky, the old saying goes, the brain falls to the ground—along with the ability to appreciate nonaesthetic standards.

And, in the eyes of high-status women, another dick is born.

▪ ▪ ▪

WITH OUR AROUSAL MACHINERY so easily tweaked by a pretty face, it's no surprise that far more men than women pursue sex outside of marriage (with the exception of that new cohort of young married women who are stepping out more often than their husbands), and that adulterous men have more partners than adulterous women. Yet when they do have an affair, women are far more likely to leave their marriage as a result. This means that men, suspiciously aware of each other's sexually acquisitive nature, will go to great lengths to "guard" their mate—a particularly unattractive behavior that decidedly falls under the asshole umbrella.

Whether powerful pooh-bahs or lowly laborers, men have a long and embarrassing but highly successful history of trying to keep a tightly clamped lid on the female libido. From confining wives and concubines in cells to veiling, purdah, foot binding, and genital mutilation, men have resorted to an extraordinary range of cruel tactics to discourage women from wandering off with a frisky, charming, and well-heeled stranger.

Some of these ancient strategies are not much different, in both spirit and deed, from the vigilante techniques deployed by other relatives in the animal kingdom. The males of many species drive off rival suitors, herd females to keep them under control, insert sperm plugs to block females' reproductive tracts, emit foul scents to repel other suitors, tenaciously attach themselves to the female after copulation, or erect a fence around their mate until their freshly deposited chromosomal bundle has had a chance to reach its destination.

Hasn't evolution, or at least the pressures of modern sexual politics, managed to temper this instinct in men? Not a bit. During the final heats of ancestral sperm competitions, our brains became permanently encoded with a variety of strategic responses, some quite unconscious and benign, to possible cues of female waywardness. Let's say your wife is out of town for a week on business with six male colleagues, all of whom make about ten times as much money as you. Even if you ejaculate every day she's away (forgetting, for the moment, why or under what circumstances), you'll still release more spermatazoa when she returns to your eager, trembling arms than you did during any of the (presumably) solo emissions. You'll also begin to manufacture more sperm designed to compete with a rival's than sperm whose sole function is to fertilize an egg. Scientists consider this a sophisticated psychophysiological adaptation to your unavoidable lapse in mate monitoring—or, put another way, to your possessive and suspicious nature.

Other monitoring mechanisms, however, are not so quaint or innocent. Consider our reactions to rape: studies have determined that while a husband or lover would seem to be the most obvious and reliable source of comfort to a rape victim, he's often the least compassionate, particularly when she's uninjured. Why? Lacking evidence of coercion, he may suspect his partner's complicit involvement—and perhaps other "infidelities." In fact, the more brutal, and hence less equivocal, the attack, the more understanding and concerned he is. To some degree, this mindset shows up in nearly every rape trial: She asked for it.

Extreme imbalances in "mate value"—one's desirability on the hypothetical breeding lot—are also a cause of some assholic male behavior. Men whose wives are substantially younger or more comely than they are are far more likely than others to keep a watchful eye on their connubial prize, threaten imagined suitors, or even knock around potential rivals. Sometimes, death does them part: federal crime analyses have documented a rise in spousal homicides as the age gap between husband and wife increases.

Curiously, women tend to have the opposite response to mate value disparities. Researchers have found that those married to men whom they perceive to be highly attractive on the open market (world-beaters, in other words) tend to relax their vigilance—an implicit acknowledgment that such a man is entitled to devote his surplus mate value to outside relationships. Keeping a resourceful but wayward partner on a long and elastic leash, the women apparently decided, is far more desirable and practical than ditching him and hooking up with a faithful man whose wherewithal is more limited.

Booting him out, after all, means having to reenter a playing field in which the odds are stacked against them.

■ ■ ■

STATUS AND BEAUTY. In a simpler, one-paycheck era, they often formed the basis of a union between an ascendant company man and a glamorous but unthreatening social X ray who affirmed her husband's dominance. Today, however, even though mate preferences remain largely the same, the social X ray is likely to have a career of her own, altering the political, sexual, and power dynamics of the marriage.

The other day, I got an unappealing glimpse of what can go wrong when these old preferences conflict in a modern marriage. After a long match, a guy I occasionally play squash with offered to buy me a beer at the bar of his club, where he had brought me as a guest. I don't know him well, but he seemed eager to untangle himself from some psychic conflict. His wife, a forty-year-old successful public relations executive, wanted a baby, their first, he told me as we cooled off. He was thinking about leaving his job as a corporate accountant and applying his number-crunching skills to a potentially more lucrative position on Wall Street—"something that would at least equal her salary," he said, eyes averted. I asked whether they had decided to remove the barriers between his sperm and her eggs. Yes, he replied, but admitted that he wasn't all that "active." Backpedaling from what I feared would be an embarrassing revelation of a physical condition I'd rather not know about, I nodded silently, but he went on. "Maybe if she spent some of her lunch hour working on her cellulite instead of her clients," he said, "I'd find it easier to become aroused."

More withholding? Is this a pandemic? I met this man's wife once, and she's as sleek and sexy as a Morgan quarterhorse. So what's the turnoff? When a man marries a woman who thinks of him as an equal rather than a superior—particularly if, at some point, she starts making more money than he does—he often feels threatened. Like the *alte kocker* with a beautiful young wife, he senses mate-value discrepancy—the feeling that his partner is more attractive on a hypothetical dating scene than he is. As her status rises, he feels pressured to measure up to her graduating standards, if not exceed them, and begins to think of her as a rival.

And who wants to have sex with a rival? Not my accountant friend, apparently. And not a lot of other men, here and abroad, who feel diminished by their spouse's dynamism. National Relate, the marriage guidance council of the United Kingdom, recently published a report that indicated a quarter of men undertaking psychosexual therapy in the British Isles are impotent, and that the increase in the last ten years is due to men losing interest because of the increased power of women. A survey of young people in a farming community told a particularly dramatic story. When couples relocated to the city, women who found jobs were no longer frigid, but formerly virile men became impotent.

In the worst cases, the uniquely male anxiety engendered by spousal competition results in physical violence; less impulsive men may respond with bullying or infidelity. When feeling less than lordly, many men typically undermine and demean their wife, from bitching about her cooking to complaining about her recently acquired, even imaginary, avoirdupoir.

Men deploy this strategy, which draws out the worst qualities of the dick and the asshole, to lower their wives' self-esteem and self-perception of her attractiveness, which, no matter how much money she makes, she knows is an important asset, at least in the eyes of a potential suitor. With her confidence shaken, she may be less likely to defect from the relationship. The tactic is a preemptive strike against a widely documented contemporary eventuality: When women are more successful than their husbands, they're twice as likely to ditch them if they're unhappy. Among all women, the most highly accomplished have the highest divorce rates.

Of course, what appears to be female ascendancy is often relative—male descendancy in disguise. Women who lose respect for their husband because of his lack of ambition or inability to carry his weight soon begin scanning the horizon for more promising candidates. The first sign of trouble, many of these women say, is that they start in some way to feel like their husband's mother, a role none of them finds the least bit sexy or romantic.

■ ■ ■

ARE SEXUAL PREDATORS dicks or assholes? The answer is complicated. In his many dalliances, Pablo Picasso's habit was to begin by exalting the women he was wooing and then, when he had tired of them, ignoring them. His passive but obvious disdain for his former lovers echoes the indirectness the bitchfesters complain about among the men they know, thus earning him a spot in the dick club. But he was also sexually adventurous and clearly possessed of a good deal more sexual stamina than most men command, which made his powers of destruction all the greater. In the end, he proved himself a major asshole.

The contemporary predator is a different animal, although his destructive powers may be equally ferocious. Consider the end-of-the-century debate that consumed Washington and the news media: Is a blowjob really sex or, say, a kind of salutation, like shaking hands? When rock-star and jock-star groupies discovered the persuasive magic of oral sex some thirty years ago, the blowjob had the power to induce a reciprocal sexual relationship, however fleeting. Groupies at least got to spend the night. Today, however, political stars as ideologically at odds as Newt Gingrich and Bill Clinton invoke biblical scripture in maintaining that when they ask a woman, or girl as the case may be, to "kiss it," they're not asking for sex per se. When formally deposed on the subject, Clinton defined sex as contact with another person's groin, buttocks, breast, or inner thigh, but excluded kissing. And because he had no contact (except through an intermediary: a cigar) with the aforementioned anatomic regions of Monica Lewinsky, he couldn't be accused of having had sex with her. Whether his penis found its way into her mouth was legally a moot point, he and his lawyers maintained, although House impeachment managers, assholes in their own right, clearly disagreed.

In thus defining sex, Clinton proved to be an eloquent front man for modern dicklike behavior, a man well-prepared, as he often likes to say, for the cold realities of the twenty-first century. And it's not easy, in such a frigid climate, to become aroused. Like Clarence Thomas, who was accused of trying to seduce Anita Hill with a sexy joke about pubic hairs on Coke cans, or Bob Packwood, whose tongue seemed to sport his most erectile tissues, Clinton seemed to get little enjoyment from his illicit dalliances. He wouldn't go all the way, insisted on holding back, and refused to take off his clothes, claiming all the while that he was "trying to be good." The first feminist president managed to introduce political correctness even to adultery.

The new sexual style for men, at least men who are or aspire to be dicks, is passivity—lie back and think of . . . resisting. From the high school boys who won't date to the bitchfest boyfriends who won't put out to the powerful politicians who want to be blown but not touched, men are exhibiting a previously unheard of collective sexual lassitude. The phallus, once a proud and eager representative of virility and strength, has become a symbol for selfishness and fecklessness. Like the person it's attached to, it often acts like a dick. A limp one.

In this climate, the big noise about Viagra, the impotence pill, is somewhat mystifying. Fifty percent of men over forty, doctors have claimed since the pill became available, have at least occasional trouble getting an erection, most of them because of some kind of physiological impairment. While a significant number of this group, most notably diabetics and long-term smokers, can't get it up for genuinely physical reasons, it seems probable that an equally significant portion have something else shorting out their arousal circuitry. One of the researchers of a study on which those figures are based found that impotent men who date and remarry much younger women suddenly find themselves sexually frisky again—at least for a while. This transformation has also been documented among elderly primates. When a young adult female is placed in the cage of a once studly old alpha male, he magically recovers his libidinal vigor. Surely these men and their simian cousins are not experiencing a sudden and miraculous regeneration of their damaged hydraulic equipment.

Let's assume for a moment that doctors are being overly generous in ascribing an organic cause to the vast majority of cases of male impotence. What could they be hiding? That over the past couple of decades the male libido has been withering, along with its erectile power, in response to the gradual liberation of Aphroditic energy? In a single generation, women have gone from being mostly anorgasmic to mostly orgasmic, many of them with a capacity for sexual pleasure most men can only fantasize about. The pressure on young men to perform, as the dickfesters complained, is immense. On older men, too: a crusty colleague of mine who, at sixty, got married for the third time a couple of years ago to a much younger woman, recently complained to me, "Sex was so much easier when you didn't have to satisfy the woman."

The only thing new about men's reaction to the surging female libido is that, in the absence of rough and primitive mate-guarding strategies, they are now powerless to contain it. So instead they withhold, passively resist it, have sex only outside marriage, suffer unconscious anxiety that results in impotence, or get no-touch, lips-only blowjobs that they won't dignify by calling sex.

It seems unlikely that Viagra will change all this. Why are men who haven't had an erotic thought about their wife in a decade suddenly popping hard-on pills? Many clearly don't have their spouse in mind when asking for a prescription. Those who aren't thinking only of themselves believe that with an erection as hard as a baseball bat, they're finally up to the challenge—again forgetting that good sex for women is never exclusively genital. For others, the pill is the perfect male aphrodisiac: it obviates the need for courtship, seduction, and foreplay, announcing quickly and simply, "I'm ready." No doubt it has come as a disappointment to many that the same resentments or lousy lovemaking that led to a couple's purchase of twin beds are still very much unresolved and, erection or no, a huge barrier to a rewarding sex life.

Impotence is simply the latest fashionable and politically—or medically—correct explanation for men's retreat from women. We won't have sex with women because we can't, the doctors reassure us, not because we don't want to. A few years ago the same lassitude was called low-desire syndrome and blamed on the ennervating pressures of juggling job, domestic duties, child care, and other responsibilities. Whatever it's called, the ugly truth about this common condition—which hits epidemic numbers, if you believe the urologists—is that many men are anxious about proving and maintaining their worth to a newly capable partner, often jealous of her success, wary of her assertiveness, and intimidated by her unrestrained sexuality. The private face of this anxiety has surfaced in the bedroom. For a lot of men, the politics of gender have become, finally, very personal.

■ ■ ■

Is it possible, sexually speaking, to be a dick *and* an asshole? Again, we might look to William Clinton. Neither his happy conquests nor his accusers, including Kathleen Willey, who claimed to be mauled by him in the Oval Office, and Paula Jones, who sued him for harassment, would consider Clinton shy. His often unwelcome advances alone would earn him asshole status. And his weaseling around whether he smoked a joint, dodged the draft, or stepped out on his wife—and the ease with which he sacrifices friends and devoted staffers in the name of lies and deceit—make him a consummate dick. Yet the sordid allegations leveled against the then president seemed only to boost his popularity, particularly with women, who are, after all, the final judges of whether a man is a dick or an asshole. The question, then, is whether he's admired because of his aggressive swordsmanship (asshole) or because he has managed to perfect a way to have sex without actually touching his partner (dick), in a way reverting to the good old days preferred by my former colleague, "when you didn't have to satisfy the woman."

Probably because of both, with an extra nod to his inner asshole. Americans expect their leaders to have excessive appetites, to act larger than life in everything they do. John F. Kennedy is still considered by many people to have been the country's greatest president ever, despite having served only a short time and having received only a so-so evaluation by historians. But with each posthumous documentation of his relentless sexual questing, his reputation has grown exponentially.

Of course, whether a politician is admired or vilified for his philandering depends in part on how he handles inquiries about his indiscretions. When the former House Ways and Means Committee chairman Wilbur Mills was caught with stripper Fanne Fox near the Tidal Basin, he acted spooked, ashamed, pitiful. Ohio congressman Wayne Hays looked foolish and hypocritical trying to explain his relationship with Elizabeth Ray, a secretary on the public payroll who couldn't type. And when Gary Hart challenged reporters to document his relationship with Donna Rice and then was photographed lapdancing with her on a yacht heading for the Bahamas, he reacted like a sullen, petulant teenager who'd missed a curfew. All three of these men were quickly banished from the political world.

Their fumbling contrasts markedly with the smooth evasions of Grover Cleveland, who was dogged by reports during his first presidential campaign that he had impregnated an unmarried woman. Although he never acknowledged paternity, he did concede that he had assumed financial responsibility for the woman's child. His election was due, in part, to his having acted in a manly fashion—circumspect but responsible. In refusing to answer questions about his extramarital love life, Clinton, too, managed to seem courtly and dignified: a gentleman, as everyone knows, would never impugn the honor of a woman by talking about their sex life. Of course, a gentleman wouldn't have an exploitive relationship with a naïve young woman his daughter's age, but that's another matter.

Perhaps the appeal of Cleveland, JFK, and Clinton is that, in an age in which a huge cohort of men are able to generate an erotic frisson only by popping a pill, these men had a good old-fashioned testosterone-fueled approach to pursuing the pleasures of the flesh. They may be assholes, but they're sort of lovable assholes.

■ ■ ■

BUT THAT DOESN'T MEAN they're any better than dicks at forming intimate relationships with the New Woman—the standup guy's most urgent challenge for the coming millennium if he hopes to propel his genes into the next generation. For women rank a man's kindness and understanding equally high on their wish list, right alongside his strength, social dominance, and ability to make a buck. They're sensitive not only to signs of resourcefulness but emotional involvement. That means that they leave their marriage not only when their husband proves to be a slacker but when they feel the quality of emotional communication in the marriage is hopelessly lacking. When a man is unfaithful, he is usually just satisfying a need for different partners and has no intention of leaving his marriage. When a woman has an affair, she's checking out alternatives. And because she tends to associate sex with emotional involvement, she's more likely to fall in love with the man with whom she finds it. Her personal bank account grants her the option to leave.

Not long ago, with the aid of some expensive wines, I spent the better part of an evening helping an old friend review the demise of his fourteen-year marriage. Along with his legal emancipation came the news that his ex-wife was planning to remarry. As the night went on, his rage intensified. He professed ignorance that his marriage had been in trouble, blamed his ex for sabotaging a long and mutually satisfying relationship, and claimed to have been emotionally swindled. He had loved his wife, he said, and couldn't believe she had so precipitously dumped him.

Since my main job was to listen, I refrained from pointing out that his wife had attempted a variety of marriage-saving schemes long before their separation, including counseling, vacations, and marathon talks. She had wanted only one thing: to see more of him and be with him more. My friend, a financial consultant and partner in a mid-size firm, often volunteered to scout out-of-town work simply because he loved to travel. When he was home, he almost always worked late, regularly missed family dinners, and usually went to his office at least one day on the weekend. They would often catch a movie and dinner on Saturday night and had a "regular, average" sex life. To him, the marriage was strong, to her, empty.

After more than a year of pressing her husband for a change, my friend's wife, an interior decorator, would take her chances on finding an emotionally gratifying connection with a man. My friend begged, pleaded, and promised to change, but he was way too late. When a man says a relationship is over, he means maybe. When a woman says it's over, it's over.

By the end of the evening, my friend was no closer to figuring out why his wife had left him. "She said she wanted intimacy," he moaned. "But we were intimate. I had no idea what she was talking about."

When women say men just don't get it, this is often what they mean. Relative social dominance, as vital as it still is to the successful modern pair-bond, can take a man only so far. All women are forever focused on *the relationship.* The standup guy, if he's to avoid falling into the asshole/dick trap, needs to acquire a special talent. He needs to be not only confidently strong and socially potent but psychologically deep—loving, available, and supportive. He also needs to be keenly aware that, when unleashed without restraint, all the unconscious behaviors, motivations, and defense mechanisms that served him well in a simpler, Darwinian universe often result in his having to spend a lot of time alone. He needs to develop emotional depth and clarity, not so he can be sensitive to all others—the mantra of an earlier New Man—but so that he can read the temperature of *the one relationship that matters* and jack up the heat when necessary. By drawing upon the zeal he has brought for so long to his assholic pursuit of sexual gratification and dominance—or, if he's been a dick in retreat, by recovering it—the aspiring standup guy can aggressively clear aside any psychological obstacles that may stand between him and his ability to work *and* love.

There's another group of men, several million strong, who claim they've mastered this. It's hard to believe—that's a lot of standup guys. But for Kate's sake, I figure I'll check them out.

PROMISES, PROMISES

...

IT'S FIVE A.M., and before he can knock a second time I acknowledge Earl Keener's wake-up call. I'm happy to be awake, having spent a fitful five hours or so eluding large tattooed men who were trying to press me between the covers of an iron-bound Bible.

I had e-mailed Earl a couple of weeks before to sign up for a Promise Keepers rally in Washington, D.C., and in true Christian spirit, Earl invited me to spend the night at his house so I wouldn't have to make a ninety-minute predawn drive from New York to the Calvary Baptist Church in New Paltz, whence the buses would depart. Bearing chocolates for Earl's wife, the director of a local preschool, and son, Jimmy, a sweet nine-year-old with huge brown eyes, I had arrived around nine P.M. at the Keeners' modest ranch home on converted farmland just off the New York State Thruway. Earl is a former metallurgist for an aluminum-can maker and now on permanent disability because of diabetes-related neuropathy in his legs, which are supported by braces. Most of his time and efforts now focus on Calvary Church—he made all the arrangements for this trip for his fellow pilgrims from the area, teaches Sunday school, and helps manage the boys' baseball team. After showing me my room and apologizing in advance for the live rock music from a nearby house that might disturb me, Earl excused himself to make last-minute plans on his computer. On another terminal, Jimmy and I played games that he'd downloaded from the Internet. At one point, I mentioned to Jimmy that he appeared to have inherited his father's knack for finding his way around a computer. Jimmy directed those big brown orbs at me and said, "But maybe I got it from my other Father, too."

I had been intrigued by the Promise Keepers ever since they emerged in the mid-nineties and was particularly interested in them now. Their message was undeniably compelling: The country has fallen into the snares of illegitimacy, poverty, drug abuse, juvenile delinquency, and sexual profligacy largely because men have failed the fundamental challenges of manhood—to take care of their families and communities. The antidote: form a few vital relationships with other men to become "godly influences" in the world, get out of debt, keep your fly zippered except around your wife, and teach your children to set up a permanent shrine for Jesus in their heart. With their emphasis on self-reliance and male responsibility, they seemed to have much in common with the New Warriors, Million Man Marchers, and other groups who encourage men to turn to each other for help in solving their problems. Their message has spread widely: three million men have attended Promise Keepers rallies, dwarfing any numbers earlier men's movement groups have managed to put up.

But their appeal seems to have topped out. This would be one of the last rallies Promise Keepers would hold before announcing that, to bolster its dwindling attendance figures, it would stop charging admission to its two-day events. How could they have grown so fast and then fallen apart so quickly? Was it because their "brotherhood of believers" had reached critical mass? Was it because they had finally been outed by religious liberals as puppets for the religious right's pro-life, anti-gay, school-prayer agenda? Or was it because what they thought was a righteous new incarnation of the standup guy was too much like the oppressive old alpha male?

That would appear to be the judgment of the National Organization for Women (NOW), which has passed a resolution declaring Promise Keepers "the greatest danger to women's rights" and commonly hires a plane trailing a banner that reads PROMISE KEEPERS LOSERS WEEPERS to circle the rallies. The same women who have long challenged men to become sexually, familially, and civically responsible creatures now worry that Promise Keepers, by vowing to become faithful husbands, engaged fathers, and active leaders in their community, are trying to reverse the gains women have made in the past thirty years. Their fears originate in a section of the handbook *Seven Promises of a Promise Keeper,* titled "Reclaiming Your Manhood." The passage reads: "Sit down with your wife and say something like this: 'Honey, I've made a terrible mistake. I've given you my role. I gave up leading this family, and I forced you to take my place. Now, I must reclaim that role' . . . I'm not suggesting you *ask* for your role back, I'm urging you to *take* it back . . . there can be no compromise here. If you're going to lead, you must lead."

On the other hand, as exaggerated as NOW's fear that a majority of women will again be shackled to the stove and bassinette is Promise Keepers' paraphrase of Scripture—specifically, a passage from Paul's Epistle to the Ephesians—to assert that "a wife is to submit graciously to the servant leadership of her husband." If the Bible says it, PK thinking goes, it must be so. Of course, the Bible also condones slavery, condemns "laying up treasure," and advises that we should turn the other cheek. Do the Promise Keepers advocate reinstituting slavery? Do they shun 401(k)s and equities? Are they pacifists?

As I search for my clothes in the pale dawn light, I decide that, for now, I'm going to hold off asking.

■ ■ ■

I FOLLOW EARL through the sleepy hamlets of Ulster County to Calvary Church, where three buses idle in the parking lot. Earl introduces me to a few of my fellow travelers—two brothers who run a local car dealership and a county agricultural agent. I shake hands with David and his ten-year-old son, Billy, who will be my roomies in Washington. We mill around in the damp parking lot, eating donuts and sipping coffee, rubbing our eyes. I chat with George, a scrubbed Marine, a munitions officer stationed at nearby Stewart Air Force Base, who's heading to the rally for a little spiritual and moral "tune-up." Former and present military are well represented here—George is traveling with his best friend, a Navy pilot he sees only every other year or so. They make fun of a brush-cut Army sergeant, who's just spilled coffee on his sweater. Everyone razzes a white-bearded old salt, Walter Smith, who spent twenty-five years in the Navy. The rest of our group includes farmers, computer techies, mechanics, builders, tool-and-die men, an accountant, a group of twenty from a bottling plant, a dozen Christian homeboys with slouchy pants and bowl haircuts, another dozen Spanish-speaking men from a church in Kingston, and two black ministers from Newburgh.

As the bus closes up and rolls off toward the capital and the forty-five thousand other evangelical Christians gathering there, my stomach churns. It could be the unsettling effects of the jelly-roll breakfast at six A.M., but I suspect my dyspepsia has more to do with my apprehension of what's in store for me over the next two days. I'm here to investigate this particular breed of standup guy, but I haven't told any of my traveling companions, which makes me ethically uneasy. I'd like to participate as much as possible, but the "message" doesn't really register with me. I love my wife, and though I lust after just about every attractive woman I meet, I have no desire to step out on her. I'm at the least a "good-enough" dad, and have no difficulty resisting preapproved credit card offers with low introductory APRs. But I am open to novel experience, and after my seduction by the New Warriors, I wonder if I'll end up in a photo on the front page of *The Washington Post* with tears streaming down my face, eyes squeezed shut, and palms open in the devotional gesture of Orans. Maybe that's what worries me most.

I doubt it, though. I've always desired the sense of belonging and identity religion provides, and have certainly been in need of its comfort, but have never found the right niche. Lately, I've been attending the learner's minyan at a nearby synagogue with my daughter Eliza, but already my interest is waning. When I was a child, I attended the Sunday schools of half a dozen different churches as my parents struggled to find a denomination that could accommodate them both. At the vanguard of a trend that would involve a lot of Jewish men of his generation and beyond, my father, who had been bar mitzvahed, married outside the faith. The thirties and forties, when he was growing up, was not a great time to be a Jew—particularly in St. Paul, which a postwar newspaper columnist once called "the anti-Semitic capital of America." Finally, he and my mother, an Anglican, found a Unitarian church with a congregation of lapsed Catholics and disaffected Jews and showed up every Sunday to hear the philosophical Whitmanesque musings of the various ministers who would drop in for a year or two from Unitarian strongholds back East. At Unity Church, which featured a large blond-wood sculpture mounted above the pulpit that, if you squinted, sort of resembled a cross, Jesus was referred to as a very good man who may or may not have been the son of God. There was a little something for everyone at Unity, but nothing too spiritually challenging. After my brother died, the little interest my parents had shown in providing a religious education for their children evaporated altogether, along with whatever faith they had in a beneficent God.

Like my dad, I just can't wrap my brain around Jesus. I attend church occasionally with my wife, but can't accept communion, participate in any of the other sacraments, or even pray. I don't really know why. Sitting in church, I'm happy knowing the twins are downstairs at the Sunday school drawing pictures of Sarah, Rebecca, and Abraham, but I had nothing to do with that, either. Like 85 percent of the other men in America, I have ceded the religious leadership in our family to my wife. She knows more about it, I figure, and does a better job—an unmanly attitude, by Promise Keepers' lights, and the source of all society's ills. "The father is the priest of the household," the Promise Keepers handbook states. "He must not, on any point, yield up his parental authority." This passage, along with the one advising men to "take back" their power, sounds to me like they were written by someone who's never been married.

Clearly, I'm going to have a hard time "receiving the message through Jesus." But, aside from the discomfort I'm anticipating from having to form prayer scrums with strange men, I'm feeling paranoid: one of the missions of the Baptists is to convert Jews, even faithless half-breeds like me. Before the bus leaves the parking lot, Earl does a roll call, his voice, I imagine, rising just a little louder on my Jewish surname. A couple of heads turn. *Bless the Lord, there's one among us.*

I feel like a sitting duck.

■ ■ ■

THE BUS RUMBLES through New Jersey, Delaware, Maryland. I had expected, in my benighted way, that the men would be singing hymns and praying in the aisles, or springing to their feet to quote Scripture, but most talk quietly. I read, doze, and chat with my seatmate George, the handsome Marine from Stewart. He's thirty-eight, has three girls— one in college—and has been married since he was twenty, the year he joined the Marines. As a munitions supply officer, George is often stationed overseas for months at a time away from his family—"a difficult time for me," he admits, his eyes falling to his lap, "a time of great temptation." He's referring, I assume, to his battle with the Devil's most effective weapon, sexual sin. George is planning to retire soon, finish his college degree and become a high school gym teacher. This is the third conference he's attended in as many years. "It's a good focusing opportunity," he says. "You get away from all the things that distract you from The Relationship. The conference also reminds us that our goal to become Christlike is something we do collectively, not just individually. When we try to do it on our own, we're not as good."

And when we try to come clean on our own, the Promise Keepers credo maintains, we're not as motivated either. Our mea culpas are even harder to pull off in the company of women. The solidarity of the stadium and the presence of forty-five thousand other self-confessed sad-sack sinners create a climate in which we're more likely to view ourselves and our lives more honestly.

George dozes off, and I eavesdrop on the conversation behind me. Jack, forty-eight, is the foreman of a construction crew. Mark, a short but powerfully built sheetrocker, is twenty years his junior. Every Friday, the two men meet at a truck stop off the New York State Thruway on their way to work to check up on each other, find out how each is doing in his plight to tread the straight and narrow, do right by his family, be a godly influence in his home, say his prayers, and keep his dick in his pants. They work together every day, but this is their formal private time, their "accountability" session. Like the New Warriors, Promise Keepers urges its adherents to form deep friendships with at least one other man so that each can help prevent the other from falling into a behavioral sink. Jack and Mark have taken seriously the Second Promise of the Christian group's creed: "A man needs his brothers to help him keep his promises." Sort of a Christian buddy system.

Today is Friday, so Jack and Mark hold their meeting on the bus. They open with a prayer, then review Jack's struggle to crawl out from beneath an ever-mounting burden of debt. "I accept every one of those credit card offers that comes into my house," he says. "I don't know how I'd get by without them."

"We've been talking about this for weeks," says Mark, "and I've prayed that you get a handle on it. Why is it so difficult for you?"

"I don't know. Ever since I took out a loan on the house last year, I've felt guilty. It was like once I did that, the floodgates just opened up."

"That house is too small for you. You should have sold it."

"That's just it. I mean, Christina should have a room where she can bring her friends and they can have a little privacy. She's embarrassed that her bedroom is in the basement, right next to the furnace, so if her friend Shelly wants to come over to do her homework my wife and I clear out of the living room so they can do it there. So most of the time Christina goes over to Shelly's house instead. I feel bad that I can't do better for her."

"Why didn't you take that money and build an extra bedroom?"

"That's just it. That's what I intended to do. But then the interest on the home equity loan was much lower than the interest on the credit cards, so I decided to pay off the credit cards with the equity loan, and had nothing left over."

"I'll help you build the room. We could do it in a month. After work and on weekends."

"I couldn't even buy the subflooring."

"I'll loan you the money."

"I don't know. If I were in debt to you, I'd just feel . . ." Jack sighs. "You're a young man. Hold on to your money."

"Are you still spending a lot of money on Christina? Giving it to her whenever she asks?"

"Yeah. I hate to say it . . . I'm afraid she doesn't love me. I feel like it's the only thing I can do for her, give her money, and buy her what she wants. In a few years, she'll be gone . . ."

"What does your wife think?"

"That I spoil her."

"She probably wouldn't mind being spoiled herself."

"I suppose not . . . I don't know, it's a mess. The other night, I went down to say good night to Christina, and she was doing her homework with the radio on. You know what she was listening to? A rock station. I said, 'Why don't you listen to classical instead of that garbage?' She doesn't like classical, she says. I told her she could listen to classical or nothing at all, and she just looks at me, like challenging me to do something. I had no choice. I unplugged the radio and took it upstairs. Now she won't speak to me."

"You've got to get domestic control of your household," Mark says.

"It's been three days."

"Get control of your household."

■ ■ ■

SHEETS OF RAIN SLAP the bus as we inch through downtown Washington, looking for our hotel. I forgot to bring a raincoat, but as we pull up in front of the Embassy Suites on M Street, the rain stops, the clouds break, and the humid air is sliced by golden tines of sunlight. Before we leave the bus, Walter, the ex–Navy man, spells out the drill: our rooms are already paid for, we won't be able to make long-distance calls from the phones, and the pay-per-view cable is locked out. It takes a moment before I register the significance of this: pornography is one of the greater temptations in the canon of "sexual sin." When I return to my room late tonight after five hours of vowing to honor the pledges I've made, I won't have to wrestle with my urge to go on a video-smut bender.

David and Billy, my roommates, and I carry our bags to our room, unpack our things quickly, freshen up, and split a soda. This is the fourth Promise Keepers rally for David, who at six-four and two-forty is a great bear of a man, and the second for his son. Billy had joined his dad the year before at Shea Stadium in New York, answering David's prayers, he says, that he would be able to find a way to draw closer to his son, "share more of the man I am, be a better role model and be better known by him." David had worried that Billy would be too young to tolerate two long days devoted to the drudgery of manly duties and the ubiquity of temptation. But he decided to take him anyway. And right at the start of the rally, he knew he'd made the right decision. "The first speaker offered an invitation," David says as he stuffs some things into a knapsack, "and thousands of men poured down the aisles to confess Jesus as our Savior and Lord. We all began cheering and applauding the decision these men were making, all fifty-five thousand of us, and the sound became deafening. Billy and I stood on our chairs to watch, and as the bulk of the men reached the front, my son put his hand on my shoulder. I realized he was trying to tell me something, so I bent over to hear him, and noticed that his eyes were full of tears. He put his arms around my neck and said, 'Thanks so much for bringing me, Dad, this is awesome.' "

Billy pops out of the bedroom wearing a T-shirt emblazoned with the message WITH GOD ALL THINGS ARE POSSIBLE on the front and DELIVERING THE MESSAGE THROUGH BASEBALL on the back. Billy is a cheerful, good-looking kid with a ropey thatch of brown hair that flops across his forehead. He's brought an extra water bottle, he says, and gives it to me. "I always come prepared," he says cheerfully, showing off a tiny battery-operated fan around his neck.

We board the bus again and head to RFK Stadium around five P.M. Inside the arena, giant beach balls float lazily in the air, punched skyward by beefy men wearing T-shirts imprinted with the biblical inscription AS IRON SHARPENS IRON, SO ONE MAN SHARPENS ANOTHER or this year's conference theme, THE MAKING OF A GODLY MAN. David, a former cop who played football at West Point, suggests we grab some seats on the field. "You get a better feeling down here," he says. "And this is the closest you'll ever come to catching a ball, even if it is a beach ball, on the fifty-yard line of RFK Stadium."

David, thirty-eight, was born in New York City but grew up in the Hudson River town of Rhinecliff, about seventy-five miles upriver from Manhattan, where his father, a New York fireman, moved his family in the sixties. David enlisted in the Army and went to West Point for three years before resigning his commission to marry his high school sweetheart. He moved back to Rhinebeck, drove a truck, and worked in a grocery store before responding to an ad for a part-time police officer for the city of Kingston across the river. With his West Point credentials and intimidating bulk, he was hired immediately. He graduated from the police academy six months later, and decided to become a full-time cop. "It started to fulfill me," he says as we sip from our water bottles and watch the stadium fill up. "I felt like I could do some good, make an impact. I wanted to help people, and I found out I was good at it."

But after a while, the work became routine: "I got tired of going into the ghetto and breaking up the same fights." So over the next few years, David worked as an undercover detective, surveilling drug activity and robbery rings—"ninety-eight percent sheer boredom scattered around two percent sheer terror." He joined the SCUBA team, then the SWAT team, and became the SWAT team leader. "I was the gas expert and the breacher—the guy who jumped off roofs on a rope or knocked down the door and went in first. I loved it." He became expert at handling each of the department's weapons, including dogs. Eight years after responding to the ad, he was promoted to lieutenant, the first man in the history of the department to rise so quickly into the top command tier. "But none of it accomplished anything, at least personally. You'd get a few brief moments of euphoria, then nothing. Eventually I saw that this discontent was a positive thing. I realized that God creates this empty place in your heart that you try to fill up with thrills and kicks, when what He really wants is for you to fill it up with Him."

Before that realization, though, David had to be "brought low." He had a four-year-old daughter, and Billy was on the way. His relationship with his wife, Marcy, a caterer, had deteriorated. "It just doesn't work well when you go home and your wife asks how your day was and you say, 'Well, I held a guy in my arms until he died of stab wounds, and I chased a guy who had tried to kill me, dropped my gun, and felt really stupid.' Or, 'I was scared to death today, trapped in a bodega with the owner who was about to be robbed, with no phone and no backup.' Or, 'I pulled a dead three-year-old girl from the bottom of a pool.' It's just not good dinner conversation.

"So I started holding that inside. You can relate those things only to other cops, you develop that blue wall of silence. The world becomes black and white, divided into good guys and bad guys. I had changed, I had become a different person, but I figured that's just the way it was."

David had also started sleeping around. "Some women are attracted to cops," he says. "And some cops, for obvious reasons, are attracted to each other." A relationship with a female coworker became serious, and Marcy found out about it. David broke off the affair and agreed to marriage counseling, "where I was brought to the point where I was introduced to a personal relationship with God. I was not seeking God, but God was seeking me."

Although he had been raised in the Catholic church, David had pretty much abandoned the faith. His older brother had been born again, and for years had pressured David to share "the joy and peace" he had found. "But I was raised in a home where 'born-again Christian' was equated with Moonie, the Hare Krishnas, or other cults," David says. "Every time I saw my brother, it was Jesus this, Jesus that. He played only Christian pop music and, frankly, it drove me crazy. It got to the point where I didn't want to see him anymore."

Plagued by guilt and filled with self-loathing, David went through the motions of trying to save his marriage. But then, while attending a three-day work-on-your-marriage seminar, something happened. "I really didn't want to be there," he says. "But on the last day, the speaker laid a transparency on the overhead projector and I started copying it down. It was a simple confession—that I didn't have the ability to control whether I sin or not. It sounded a lot like the first of the Twelve Steps: 'God, I am a sinner and powerless to do anything about it.' It hooked my attention. The final part, which I now know to be the Sinner's Prayer, was: 'Will you take control of my life? I trust you enough to enter a relationship with you and trust you'll do the things I can't.' I read that and said, 'Hmm, that's pretty interesting,' and copied it down. I realized the third time I said it, I prayed it. In that moment, I realized that what I wanted out of life I couldn't have until I had this. Then I would trust God to fill in all those empty places and unravel the mess I'd made.

"I knew instantly that something had happened to my attitude, but I didn't recognize it as being born again. For the next couple of months I would read that notebook, the Sinner's Prayer, at lunchtime, then read the Bible. I read it from front to back with no real design. I could sense that I was changing—I didn't hate myself so much anymore, for one thing. Then one day, I had a young recruit with me—I was a training officer—and we were directing traffic around the scene of a fire. A car came by, ignored my directions, drove through a puddle created by a firehose, and completely drenched me. And I said, sort of quietly, under my breath, 'Damn!' The recruit, whom I'd been training for a couple of months, looked up at me and said incredulously, 'You know, that's the first time I've ever heard you swear.'

"And I just looked at him. I'd had probably the foulest mouth in the department, but without being aware of it, I'd changed. God was sending me subtle signs. I became aware that I was no longer that person I didn't like so much.

"Marcy and I had been talking about getting back to church. With the baby coming, it was one way we could get our life back together. So one Sunday we decided to go. Drove downtown right past the Catholic church—she had been raised Catholic, too—and without saying anything to each other drove straight to Calvary. It seemed the thing to do. I don't know how it happened, this was the kind of church my brother had been going to, and I'd spent all those years mocking him. Before that, I would never have considered joining a Baptist church. Inside, the pastor asked if there were any visitors, and I raised my hand and filled out a card. That afternoon, the pastor called and asked to come over, and we said fine. We talked, we told him what we'd been going through, and he was very kind, very compassionate. Toward the end of his visit, he asked my wife if she'd like to pray with him. They got down on their knees, and he led her through, of all things, the Sinner's Prayer.

"Well, I just lost it. I burst into tears. In that explosive moment, I understood that what I had found was a relationship with God that filled all those empty places in me. I felt tremendous relief that I now understood what was going on in my life, that I could stop chasing after the things I couldn't have—I could stop chasing the wind, as Solomon says. I was created for a relationship with God, and that doesn't take any effort or wisdom, just an acknowledgment that I'm in the relationship, and that it's good.

"But I also felt like, Oh no, I'm one of *them*."

• • •

DAVID'S STORY IS IMPRESSIVE. Here's a big, brave, intelligent man, a cynical but at heart still sensitive cop who falls on his face, gets dusted off by God, and saves his marriage. Whatever works, I say— surely there are different paths to becoming a standup guy. I'm beginning to think a lot of people have the wrong impression about this group.

Around six, the band cranks up. The music is surprisingly good, the foot-stomping hybrid of gospel, country and western, and rock that has propelled Christian pop onto the mainstream charts. A Jumbotron mounted above the stage broadcasts the lyrics, and everybody sings along.

> *And though this world with devils filled*
> *Should threaten to undo us*
> *We will not fear, for God hath willed*
> *His truth to triumph through us.*

I leave David and Billy and wander around the stadium, procure a greenish hot dog for four bucks and choke it down. When I return, the Jumbotron is showing the first segment of a three-part video about a new accountability group: three men gather in a restaurant to talk about their ongoing struggle with their base desires. They ask each other about their wives, children, jobs, whether they've been saying their prayers. The segment ends with the three men heading in different directions—one to a church to pray, another to a porn shop, the third to a pay phone to call his wife and tell her he has to work late.

A parade of speakers comes and goes, rapping about workplace ethics, racial harmony, and financial responsibility. They all look remarkably alike in their blue polo shirts stitched with the Promise Keepers insignia and khaki pants—Dockers, probably. The resemblances are beyond sartorial: all are middle-aged, pleasant but nondescript, sandy- or gray-haired, and athletic. It's spooky: they all could have the same mother. Sports metaphors and clichés ricochet around the stadium, caroming off the mezzanine placards bearing the names of men who performed dazzling athletic feats in venues such as this one—Walter Johnson, Red Auerbach, Vince Lombardi: "You ain't going into the end zone without the Holy Spirit." "No relationship of substance can be sustained if you're racing down the speedway at a hundred-fifty miles an hour." This is what it means, I guess, to deliver the message through sports.

Each of the speakers drives home his remonstrations with force and clarity: "Men, end your isolation from each other now. Be the servant who leads. A man's man is a godly man. A godly man at work demonstrates character, skill, and competence. Invest in your children. Your wife is a gift from God. Be a man of influence: motivate others by using rewards instead of punishment. Never underestimate your ability to heal your community. Reach out to men of other races . . ." About midway through his talk, each typically interrupts himself, overcome by the power and truth of his own words, and asks the men to huddle up in prayer for a minute or two.

Around eight o'clock, as the stadium lights heat up, attendees who have avoided committing themselves to Jesus are invited to do so now. As the band provides a sober and meditative aural backdrop, thousands of men, many accompanied by their sons, move into the aisles to fill out forms that make them official Promise Keepers and link them to the larger network of evangelical Christians. After testifying, each is given a Bible and sent back to his seat, forever changed and chastened, he's told, by his membership in the bold and powerful brotherhood. Fathers hug their sons, brothers embrace their brothers-in-law, many break down in tears.

As I stand with David and Billy watching the men signing their covenant with Jesus, I sense much of my cynicism and apprehension about this event diminishing. Despite the massive marketing of books, tapes, T-shirts, videos, and other PK paraphernalia; whatever their connections to the Christian-right voting blocs whose politics I generally disagree with; regardless of the personal wealth that's undoubtedly being created for PK leaders (what's new about Baptists ripping each other off?); I'm genuinely impressed by the connections men are making with each other here, by the sincerity with which whites and blacks reach out to each other, by the physical affection sons and fathers show for each other, and—I'll admit—by the "message": the exhortations to lead, protect, be honest, faithful, responsible, loving— a credo, in fact, that has traditionally defined masculinity in every culture around the world and is not at odds with the profile of the new standup guy. I've heard nothing about throwing the little woman back in the kitchen. The NOW hysteria seems unwarranted. Every man I've met here tells me his wife has a job. So shoot me: I could easily be a Promise Keeper, except for that little problem I have with Jesus.

David seems to sense that I'm weakening. As the choral group—all of whom wear T-shirts proclaiming REAL MEN SING REAL LOUD—chimes with churchy fervor, David tells me more about his born-again experience, which he clearly finds inspiring in the retelling. "There's a thing we're all after," he says, flashing a knowing look. "We want to be loved and to give love. And we want to be significant. Those are the two basic needs we all have. But what I learned is that those things were unattainable until I entered into the only relationship I could have that automatically provides those things. As a man of God, I know I don't get the things I desperately need by chasing them. They come as a gift after entering into a relationship with God. He won't fail me, He won't die on me, He won't leave me, turn His back on me, or hate me for anything I've done. I can place everything I need right there at the foot of the cross.

"My goal is to become Christ-like, not David-like. For example, when I spend all my energy trying to be a good dad, I do it on my own strength. I'm David-like. But when I become Christ-like, being a good husband and father is automatic. The things in my life now that make me loved and significant come when I stop wanting them."

I nod dumbly. Neat trick. I take it back. I'm not there yet. This could be a long evening.

. . .

NEAR TEN P.M., Bill McCartney, the Promise Keepers guru, struts from the wings of the stage and grasps the microphone. It was he who, in the spring of 1990, was struck by a vision of stadiums filled with once wayward men beseeching Jesus to guide them toward a more honorable and responsible life. McCartney is an ideal figurehead: tall and rugged, son of a Detroit autoworker, and a former alcoholic with a wandering eye, McCartney cleaned himself up, got a job as the coach of the University of Colorado football team, transformed the once hapless Buffaloes into an Orange Bowl victor in 1991, and was voted Coach of the Year. In 1994, he walked away from a fifteen-year contract that was paying him $400,000 a year to devote himself full-time not to Promise Keepers but to his long-suffering wife, Lyndi, whose severe depression had been evident to everyone but him.

McCartney opens by telling a story about a man named Ivan, an Hispanic Vietnam war veteran he met in Denver. Ivan's life is in ruins: he's living on the street, his children hate him, he's totally isolated, trapped in a living hell. Ivan, McCartney says, has never been able to accept what happened to him in the jungle. He had befriended a group of Vietnamese village children who visited him and his platoon members every day to peddle candy. Ivan had developed a close, almost paternal relationship with one of them, a little seven-year-old girl named Kim. He held her on his lap, told her he loved her, gave her presents to take back to her family. He looked forward to her visit every day, her bright, smiling eyes; the way she cheerfully skipped along ahead of the other children as she made her way into the soldiers' encampment.

One day, Kim came over the hilltop to their camp, but this time she was alone. As the men trained their binoculars on her, she opened her blouse, revealing to the soldiers the rack of explosives wired across her chest. "She was saying, 'Take me out,' " McCartney says. "Take me out now because if I get any closer I'm going to take out all of you." Ivan was one of the men who shot her, triggering the explosion that atomized her tiny body. "To this day, Ivan is in pure torment," McCartney says. "He can't receive what Kim offered: his life. She gave her life so he could live." He pauses, waiting to deliver the kicker. "Of course, that's what Jesus did. He gave His life because He fell in love with you."

Forty-five thousand men sit silently. Then McCartney starts up again, his raspy tenor bouncing and booming around the stadium, his words instantly appearing on the huge screen as though the Jumbotron has a direct feed from his neocortex. As the host of this pious party, the pasha of PK, he can address whatever topic he wants, and he touches upon them all. "Get out of debt, men," he admonishes. "Be ethical at work. Be a godly influence at home."

He builds toward his favorite topic: sexual sin. McCartney knows something about this devilish business: many of the football players on teams he's coached have tended toward the kind of destructive behavior he now rails against—twenty-four of them were arrested during one three-year period. And his daughter Kristyn gave birth to two children by different fathers, both members of her father's football team. McCartney, who exhorts men to "treat your wife like a goddess," admits he ignored and mistreated his wife for nearly thirty years but realized his sin before it was too late. His epiphany? A pastor visiting his local church in Colorado had said, "You want to know about a man's character? Just look into his wife's face." When McCartney turned and looked at his wife, Lyndi, he saw nothing but pain and torment. He had produced and spoken at ten PK rallies, telling men that he conceived of the organization as "an answer to the cry of women's hearts," before he was able to hear the sobbing of his own wife's.

"Sixty-two percent of all men in our country are living in sexual sin," he's saying now as the stadium crowd begins to murmur. "Recently, fifteen thousand of them confessed to it at a Promise Keepers conference in Detroit." Cheers greet the news. "Men, give up lust, adultery, pornography, fornication, homosexuality!" A chorus of amens from the crowd. "When you watch TV and get aroused by it, turn it off!" Louder affirmations. "The only sex you can have is with your wife! If you're single, get married!" Yess!

"Remember, men: your wife is a gift from God," McCartney yells hoarsely. "Your wife is your greatest asset. Dress her up so she can walk before you like a goddess! And when you leave here tonight, make the phone call to break off the ungodly relationship that's keeping the two of you apart!" The crowd roars.

"God bless you, men. And make the call!"

■ ■ ■

BACK ON THE BUS following McCartney's jeremiad, we're all accounted for except one—Frank, a thirty-five-year-old accountant. I'm eager to get back to the hotel and catch a few minutes of the Bulls-Jazz playoff game, and a few others in the bus have the same thing in mind. With the pay-per-view in each of our rooms locked out, and the idea of a nightcap anathema to the Baptist teetotalers, the game is the only diversion permitted before turning in.

We wait ten minutes, fifteen, twenty. As Billy nods off in the back of the bus, I ask David whether sexual sin is really such a big deal for men at the rally. "Huge deal," he says. Then, lowering his voice, he adds, "Coach isn't just talking about fantasizing about a coworker or watching pornography. He's talking about adultery and abuse. In my case, I struggle with temptation every day. I won't have lunch with a female client. If there's business to discuss, it's in her office or mine. I just can't be cavalier about it. It's not so much that looking like sinning is sinning; if I put myself in a situation where temptation could exist, it probably will, and I don't want to be around it. And I don't want other people to stumble, either. I have lots of female friends, but I'm not going to get in a situation where I'm in an intimate dialogue with one when no one else is around. We're good friends with our neighbors, but if he's out of town and my wife is out shopping, it's inappropriate for me to go next door and ask to borrow a hammer or something. If I'm at the tennis club and a woman friend is sitting there having a Coke, I'll chat with her, but while standing up. To sit down—now we're engaged. If you don't expose yourself to temptation, you're probably not going to end up with a sin. I distrust myself enough that I won't even give myself the opportunity."

Finally, Walter, the retired Navy captain and our bus leader, suggests a vote on whether to leave Frank to fend for himself at the stadium. If that's our decision, we should all share in the responsibility for it. We all agree. To hell with Frank, I almost say before catching myself. As the bus pulls out of the parking lot, someone notices a man running behind us, arms flailing. We stop, and Frank boards the bus, too exhausted to speak.

I can't resist. "Must have had more than one call to make, eh, Frank?" I say. Howls of laughter fill the bus. Heads turn to identify the quipster. *It's the interloper in the rear.*

. . .

THE NEXT MORNING, we eat, pack, and check out of the hotel in time to get to the stadium by seven-thirty. Anticipating rain, many in our group find seats under the stadium overhang, but Billy, David, and I head for the field along with the homeboys and a few others. Beneath their slouchy, hip-hop defiance, these kids are well-mannered, wholesome, enthusiastic, and get on well with the older pilgrims. "I'd rather be at a Dave Matthews concert," says one, "but this is almost as good."

David and I sit next to Walter Smith and his son-in-law, Harlan, a janitorial supervisor at a hospital in Ithaca. At eight o'clock, two Jews for Jesus walk on the stage, relate the stories of their conversions, and open the day's events by blowing the shofar. Five minutes later, the PK band is smoking, the homeys are on their feet clapping and dancing, and we're sailing away on a magical Christian carpet ride.

The program opens with the second video segment about the accountability group. The man who was headed to church prays for the others, hoping his entreaties will save them from sexual sin. The one who went to the porn shop disgustedly throws his purchase in a trash container after leaving the store. The third argues with his lover in a telephone booth, the camera zooming in, soap-opera style, on his tormented face as the segment ends.

Bill Hybels, the former chaplain of the Chicago Bears, mounts the podium to talk about manly friendship and the need, as McCartney says, for "a masculine context that allows men to come clean." As he drones on, I ask David what he and his accountability partner talk about. Every Monday morning, he tells me, David meets his partner at a McDonald's near their offices. They grab their Egg McMuffins and coffee, say a prayer, and update each other on the previous week's concerns. "There are no ground rules," says David. "We talk about sex, finances, kids, work, whether we've devoted enough time to prayer. As you get to know your partner, you invite him to hold you accountable for your actions. Proverbs says two is better than one, and a chord of three strands is not easily broken.

"Left to my own devices, I'll do only that which I'm self-motivated to do. What I'm not self-motivated to do is tell other men my darkest secrets and let them guide me through them. You sit down, get transparent, and peel off your mask. You'll meet for a couple of weeks, and then one of you will say, 'Look, I haven't been really honest,' and you peel off another mask, and that continues. You're not encouraging each other to get in touch with your feelings but encouraging each other to be what God wants you to be: more Christ-like. So you talk about the areas of your life you're not proud of and the next time you get together you say, 'I've been praying about that thing you told me about. How are you doing with that?'

"Accountability is about wanting to be better than you are and expecting your partner to hold you to that. If I'm doing well, I expect you to encourage me; if I'm doing poorly, I expect you to challenge me and get in my face about it. It's not the same as friendship, because often you won't see your partner outside of church or the accountability session. But you develop a language with each other that you slip into immediately—like the close friend from high school whom you see once a year? It's like that. It never changes. You develop a closeness that is intentional and purposeful and that's designed to change you, not just let you be okay with yourself. And change can be painful. But when you recognize it as being necessary for the things you want, then it's not so bad."

Hybels now asks the men in the stadium to huddle up in groups of two or three and pray for guidance on how to form the special friendship that will help us become godly men. David leans over and puts his arm around Billy, talking to him softly, so I hang with Walter and Harlan. I have no idea how to handle this. I've never prayed before and have never felt like doing it less than now. We put our arms around each other's shoulders and bow our heads toward the center of the little ring we've made. Walter thanks the Lord for the accountability group he's formed with two other retired Navy men who have also realized how fortunate they were to have wives to raise their children while they blithely sailed around the world for a quarter century. Harlan says he's tried to interest men who work with him at the hospital to form a group but hasn't been able to. He prays this will happen. I'm not sure what to say, but come up with this: while I'm not a member of an accountability group and haven't tried to put one together, I do have important friendships with men I've played music with every week for the past twenty-five years. On those nights, we find plenty of time to talk about our children, our home life, our difficulties at work. It's not a formal accountability group, but it offers something of the same kind of comfort and support.

Walter floats a prayer. "Lord," he says, "I want to thank you for introducing me to these important men, for giving me the opportunity to help other men in my life, and to be helped by them. I pray that you'll find a way for Harlan to form bonds with men who will help him in his life, and thank you for granting Mike the friendships, the music, for twenty-five years, that have given him such happiness."

Yes. Thank you, Lord. And thank you, Walter, for making it easy. I mean it.

. . .

JUST BEFORE THE lunch break, as dark, glowering clouds gather, James Ryle, the team pastor for Coach McCartney's Buffaloes, walks on stage. He's scheduled to talk about fatherhood, the program says, but begins with the obligatory sports metaphor. He holds up a brown, scruffy, shapeless object that turns out to be a deflated football. "We're like this football," he says. "We've got the potential but we're empty. How far in life can you go without God? You can not go far without God any more than a football can go far without air. We're looking for men who are ready to be filled with the spirit of God so that God can give you shape, and in your shape you can go the distance! How does that happen? It happens with a life-shaping encounter with the truth. That happened to me several years ago and I'd like to tell you a little bit about it."

When he was two years old, Ryle tells the rapt crowd, his father was found guilty on two counts of armed robbery and sentenced to the Texas state penitentiary. "Not knowing how to handle five kids, my mother put the three youngest of us in an orphanage," he says. "So I grew up feeling unwanted and unloved, and those are powerful emotions that can drive you to do stupid things to get attention. And I did stupid things. I lied, I stole, did all the drugs available—anything so people would think I was impressive."

When he was seventeen, a runaway, he was in a Labor Day car accident in which a friend was killed. Ryle was charged with negligent homicide. Hoping to raise enough money to hire a lawyer, he began selling marijuana and was busted. "This was in Texas in 1969," he says. "Are we communicating here?" Ryle was sentenced to the Texas Department of Corrections, where he was born again.

Ryle became a preacher especially devoted to helping young men tread the straight and narrow. A few years later, in his wanderings around Texas, he ran into his father, with whom he'd maintained sparse contact after both were sprung. The older man told his son that he, too, had thought of becoming a minister when he was in his early twenties. " 'Why didn't you?' I asked him," Ryle says. "And my father replied, 'Son, every choice I've made in life, every decision I've made, has been the wrong one. My life has been a series of wrong choices.'

"Then my father asked me what prison I'd been in, and I told him. I watched the blood drain from his face. 'Son,' he told me, 'when I was in the state penitentiary, I got on a work detail that helped build that prison you were sentenced to.' "

Ryle waits for the full biblical weight of his words to settle upon the crowd. Then, in a booming voice, he says, "The Lord said, 'I have set you free from a prison your father built.' Men, set your own sons free!"

As the crowd roars, the band kicks into Bob Dylan's "Serve Somebody," and David, his arm around Danny, talks about his own dad. His father was the son of an alcoholic who beat him mercilessly, and consequently, says David, his father was never able to show any feeling except anger. "I inherited his quick temper," he says. "But I recognize it now and can say to myself, 'You're doing that thing again.' But I never doubted my father's love for me, even though he never told me he loved me. It's something I try to tell my children regularly. So, as a father, I feel like I'm trying to pass on a legacy, break a legacy, and create a brand-new legacy all at the same time.

"Being a father and knowing, watching, and enjoying my kids has taught me more about my relationship with God than anything else. I can see in His model the perfect relationship between father and son, and that's what I want to emulate. When my kids do something to disappoint me, I suddenly understand how God must feel. When I fail and feel really badly about it, I think about how I am as a dad when my kids fail, and I feel really badly. I just want to hug them and say, 'It's okay, we'll make it better, together we'll work through this'—and that's exactly how God is feeling about me.

"So through my kids, I've learned more about how He feels about me, how I should be about Him, than I think I ever could have without kids. We'll do things to God that we won't tolerate from our own kids. When you think about it that way, the relationship becomes very real."

■ ■ ■

AT NOON I LEAVE the stadium and join a long line outside to get my special PK lunch: water, turkey sandwich, and a cookie. Truly ominous clouds have been forming for the past hour to the west, and I grab a plastic garbage bag from a heap near the box lunches as an emergency raincoat. I wolf down my sandwich and cruise the cavernous tent where PK audiotapes, books, T-shirts, and other knickknacks are sold. Business is brisk.

At one-thirty, I'm back in the stadium, sitting next to David and Billy. A light misty rain has begun to fall, and technicians hang plastic tarpaulins above the stage to protect the musicians and equipment. The emcee looks skyward and announces to the crowd, "This is nothing. In Alabama the heavens opened, blessing us with God's good rain for the entire two days. Lord, bless us with Your rain!"

I wonder whether it's such a good idea to be goading God like this, for He seems to be responding. The rain is falling harder now, and I pull the garbage bag tight around me. David and Billy have their ponchos on and are standing, clapping to the music, which has kicked into an upbeat, spirit-rousing tempo.

> *If the Lord had not been on our side*
> *All our enemies would have swallowed us alive*

Other men, shirtless, toss frisbees and minifootballs in the aisles, belly-flopping onto the soggy turf after feigning a spectacular over-the-shoulder catch—Montana to Rice!—and skimming along its surface. I'm reminded of Woodstock—surely some of these men were there—only without the drugs. Or the sex.

The rain washes over us, warm and soft and enveloping. Many men flee to the seats beneath the stadium overhang. Others strip to their shorts and wrestle with their kids in the mud. My plastic bag is no match for this monsoon; my shirt, shorts, and underwear are soaked, and water pools in my shoes. I step out of the bag, turn my face to the sky, and give myself up to the silky rain and the music.

> *If the Lord had not been on our side*
> *All the raging waters*
> *And the mighty flood*
> *Would have swept over us*

The band is really cooking now, cranked with gospel fervor and rock-steady, laboring to keep everyone's spirits up, the vocalists locked in an impassioned call and response. I find a comfortable midrange harmony and join in, clapping and swaying.

If the Lord, if the Lord
If the Lord, if the Lord
If the Lord had not been on our side

The rain, even harder now, washes away all color and detail. Everything is a gray blur. There is only the music, and my voice rising above all others, locked in rhythmic refrain.

If the Lord, if the Lord

The music lifts me up, gently, and I float effortlessly, like a hawk riding a thermal. I feel oddly peaceful, safe, soaked, and warm. I might be crying. Someone, something, may be knocking on my carapace. For the next half hour I ride the music, sensing some of the hard parts within me, the calcified resentments and stubborn pride, dissolving in the torrential storm.

This, I suppose, is as close as I can get to a baptism.

■ ■ ■

IT'S NEARLY MIDNIGHT; we're somewhere in central New Jersey, and the thrum of the bus engine has lulled most of the men to sleep. David snores in a seat behind me. I'm relieved the weekend is over, but glad I went. I think I managed to get a handle on the Promise Keeper message, and why it appeals to so many men. For much of the weekend, I couldn't help but think: What's not to like? The talk about "taking back" spiritual power from women—none of which I heard at the rally, by the way—may be antediluvian, but who really takes this seriously? Does it matter who drives the kids to Sunday school? Besides, I know plenty of women—smart, well-paid, well-educated women whose husbands have bailed on them—who would welcome any measure of masculine power and energy back in their home. Some men need Jesus to help them be a better father and husband, racially tolerant, and a moral leader in their community. Some men need the structure of an accountability group to form a trusting friendship with another hostile force of nature. "Treat your wife like a goddess." What's wrong with that? Maybe the real enemies of the Promise Keepers are those who abuse women, neglect children, foment racial hatred, and undermine their communities.

So can I report at last that I've found the standup guy? Well, no. Most of these men continue to screw up badly or they wouldn't be here. According to McCartney, a majority regularly step out on their wives. Others can't handle money or their kids, are drags on their community, or, as David reveals, are physically abusive at home. I can't help but think that, as genuine as their desires to reform may be, what they're really looking for is forgiveness. Show up at a rally once a year, toss a few footballs, emote a little, confess your frailty, and be on your blessed way. It's short-term group therapy—really short-term—and the only kind men can stand.

For all its merits, the evangelicals' vision of the standup guy is also exclusionary, as is much of the politics of the religious right: unless you buy into Jesus, you can't join the club. Even my new friend David told me he was deeply sorry that after I shrugged off the mortal coil I wouldn't be joining him in heaven. And there's something a little spineless and unmanly about feeling that you're simply not strong enough to resist new credit card offers or the come-hithers of the new office temp. David feels like he's just one hot daydream about his neighbor away from veering out of control. He can't even sit next to a female business acquaintance at lunch without fearing that he'll try to take her blouse off.

So where do I look next? Gazing out into the orange haze of the New Jersey oil refineries, surrounded by a few dozen standup wannabes, I remind myself that the reason men are turning to each other to bolster their personal power in the world—at New Warrior retreats, cocktalk marathons, one of the thousands of weekly talk groups, or even (though attendees wouldn't see it this way) at Promise Keeper rallies—is a very old one: they're trying to make themselves more desirable to women. For as long as there's been a human pair-bond, women have been the ones to call the final shots on mate selection.

Which means that women have some very firm ideas about what constitutes a standup guy. It might be instructive to take a close look at what they are.

WHAT WOMEN
REALLY WANT

. . .

Iᴛ's ᴇɪɢʜᴛ ᴀ.ᴍ. on a Monday morning and, buzzing with anti-inflammatories to minimize the soft-tissue paralysis I'm guaranteed to be suffering by noon, I lace up my hockey skates and adjust the fifteen pounds of protective equipment I've strapped, taped, and velcroed onto my creaking body, which is already howling in protest. I'm surrounded in a malodorous locker room at Chelsea Piers, a magnificent sports complex in lower Manhattan, by my frisky, youthful teammates, all but a few of whom are New York City firemen, about as noble and manly a group of guys as you could hope to assemble in one room. Some of them have just come off a graveyard shift and chatter noisily about the pasta sauces, ragouts, and vats of stew they've prepared for the coming week at the firehouse, meaning they had a quiet, alarm-free night. Others will be heading to various stations around the city after our game. Some will probably get paged during the contest and have to leave to rescue trapped infants from four-alarm infernos or bridge painters dangling by their safety harnesses from collapsed rigging high above the East River. We all knock helmets in the Police and Fire Hockey League, which includes teams from the police department, FBI, and Drug Enforcement Agency. Hockey is popular among the firefighters, and they signed up too many guys for one team, but not enough for two. So I and a couple of other ringers were recruited to round out the second team.

As they do for a lot of men, sports to me present allegories of real substance. The minidramas that unfold over forty-eight or sixty stop-time minutes on a court or rink, over nine innings on a field of dreams, or during a deranging five-set tennis match in hundred-degree heat reveal much about their dramatis personae. Courage and composure, guile and grace, strength and skill—many of the same talents essential to prevailing in nonsporting milieus—are on display to be disparaged, admired, or rewarded. Being a member of the cast, as opposed to just watching the drama, is the fun part: every new game situation presents a different test, and I love being tested, even if, just as it was in childhood, it's only pretend.

It's no secret that the most successful men are intensely competitive—although simply being competitive, as I'm willing to testify, doesn't necessarily guarantee success. Today, however, a man who loves to compete—or, in anthropological terms, sees other men as "hostile forces of nature"—is not always admired. Although men are still allowed to ritualize their urge to bang up against each other on the playing fields, manly aggression is routinely knocked in many real-life venues, particularly those inhabited by the arbiters of the new politically correct behavioral codes. Among the ways men have been asked to change by gender rhetoricians, this one has flummoxed them more than any other, causing many young men, in particular, to shrink from manhood's larger contests. If the alleged contemporary female preference for sensitive men were true—if Kate and her girlfriends really did crave the metaphysical-poet type, as they claim—this new bias would have to rank as one of nature's great reversals, for women have always encouraged tough and forceful engagement with the world. Evidence of their complicity still abounds, and sometimes this plain truth is drilled into you even on the hockey rink.

This morning we play the FBI, the nastiest and most viciously competitive team in the league, although the drug cops are not exactly known for their gentility on the ice, either. Clearly, there's some kind of hierarchical thing going on here, a federal versus local rivalry at work. The FBI goons have gleaming, perfectly matched uniforms in the colors of the flag, naturally, with the stars and stripes emblazoned across the front of their jerseys; all new equipment; a row of expensive new sticks stacked behind their bench; even a team manager, who proffers high-carb sports drinks to the players after a shift. Our federal tax dollars at work. The rest of us wear twenty-year-old pads and skates salvaged from our high school or college teams and pull on shirts-and-skins-style sleeveless pullovers to distinguish us from our opponents. Someone tried to take up a collection to buy matching jerseys imprinted with our team nickname, the Hosers, but no one was interested in coughing up the twenty bucks apiece.

Many of the feds were recruited from Ivy League or Big Ten schools that had terrific hockey teams, so in addition to being talented players, many of them are gifted in the IQ department—and with all their supercop psychotraining, they aren't above messing with the heads of their opponents. Their second-line center, a short, quick man with disturbing cobalt eyes, disgorges a stream of trash talk before each face-off. "I know where your sister lives," he'll say with a smirk, his implication totally mystifying. Or, "Still keep up with your old Yippie pals?" (I'm the only one old enough in the league to even remember the Yippies.) But every once in a while, he'll astound me with a bit of personal knowledge, indicating he's done some real snooping. "So, how are the twins?" he'll ask just before the puck is dropped, then win the face-off easily. I wonder how he even knows my name, much less the fact that my youngest kids are twins.

This morning, our third game this season against the feds, I'm whipped. I've been staring at a computer screen all weekend trying to honor various deadlines, and I haven't gotten much sleep. But on my first shift, parked in front of the net, I score by tipping in a shot from the point, having eluded for a split second my chatty nemesis, whose job was to cover me. On my second shift, I thread the puck through the opposing defensemen to my left wing, who scores, and suddenly we're up by a pair over the feisty feds, who dominated us in the first two games. Feeling a little cocky, I decide to engage my noisy opponent before the ensuing face-off. "I hear your wife is going to have a baby," I tell him, having overheard him gush about his incipient parenthood in the next locker room. "Who's the father?" Shifting into robocop mode, he effectively tunes me out and controls the face-off.

This is supposedly a no-checking league, although plenty of hitting goes on. My opponent is a master at staging an apparently inadvertent collision, and on my third shift he's looking for me, although I don't know it at the time. I don't have his training in mind reading and constantly watching my back. As I circle at center ice about to receive a pass—a screw-your-buddy pass, it turns out—he lunges for the puck, and for me, burying his shoulder in my solar plexus. He may not be big, but like a lot of hockey players he has a low center of gravity, with meaty thighs and a powerful butt, and he levels me, sprawling backward as he pretends the hit was just one of those unavoidably random atomic events in a high-speed game. The referee looks at the two of us laid out on the ice, apparently decides no malice was intended, and lets play go on. The feisty fed springs to his feet and rejoins the play.

I lie gasping on the blue line, hoping my neck bones will remember where they're supposed to be and reconfigure themselves in something that resembles a natural alignment, my retinal rods quivering and sprinkling little points of light across my visual field. As I drag myself back to the bench, calling out for a replacement, I laugh at the silly thought bobbing on the surface of my foamy brainpan: This is all women's fault.

■ ■ ■

THE IDEA ISN'T that silly, actually. Evolutionary biologists think of men as a vast breeding experiment run by women, because everything we do in relation to them, and often with and to each other, provides clues to our desirability as mates. In this view, we evolved in response to women's preferences. Men are naturally aggressive, obsessed with dominating each other, and inclined to take risks, because over the eons during which the male brain was laying down its circuitry, the benefits conferred by these traits helped us get the girl. The dickfesters and other men who feel overlooked by desirable women need to get with this simple evolutionary plan. Join a hockey club and practice your dominance technique. Fight for the big job. Stay competitive. Because women are watching, and comparing notes.

Of course, "dominance" is a loaded word in today's touchy social climate. Men's healthy desire to leapfrog over rivals, along with our affinity for pissing contests, wars, and the Super Bowl, is often maligned, in male bashspeak, as "testosterone poisoning." But if that's the case—to take the breeding-experiment metaphor a step further—the estrogen-afflicted are helping to skew the data. Some of the wiser feminists know this and are willing to admit it. "Male oppression is not just attributable to men," says Felicia Pratto, a psychologist and feminist scholar at Stanford, "but to a cooperative relationship between men and women."

Is this feminist heresy? How do women participate in their own oppression? Like everything else, it starts with sex, says Pratto. As do most other female animals, women expend more effort (and thus risk more) than men in launching their kids—and are therefore pickier about choosing an ambitious and prosperous mate who will keep the nippers well fed, clothed, and tutored at the finest academies. According to evolutionary theory, men have responded to this selective pressure by learning to monopolize the material wealth their partners would want or need—thus making themselves attractive—and by keeping those goods out of the clutches of other men.

So over time, this adaptation to female choosiness helped mold a male noodle specially equipped with the desire to keep lower-ranking men in their place, accumulate disproportionate wealth, and back political causes that keep a lid on women's power. Men who were particularly apt at hip-checking rival suitors into the tarpits while bearing food, furs, and the deed to a capacious and well-appointed condo fathered and raised more children, who inherited a special talent for beating down others.

The gender differences in what Pratto calls "social dominance orientation" explain why men favor ideologies that squash social groups unlike their own—wage and income controls are a favorite hobbyhorse—while women wave the flag for social equality. Men are far more supportive of defense spending, the use of troops in foreign countries, and the death penalty, while women tend to back funding for welfare, education, health, and programs for the poor. A man's obsession with status also predicts the career he chooses. Men overwhelmingly hold jobs that enhance their hierarchical positions—three quarters of all lawyers and judges and more than 90 percent of police (and 100 percent of hockey-playing FBI agents) are men—whereas three quarters of all social service providers are women. Along with their political views, this makes men, in Pratto's view, "rankers" (*My salary/house/dick is bigger than yours*) and women "linkers" (*Peoples of the world: Unite*).

As disloyal as it may be to say it, Pratto knows that women continue to be actively involved in tweaking our obsession with status and rank. By preferring and selecting trophy husbands (the bitchfesters' résumé man), they encourage male competition, which in turn reinforces social stratification and the sexist cultural practices that enable it. Surveys of accomplished women, including those who call themselves feminists, indicate that they seek even higher-status men for themselves and their daughters. And, though the practices are supported by men, it is upper-class women in India, China, and much of Africa who impose veiling, footbinding, and infibulation on young women to make them "marriageable" to a man with a fat wallet. The obvious benefits that accrue to both mother and bride go a long way toward easing the guilt they may feel for having to cooperate in their sisters' oppression.

It's an old story, succinctly articulated by the very modern slacker/cartoonist Holden in the movie *Chasing Amy:* "Life is about money and chicks." History is filled with colorful examples of how cultural success (money) translates into reproductive success (chicks). Moulay Ismail the Bloodthirsty, the emperor of Morocco from 1672 to 1727, had 888 acknowledged offspring, produced by a harem of five hundred women that was managed by a senior wife. In the royal courts of China and the Middle East, the harems were even larger. The Arabian caliph al-Mutawakkil, who ruled his kingdom from 847 to 851, reportedly had four thousand concubines. The Egyptian Abdur Rahman III topped out at 6,300. As Holden might say, the more money, the more chicks.

Dominant men don't have to enslave women to mate with them, though, as Pratto knows. From Thomas Jefferson to Bill Clinton, Louis B. Mayer to Jack Nicholson, Babe Ruth to Magic Johnson, Nabokov to Picasso, overachievers have been magnets to women. Social dominance theory is writ large in a man like Sir James Goldsmith—a corporate raider and one of the richest men in the world. Among his several palaces, the tycoon has built a huge compound in Mexico, where he's surrounded by ex-wives and current and former mistresses, one of whom he has married (others have borne him children). Once, on vacation in Sardinia, his wife and children were lodged in a seaside villa, his mistress across the water. Goldsmith went back and forth by speedboat, keeping everybody happy.

"When you marry your mistress," Goldsmith has said in the tradition of Moulay Ismail, "you create a vacancy."

■ ■ ■

I CAN ALMOST HEAR the bitter fulmination issuing from distaff readers and PC-poisoned men: Just because men evolved under competitive pressure to kick ass with more authority than the next guy doesn't mean they have to obey their inner primitive in these enlightened, postfeminist, theoretically queer times. Men like Goldsmith are unenlightened throwbacks, men like Clinton sex addicts, and Jack Nicholson is "unmarriageable." Men can change. Men have changed.

Maybe on the surface. But a probe into the murkier depths of his brain reveals that even the impassive New Man spends a significant chunk of mental energy fantasizing about glorious victory and dreading ignominious defeat. No matter how often he gets in touch with his feminine side during the day.

Since 1953, when rapid-eye-movement (REM) sleep, or the dream state, was first recognized, about thirty studies have dissected gender differences in dreaming. Generally, women's dreams are set indoors, typically in the home, and involve relationships and loss—what you'd expect of linkers. Men are more likely to dream about fighting, protecting something, or competing—outside, of course, where the rankers won't wreck the furniture. Even though men get banged up almost nightly, women tend to be victims much more often and feel emotional pain in their dreams much more acutely. In analyses done by psychiatrist Milton Kramer, male subjects had more single characters and strangers in their dreams than women did, and those figures were more likely to be men. Men also typically dream in black and white and are more concerned about large sizes, fullness or emptiness, straightness or crookedness, and old age.

The worries that percolate up from the sleepy wild kingdom are just more evidence of our obsession with dominance—hence our fretting over largeness (physical and phallic) and the diminution of power that accompanies old age. Achromatic dreaming probably reflects the fact that men have more rigid boundaries—between thoughts and emotions, right and wrong, sanity and madness—than women do. And our preoccupation with shapes and quantities, say analysts, may reflect our greater interest in spatial patterns and concern about navigating successfully through a highly competitive world in which other men are considered hostile forces of nature.

Curiously, these differences transcend time and culture: a comparison of the dreams of college students in 1950 and those in school today found the sex differences to be identical. Despite feminism and the sexual revolution, despite political correctness and all those New Age moms who are mustering the "courage" to raise "good" sons, dreams suggest that men are still primarily concerned about pounding a male rival, women about the home and family. In fact, men on opposite sides of the world dream more like one another than they do like women in their own neighborhoods. That you, a Burmese pygmy, and a Mongolian shepherd are all fretting about large strangers trying to block your path home suggests that Freud was right: Anatomy is destiny.

If you have a penis, you're a ranker.

■ ■ ■

ANOTHER MONDAY MORNING, another scrum with the goons from the FBI. Two weeks ago, after we played this team, I made the mistake of telling my wife about my feud with the scrappy federal agent. She examined my scraped and swollen lip, which interfered with my opponent's elbow during a corner tussle, and threw me a look—that look—which she used to back up with the following admonition: "Don't be stupid. You know how you can get. I really don't want to have to raise our kids by myself." Now, of course, she only has to give me the look, and I say the words for her.

Last year, after a twenty-five-year layoff, I started playing hockey again. I was asked to coach my son Tom's mite team, and gradually got drawn back into playing. As I slowly rediscovered some of my skills, I remembered why I was so attracted to the sport as a young boy and up until my last game in college: it's played at an exhilarating pace and requires split-second reactions and decisions. Its constantly shifting geometry focuses my mind in a way that no other activity—save, say, sex—does. It's got speeding missiles and moving targets. Its greatest appeal, though, is that it satisfies my desire to experience, however artificially, danger. To my middle-aged mind and body, that danger is relative but real—and to my usually underaroused metabolism, absolutely necessary to feeling alive.

When I was twelve, my father, then a trial attorney, knew this about me and decided in his wisdom to send me to a boys' school with a good hockey team. Dad figured that the key to reforming my youthful talents, which demonstrated special aptitudes for hopping trains, stealing cars, and busting my nose on the rink, was good old martial discipline—and a lot of exercise. "I'm doing this for your own good," I remember him saying, reciting the popular parental mantra, which was also invoked while delivering corporal punishment. "If I don't, you'll end up dead or in jail."

Dad believed my waywardness was due at least in part to the company I kept—my pals were all tough, working-class, Irish Catholic kids, whose penchant for mischief certainly equaled my own—never suspecting my affinity for trouble and risky adventures might have been innate. Today, he could get a pretty good sense of how attracted I am to activities with a higher-than-average probability of making me a paraplegic or my wife a widow simply by measuring my resting pulse rate. Seventy beats per minute is normal; sixty is common among well-trained athletes, mountaineers, and other Xtreme sports fanatics; fifty is typical of test pilots and serial killers. Recently, during a routine physical, I clocked a forty-eight.

A reptilian nervous system is the physiological hallmark of what psychologists call the Type T (for thrill-seeking) personality. Type T's chase risk, uncertainty, intensity, and novelty just to arouse themselves to the level everyone else is at when they get out of bed in the morning. As my father intuited, low-idlers may live fast but often die young. One in five fighter pilots, for instance, will have to eject from a doomed plane, and one in twelve will die on the job.

Among this group of thrill-chasers—in America, about 20 to 30 percent of the population—men far outnumber women. Psychological tests reveal that we score twice as high as they do on measurements of aggression and impulsivity—a combination researchers uncharitably refer to as "psychoticism." Like astronaut Buzz Aldrin, who dozed while waiting for hundreds of thousands of gallons of hydrogen fuel to ignite beneath him and hurtle him toward the moon, they are almost unmoved, both psychologically and physiologically, by potentially fatal risk.

This particular trait is key to understanding the connection between the sangfroid of the *Top Gun* joyrider and the cool, impassive hostility of the Boston Strangler. The only thing that separates them, as my father intuited, is socialization. Personality researcher David Lykken, a psychologist at the University of Minnesota, says, "The hero and the psychopath are two twigs on the same genetic branch."

Type T's inhabit extreme characterological outposts, but many other men are also blessed with an inherent desire to take risks that far exceeds most women's. On psychological tests, this trait is measured as "harm avoidance." "Psychoticism," or this wicked cocktail of aggression, impulsivity, and risk-taking behavior, nudges us toward the achievement contests, the endpoints of which, of course, are the female prize.

Male risk-taking may have evolved to facilitate a baser instinct, but it's a trait that continues to serve the commonweal. The loftiest expressions of this innate urge are documented daily. Every year, the Carnegie Hero Fund Commission reviews eight hundred to a thousand incidents of selfless bravery in America and awards the 10 percent of the rescuers they deem truly heroic a medal and a stipend. Since the awards were established in 1904, more than 90 percent of these citations have gone to men. Many of the players in the Police and Fire Hockey League—even some of the rabid FBI agents—would be candidates for citation were it not for the fact that part of their job description is to save lives.

Women often complain that men are insensitive, but like most hardwired traits, emotional restraint has real advantages, particularly as a subtle courtship device (just ask any woman how she feels about a firefighter in rescue gear). In the more overtly competitive eras of our dark evolutionary history, the ability to suppress fear had obvious adaptive utility. Today, the ability to stay cool under attack—one of the largest gender differences to emerge in research done by personality researchers—still serves men well: in cutthroat boardrooms, a negotiator who reveals his emotions wages a losing battle. And when facing life-or-death situations, a tendency to act first and feel later is an almost godly gift. After seeing a man and his four-year-old son sucked into deep, cold water after slipping down a cliff on the Oregon coast, Christopher Hockert, a thirty-five-year-old glazier from Grant's Pass and a recent Carnegie Hero, shed his boots and jacket and dived in. "I didn't really think about it," he said. "I just figured if I didn't succeed, at least I could save myself, and I could always say I tried my best."

In sync with the grand design of the breeding experiment, the ancestral female was really helping herself by selecting those among us who could best keep their cool.

■ ■ ■

TODAY, I'M LOOKING to be a hero too, albeit one of the pretend sort, but heeding my wife's warnings, I hope that my nemesis will find a way to lay his psychoticism on someone else. On our first shift, though, we're up in each other's faces again, and this time the jousting gets nasty. Forechecking him behind the net with my elbows high, I clock him on the chin, and he pops me back. We bark at each other, grab each other's jerseys, push and shove and snarl until the referee separates us and ushers us to the penalty box. Pretty stupid stuff, even for rankers.

The rest of the game, though, is brisk and clean. In the second period, I bring the puck up the ice and neatly stickhandle around him. "Nice move," I hear him say. In the third period, he spreads our goalie and stuffs the puck between his legs on a beautiful deke. "Nice move," I tell him as we line up for the face-off. Somehow, the redoubtable Hosers have managed to stay close to the feds, but thirty seconds into sudden-death overtime, as though they've been toying with us, they put the game away with another goal.

During the customary postgame handshake, my rival apologizes for the elbow he threw. "Me, too," I tell him. It's a friendly league, but sometimes we fall back into the habits of our youth, when the game seemed to be exclusively about dominance. "Hell," I tell him, "I instinctively hip-check my wife when she tries to pass by me in the kitchen." He laughs, and as we skate off the ice, we talk about our more glorious hockey past. He played at the University of Michigan, just missed the final cut for the 1980 Olympic team, and played pro in Europe for a couple of years before joining the FBI. He's an investigator for the Justice Department in New York's southern district office. He introduces himself, and we shake hands again. His name's Fred.

As we head off to our respective locker rooms, Fred apologizes again. "Sorry about the elbow," he says. "And I'll apologize in advance for the one I'm going to give you next time."

■ ■ ■

NO BIG DEAL. An elbow to the jaw is an honest, direct form of communication, easy to read and easy to respond to. At least I know it's coming. There's no subterfuge, no hidden intent, none of the lingering toxicity of passive aggression—the leadership and courtship styles du jour. It's easy to forgive, too. He's just being aggressive, as he should be.

A dirty word, "aggressive," but again, a reliable measure of a man's social dominance—and thus how attractive he is to women. In the past few years, curbing male aggression (and encouraging it in females) has become kind of a clarion call among feminists and New Age men. In nearly all studies of aggression, the subject of more research than just about any other human behavior, boys and men demonstrate far more confrontational behavior and rough-and-tumble play than girls and women, and are responsible for almost all violent crime. According to a well-known feminist jeremiad, our inherent pathology—our "psychoticism"—taints even our most artful creations: the rhythms of Beethoven's Ninth Symphony, as we've all heard, are really the tympanic expressions of male rage and the universal urge to rape.

Although men are overwhelmingly responsible for all murders, muggings, gang violence, rape, and spousal abuse, violence is an aberrational by-product of aggression. "We wouldn't have so much of the behavior if it didn't work not only for the individual—as a means of maintaining one's autonomy and the integrity of one's life—but for the species," says Robert Cairns, a psychologist at Duke University who has studied aggression for three decades. "It's not just a virus that's been inserted into our behavior."

An early-life example: Boys, rankers manqués, learn the efficacy of an aggressive problem-solving style—confrontation—almost the moment their first toy is snatched from them. The up-front approach, which initially shocks everyone in the play group, including first-time moms, resolves conflict quickly. The strategy serves him well throughout his life: when a dispute has been settled, boys and men are much more likely to make up afterward, as opposed to girls, whose grudges can last indefinitely.

In fact, according to Cairns, girls may actually be meaner—agents of a different, and sometimes more destructive, aggression. Around age ten, they develop a powerful, sophisticated social weaponry that, although not physically assertive, uses alienation, rumormongering, and ostracization to vanquish a rival. This style of passive aggression can emotionally devastate the victim, who often has no idea why, or even by whom, she's being attacked. The junior linkers' strategy of organizing informal social networks as a way of ganging up on a peer not only prolongs conflict but kindles larger in-group discord. As girls enter adulthood, they become even more skilled at using gossip, aspersions, and social ostracization to assault their adversaries. Margaret Mead once remarked that women should stay off the battlefield because they'd be too brutal. Unable to handle direct confrontation, they'd end up blowing everyone away when more modest strategies might suffice.

All linkers, large and small, seem to know this about themselves and go to great lengths—a classic female weakness—to avoid conflict. In a famous study of kids' games, researchers found that girls played less competitively in smaller groups and their games were shorter, partly because they were unskilled at resolving disputes. When a quarrel began, the game typically broke up because no one made an effort to resolve the problem. Boys, on the other hand, quarreled all the time, but not once was a game terminated because of a dispute, and no game was interrupted for more than seven minutes.

Despite its bad press, aggression, skillfully and maturely deployed, sets the stage for manly cooperation. Whether on the ballfield or in the boardroom, in the Marines or in the mailroom, boys and men quickly run up against each other to establish a hierarchy and create an ordered environment in which they can work together best. To the female sensibility, this jockeying for position and rank is just another pissing contest (although they quietly pay close attention to the results). But to rankers, who learned from women a long time ago that all men are not equal, a hierarchy is a tool of cooperation and social integration. Even picking a fight, many psychologists say, is a common way for men to relate to each other, check each other out, and some- times—mystifyingly to women—take a first step toward friendship.

Of course, the key to making this work is having women hover around the edges of the competition—the breeding experiment— implicitly offering themselves as the prize. Without them, the conse- quences of male hierarchical jostling can be dire, not just for the men involved but for society as a whole. Lost in the debates about the root causes of violence in America is the simple fact that most acts of aggression are committed by single men. Marriage has long had a civ- ilizing influence on the energies of young rankers: disproportionate gender ratios and the absence or presence of family life have more to do with historical rates of nasty aggression in America than "testosterone poisoning." In the nation's early days, when the number of men far exceeded the number of women, homicidal fights were common in towns like Sutter's Mill, where the ratio of men to women was twenty to one. Within six months after their arrival, a fifth of the men were dead. Other frontier towns, like Leadville, Colorado, had homicide rates eigh- teen times that of Boston, which had more even gender ratios. In the Western towns that were settled by families, however, there was little violence and premature death. These correlations have persisted throughout the nation's history. By 1950, the percentage of unmarried men was about the same everywhere, and the rate of violent death fell to very low levels. With the decline of the family, the rise in illegitimacy rates, and competition for scarce jobs, the inner cities have become modern frontier towns, and rates of aggression have again soared.

Sometimes the results of women's breeding experiments don't turn out as planned.

■ ■ ■

DOMINANCE HAS MANY LOOKS, and a lot of them are on display in the locker room I get dressed in before my Monday morning adventures on the ice. There are the police department's "twin towers," two huge defensemen who would seem more at home on a basketball court. There are a lot of strong brows and square jaws among the kick-ass FBI, and the noble firemen have an upright bearing, with their shoulders straight and heads held high, and move with a general ease that communicates a sense of calm and self-assurance. Which is exactly what you might want from a guy who's rappelling through your skylight to rescue you and your infant twins from your penthouse blaze.

The dominant look can take a man far. An analysis of the class of 1950 at West Point showed that the most reliable predictor of a soldier's future rank was a formidable appearance—a muscular face, strong chin and brow, and good skeletal structure—"a gestalt kind of thing," according to sociologist Allan Mazur, who did the study. (Among modern military leaders, the Eisenhower and Powell mugs fit the mold.) Though the cadets' Schwarzenegger look provided few clues as to how they'd do in mid-career, they accurately predicted who would eventually become generals.

The powerful look also predicted another Promethean quality: the generals, on average, fathered one more child than their pudgy-cheeked, weak-chinned classmates. Studies of adolescent boys have also shown that facial gestalt predicts their skill as lotharios. Lads with the look of leadership attract the look of love and tend to have sex at an earlier age than those who are merely babes. To the discerning female eye, male sex appeal registers as perfect body symmetry, not only of the face but of feet, ankles, hands, wrists, and elbows. One survey discovered that women with finely balanced partners were more than twice as likely to reach orgasm during intercourse than those with less symmetrical mates.

In favoring the Dick Tracy types, women are unconsciously choosing genetic resilience. The heavy lower face typical of the perfect male specimen is a visible record of the surge of androgens that helps morph a skinny lad with a weak chin into a meaty federal agent with a big slapshot. Because the hormones required to produce the Mark Messier–like mandible are biologically expensive—they tend to compromise the immune system—evolutionary biologists think a strong jaw is an honest advertisement of a superior ability to fight disease. To be the kind of standup guy who can resist not only rivals but parasites, you need a superior immune system, which presumably you will pass on to your children.

Women's preferences for these physical characteristics show up consistently across cultures. In Spanish countries, the man who turns heads—the *hermoso* man—is not necessarily Leonardo cute but rather strong and powerful and inspires fear and respect. In the Mediterranean, the most desirable men are likened to savage animals—bulls, bears, and rams. Even in exotic cultures—among the numerous tribes in northern Africa that occupy what anthropologists call the "Narcissus band" or "male beauty belt," for instance—manly attractiveness depends on skill and prowess. Although all the men are obsessed with their comeliness and apply makeup and body adornments to lure female interest, the most favored are those who are also warriors and political leaders.

Not that the pretty Afro-Adonis, whether a warrior or a wimp, goes unrewarded for his physical splendor. The Wodaabe tribe of northeastern Nigeria considers men the most gorgeous creatures on earth; to dignify the honor, most carry pocket mirrors and combs at all times. In the annual *gerewol* ceremony, a weeklong celebration of male resplendence, young men gussy themselves up as the anointed boy toys of the community and parade before the women languorously. In a reversal of the American beauty pageant, they line up before the female judges, draw themselves up to full height and, with teeth gleaming, bodies undulating, and eyes rolling seductively, strut their stuff. One by one, the young men are selected by a judge who succumbs to his physical charm, and she's led to his sugar shack for her reward.

So women prefer a certain look—and heft. Not surprisingly, men worry most about their height, and with good reason: how tall a man is has a significant impact on the quality of his social relations, employment opportunities, political success, earning power, and the physical attractiveness of his partner—in other words, just about everything that's important. A study of personal ads found that 80 percent of women want a man at least six inches taller, and all women want a man at least four inches taller.

Of course, whether it's a strong brow, square chin, or symmetrical feet, they don't always get everything they want. But then, who does?

■ ■ ■

IN TAKING THE MEASURE of a man's potential to make his mark in the world, women don't look exclusively for assertiveness, his willingness to risk all, and an iron jaw. They're also interested in how skillfully he negotiates the social hierarchy he's a member of and how he interacts with and is treated by other men. They're particularly on the lookout for a potent combination of dominance and extroversion, drives often found in leaders who have a very appealing common touch. In the inventory of personality traits, men are usually more generously endowed with this quality than women. Those who are so specially blessed tend to become politicians or heads of corporations. The leaders of societies are seldom the toughest guys, like Saddam Hussein, but those most skilled in schmoozing and making deals, like Bill Clinton and Tony Blair.

What happens when you put together a group of guys—on a hockey team, say—who by all other measures would be considered productive, fearsome, dominant men, but are otherwise lacking in such political savvy? Just this morning, my buddy Fred found out when his collection of feral federals played our spunky Hosers, who finished second in the league standings, in the championship game. The feds, cocky after going up by three goals in the first period, took a couple of cheap penalties in the second, lost their lead, and began arguing with each other. They scored two goals to start the third period, but quickly got two more penalties and began bickering again. At one point, unbelievably, a fight broke out on their bench, and two of their players left the game in disgust. We beat them with a goal in overtime, 7 to 6. It was a particularly gratifying victory, since we all hated them.

After the game, I asked Fred what happened. "A leadership problem," he said. "Some of our guys can't distinguish their friends from their enemies."

Not a problem for highly evolved, dominant, extroverted men. But, oddly enough, it turns out that this leadership style emerged way back in our unevolved past. Dominant primates also tend to rule their troops by consensus rather than fiat.

In the monkey world, the main leadership strategy is political—primate pooh-bahs build coalitions with their neighbors instead of flattening their competitors. "The monkeys who rise to the top of the heap are good at taking turns, helping others perform tasks, and assessing potential allies," says J. Dee Higley, a researcher at the Laboratory of Clinical Studies in Poolesville, Maryland. "And when there's trouble, they seldom have to resort to direct aggression to stop it. They simply glance at a couple of their disciples, who suddenly come up behind them like a police force to quell the problem."

In primate society, a constituency depends on two other characteristics. When they sense others are particularly needy, the most successful males are willing to groom their ailing friends—that is, pick fleas from their pelts. (More elaborate back-scratching, of course, is performed daily in the power corridors of corporate America.) Executive monkeys are also good at making up after a spat: they're quick to get back to the business of nit-picking, which repairs weakened bonds.

In contrast to the smooth operators at the top of the social pyramid, the surliest monkeys at the bottom show little concern for others' dermatologic comfort and spend most of their days alone. Their interactions often consist of impulsive fights with older and bigger monkeys; like human teenagers with authority-figure problems, they often act rashly and foolishly when challenged. These hot-tempered loners also seem unable to pull back once a fight starts, even when outnumbered. Not surprisingly, they're more likely than less irascible members to be driven from the group or meet an early demise.

Neurochemical analyses by Higley's team link the peevishness of the attitudinal monkeys to low levels of the brain hormone serotonin (which inhibits impulsive behavior) and the diplomacy skills of the socially sophisticated monkeys to high levels. (In general, female primates, including humans, tend to have more serotonin than males, which may contribute to their greater overall interest in linking.) These findings parallel what's known about the chemical's influence on human leadership: men who occupy the corner office tend to have higher blood levels of it than those who don't. Some people are genetically predisposed to have higher or lower levels of serotonin than average, but other research shows that the further a man rises, the more serotonin he manufactures—a wonderfully self-propelling bit of personal chemistry and a biological vindication of his competitiveness.

Abundant serotonin helps ensure another kind of popularity as well. Higley's research shows that females have an uncanny knack for pegging the Prince Charmings and the Dastardly Dans. Shortly after two males of contrasting temperament are put into an all-female cage, the monkey gals are typically "falling all over themselves" to groom the high-serotonin schmoozer, even though neither male has done anything overtly to woo or reject the girls.

The monkey gals just have a way of knowing who's going to rise to the top. Human gals, keenly aware that a standup guy is both dominant *and* affiliative, do, too.

■ ■ ■

AH, BUT AGAIN I imagine that chorus of protest, this time perhaps from the bitchfesters. Yes, Kate would acknowledge, up until the very recent past the surest way women could acquire power was to marry it, but we are now in the midst of a cultural sea change. As they continue to shrug off the cloak of male oppression and increase their access to power and wealth on their own, women are acting more like men, both in the boardroom and the bedroom. Furthermore, Sarah would argue, as their independence grows they'll be less interested in judging a man by his ability to rise above other men—and women— and they'll acquire for themselves the pelf that historically has attracted them. When you're making big bucks of your own, a cute surfer with a nice bod and good sense of humor will do.

Surely, part of what Kate would argue is true. Women have discovered the expediency—if not always the gratification—of acting sexually aggressive, even if they often resort to such behavior, as the bitchfest participants admitted, only out of necessity and even then reluctantly. But her vision of lady doctors and lawyers marrying beach bums and potters is unlikely to be realized anytime soon, and probably not ever. Current surveys show high-powered women want superpowerful men: recently, when asked what traits they sought in a husband, fifteen women's leaders, all of them veterans of feminism's earliest skirmishes, routinely used high-status words like "very rich," "brilliant," and "genius." Even Kate and Sarah's mate test—their lucky candidate had to have read John Donne, cultivated a sophisticated international palate, and studied classical music—was a poorly disguised status check. Broader surveys of the world's industrialized nations show that today's financially successful women continue to demonstrate the universality of this fundamental mate preference: they want men who are more successful than they are. Even in Sweden, the most gender-equal society in the world, these partialities hold true. That's not to say the issue isn't fraught; as one highly accomplished woman told me at a dinner party, "Ideally, I want my husband to make one dollar more than me."

However modern, that's a formula for marital happiness that leaves only a small margin for error and a lot of room for conflict. Of course, from the long view of evolutionary biology, conflict between the sexes is as natural and inevitable as their essential differences—between the male need to seek status and rank and the female need to link. Together, men's and women's pursuits of their respective agendas act as an engine of evolutionary change, as each party struggles to outmanipulate the other. When one party introduces a new strategy, it sets off what biologists call a coevolutionary arms race. To stay in the game, the other sex is required to work out a new defense.

But it's precisely because men have yet to work out an adequate response to feminism—and devise a formula for marital happiness that's also acceptable to modern women—that the gender war continues to slog along. Certainly women over the past thirty years have adopted a new strategy—they've refashioned themselves, redefined the nature of mutual dependence and partnership, and changed their expectations of their long breeding experiment. Many men's "new defense" has been to let their wives and children fend for themselves or to withdraw from the mating pool altogether. Even those of us who are attracted to and marry accomplished women still often confuse them with rivals, other "hostile forces of nature," and aren't entirely comfortable when they make one dollar more than us.

So what would the standup guy, wherever he is, recommend as an appropriate and strategic "defense," however overdue it may be? For men who have retreated from the mating contests, the best defense is a good offense: they need to reaffirm the value of their natural aggression and desire to take risks, and reenter the competitions that determine who gets the girl. As the former astronaut Walt Cunningham told me recently, "When in doubt, act." The rest of us need to adopt a new code of behavior that enables us to indulge our innate ranking proclivities without alienating the linkers we're aiming to attract.

We need sexual manners.

SEXUAL MANNERS

. . .

WHEN FEELING A LITTLE insecure and in need of manly affirmation, the spouses of Washington's female power elite ring up Jim Schroeder, a Washington attorney and the husband of former congresswoman Pat Schroeder, to inquire about the quirky quasitherapeutic fraternity he founded back in the eighties called the Dennis Thatcher Society. Named in honor of the good-natured, happily low-profile husband of the former British prime minister, the club was Schroeder's clever response to endless questions from the press about how he coped with marriage to a powerful woman—the "feminist congresswoman," as reporters referred to her. Sadly, Schroeder has to report that the society has since disbanded.

Schroeder had brainstormed the idea with Charles Horner, whose wife, Constance, was a director at the Office of Management and Budget (OMB) and who was receiving similar inquiries about how he tolerated life with his manhood under constant threat. Applicants would be admitted, the unwritten bylaws allowed, if they could satisfy one essential requirement: "Your wife had to have a job that was more important than yours and one that you wanted." Eventually, they recruited James Woolsey, whose wife also worked at OMB; Dick Cheney, who was married to the head of the National Endowment for the Arts when he was just a lowly congressman; and the spouses of Supreme Court justices Sandra Day O'Connor and Ruth Bader Ginsburg and other congresswomen. "The idea was to get together once a year at a club where we could have a few drinks and sign our wives' signature to the bill," says Schroeder. "We were told we were supposed to be suffering because we had powerful spouses, so we did our best to create that impression."

Depending on Washington's political vagaries, members were alternately admitted, kicked out when they got better jobs, and reinstated when they lost them. "When Dick Cheney became secretary of defense, we had to let him go," Schroeder says wistfully. "We had to do the same with Woolsey when he was named CIA director." Schroeder wouldn't be surprised if the unemployed Bob Dole, whose wife, Elizabeth, until recently headed up the Red Cross while he testified about the wonders of Viagra, were to resurrect and possibly even rename the club. Like Dennis Thatcher, he may soon, after all, be the First Husband.

"The incredible thing was that there was just nothing there," Schroeder says. "It's not like we commiserated about how wrongly our lives had gone. We all had good careers; we were supportive of our wives and had strong marriages."

The Schroeders, who married in law school, moved to Washington from Denver in 1972, feminism's most strident era, with their kids, then two and six. "The conventional wisdom, particularly then, was that it's difficult for men to follow their wives around," he says. "But what is marriage, if not respect for your partner's goals and career objectives? Inevitably, particularly if you have children, somebody has to compromise and recognize that they're in the subordinate career slot. Inevitably, somebody has to adjust to meet the demands of the overall group. And that strengthens a marriage and a family."

■ ■ ■

JIM SCHROEDER MAKES the power marriage sound easy, though he knows it's not. Other couples he knew who had married in law school couldn't insulate their relationship from competitive strife and divorced not long after getting their first jobs. The rivalry among today's young professionals, he knows, is much more ferocious than when he and Pat were newlyweds and is as responsible as thorny sexual politics for poisoning the romantic aspirations of the young. Despite the model of love, partnership, and mutual respect he and his wife embodied, even his own children, now in their early thirties, have "majored in lack of commitment," he says.

With the coevolutionary arms race at full tilt, how do the bitch-festers and dickfesters declare détente? How can Kate and her friends bury the hatchet and get back in the dating-and-mating game with young men who have yet to fulfill the potential promised on their "résumé"—but will? How do the dickfesters ditch their passivity, and their dick status, and set out to become a standup guy without assuming the trappings of the old alpha male—that is, becoming a bossy and selfish asshole? How do older men who got married in the one-paycheck era satisfy their need to demonstrate assertiveness and confidence in a relationship with a now equally accomplished mate who, after raising their children, has discovered a unique talent for making money? Amid the strafing and crossfire of this protracted gender war, how can couples learn to see that the different needs, goals, and talents each partner brings to their union are dynamic, complementary, and ultimately liberating sources of strength, not divisiveness? That the popular notion that everyone is the same, a noble concept when applied to equal rights or wage scales, is the wrong template for viewing heterosexual relations and marriage?

There are no pat answers or easy formulas, particularly at this transitional moment in the culture's gender experiment. For one thing, men born before the 1980s harbor discrepant models of what a relationship should be. Consciously, we want a woman who is our equal, someone we can talk to man-to-man. But we also have a deep unconscious need to have our potency mirrored and bolstered by our wives in the same way our mothers did for our fathers. Women, too, have a built-in conflict between wanting a powerful and heroic man who wears the pants in the family the way Dad did and being angered by and envious of such power. On one level, they want to affirm their mate's worldly dominance and strength, but on another they may find it demeaning to do so. It's not surprising that the interlocking needs and desires of men and women, whether single or married, can be at cross purposes, not only within themselves but with each other. It's not easy for men to admit to wanting the soft Mommy when they're getting too much of the chairman of the board, or for women to confess longing for the stoicism and put-your-foot-down decisiveness of the Man of the House when being smothered by the cloying agreeability of an Alan Alda wannabe.

Couples can start to sort out these conundrums by observing what I call sexual manners. Some sexual manners are eternal, although most men can always benefit from a refresher course in the more mundane rules of marital propriety: Never suggest that your mate may be moody, ornery, or weepy because she's getting, or already has, her period. Never grab her crotch first thing in the morning—or any other time, really—even though you may be praying that she grab yours. Never consider offering any response but the obvious one to her question, "Do I look fat?"

The new sexual manners, though, are intended to depoliticize gender differences and prevent relationships from lapsing into a competitive free-for-all. They require understanding that while some things change, others remain the same. They mean coming up with new ways to address ancient needs. They mean supporting modern political and economic gender justice while honoring the prehistoric, sometimes anachronistic, impulses, instincts, feelings, and desires that have ever animated men's and women's private lives and dealings with each other. They often require holding on to two different, and apparently conflicting, values. Like other forms of good manners, they're often expressed better by actions and attitudes than by words.

As the modifier implies, sexual manners recognize and honor the differences between men and women that are at once intriguing and mystifying, irritating and predictable. They can be as simple as a wife understanding that her husband, no matter how "evolved" and theoretically supportive of equal partnership may still derive much of his self-esteem from his ability to provide for his wife and kids, even though she may make as much or more money as him. They can be as sophisticated as a man resisting his deeply engendered impulse to counterattack when his wife expresses unhappiness with his behavior, instead recognizing that her entreaties are not expressions of malice but of an equally deeply engendered desire to strengthen their connection—to link. In short, sexual manners acknowledge the fact that men and women often do not seek the same things from their professional life; that their notions about what constitutes intimacy are frequently at odds; that they want different things, at different times, from sex; that, as parents, each partner has comparative advantages over the other; that, as roommates, each may contribute to the upkeep and maintenance of the domestic commonwealth in ways that the other doesn't recognize or appreciate.

For single men in retreat, sexual manners require them to short-circuit their primitive instinctual impulse to demean or avoid women who are ambitious, successful, assertive, and seemingly as indomitable as they are—or should be—and instead view them as highly desirable potential partners. This means men have to be even more relentless in their pursuit of status, for women, however capable of taking care of themselves, will never marry down. As the culture embraces standards that enforce gender equality in virtually every realm, sexual manners demand that fundamental, ancient mating protocols be preserved: Men must pursue and women must choose. With few exceptions, women who ignore mating rules worked out over eons of evolutionary history and boldly chase a man to the altar will eventually be looking for another.

Properly observed, sexual manners help foster the kind of trust, intimacy, mutual dependence, and respect that underlie dynamic and loving partnerships. For men, the potential rewards of the sexually well-mannered relationship have never been greater: the prosperity of a two-income family, the opportunity for greater involvement with one's children, and the richness of an erotic life with a physically assertive mate.

Which brings us to the fun part. For novices, the best place to begin practicing sexual manners is in bed.

■ ■ ■

WHAT DOES WARREN BEATTY KNOW? The sixty-year-old lothario, even though now married, still has an incomparable reputation for his seductively slow hand. His lovers are a devoted lot: they almost universally refuse to discuss him or their trysts and only obliquely (but reverentially) acknowledge his magical lovemaking skills. What's his secret? My money says he's capable of focusing entirely on his partner's pleasure, which requires a special macho talent: he can imagine what it's like to be a woman. It's not enough to be selfless in bed; what puts you in the standup leagues is an ability to see the world from the other side. Aspiring practitioners of sexual manners would be wise to adopt this perspective and use it to examine all facets of their relationships with women.

Because of their superior relational skills, women may already have more experience at opposite-sex fantasizing than men. Try an experiment: Toward the end of your next dinner party, when your guests are appropriately lubricated, ask the women at the table what they'd do if, for a polymorphous twenty-four hours, they were magically endowed with a penis. You may be astounded to learn that they've thought, well, long and hard on the topic. A typical answer from my investigations: "The first thing I'd do is go to the gym and lift some really heavy weights. Then I'd go out on the street and punch the first person who hassled me, just to know what that feels like. Then I'd go home, arouse my partner for about ten seconds, and have jackhammer sex. And fall asleep immediately afterward." Other musings commonly involve masochism and rape—old chestnuts from the female preconscious—only in these fantasies they're the ones who are pouncing.

In a more benighted and sexist epoch, these reveries would have warranted a diagnosis of penis envy. A hundred years ago, Freud suggested that when a little girl discovers that she lacks a penis, she naturally and normally retreats into a passive, dependent, and masochistic pattern of behavior. (The übershrink excluded his properly enlightened female disciples from this fate, of course.) His theory of feminine psychology has long been discredited, but that doesn't mean women don't often dream about what it might be like to have—or be—a dick.

The nearest equivalent in men—vagina envy?—has been observed among Basque peasants and certain Brazilian tribesmen. While most men are at least a little envious of women's ability to have babies and nurse them, these avid worshippers of female fecundity ennoble the longing in a torturous ritual called couvade. During their mate's labor, the men take to bed as if about to bear the child and, working themselves into a state of extreme discomfort and agitation, submit to fasting, purification, and taboos. Some identify with the mother so successfully they claim to be able to feel the baby being born. Of course, the laboring moms find this laughable, and would be delighted to have the father of their child learn what it really feels like.

But how many men have contemplated having sex as a woman— not just to be jackhammered for three minutes but to be unselfishly ministered to by, say, Warren Beatty? Have you ever imagined what it would be like to experience arousal not as an instant shunting of blood toward highly enervated tissues that swell and throb with excitement within three seconds of eye-locking onto a Calvin Klein underwear ad, but as a slow, incremental buildup, a gradual capitulation to the intimate "trusting state" in which deep female emotion potentiates sexual desire? Have you thought what it might be like, as the love god continues to sprinkle his stardust, to experience the preorgasmic "plateau"— the anticipatory quivering of pelvis and thighs, the apneic breathing, nystagmus, and free-fall into an altered state that immediately precedes orgasm—and then the aftershocks, solitary shudders, and serial flexes that gather again into a second round of rhythmic contractions?

If you can pick the woman you could have sex as, you may as well fantasize about one who's multiorgasmic (about a third of all women) and capable of having not only the common clitoral but vaginal kind (about 10 percent of all women, but even among them, only rarely). The knowledge you'd have acquired after being swept away by the oceanic would help you understand why women quite naturally associate sex with love and why those who regularly "shed into oblivion" with the aid of their husbands report having the happiest marriages. And you'd understand why the partner of a woman who is regularly filled with pleasure gets everything he wants, and more, from his grateful mate.

If you get a second chance to road test the female apparatus, though, you'd be wise also to have sex as one of the 20 percent of women who never climax. Then you'd begin to understand the loss of personal autonomy that accompanies penetration, what it's like to have sex when you don't want to, and how important it is not to have sex when you really don't want to—feelings that all women have at least some of the time. You'd also know why female arousal proceeds at a glacial pace compared to men's: it takes a while to be comfortable with the idea of having your insides poked by an avid partner.

Which means that sexual manners of the erotic variety require a man to learn how to take no as an answer without bargaining, wheedling, forming a grudge, or plotting revenge and to stop thinking of his sexual partner proprietarially and his own avid sexual needs as preferential. By pressing to have his urgent demands satisfied, the selfish lover runs the risk of shutting down his mate's delicate arousal system altogether—every man's nightmare and a sign that he's doing everything wrong and on thin ice. The respectful lover, on the other hand, may find that he sometimes has to go to sleep a little frustrated but awakens in the morning the recipient of a quick sexual favor from an appreciative and newly revived bedmate (assuming, of course, that she too is sexually well mannered).

Your selflessness can redound to your advantage if you do a little sleuthing to determine when your mate is most interested. Women's arousal patterns vary (except for those on the pill, which flattens out the peaks and troughs of sexual desire). As measured by frequency of masturbation, vaginal blood flow, and testosterone levels, the hot point should logically be midcycle (starting a few days before and ending a few days after ovulation). Yet dozens of studies indicate that this is when women have the least sex (although they report a terrific sense of well-being). Their most active time: four to six days before menstruation, when testosterone is dropping, and four to six days after, when it begins to rise.

Sex researchers aren't sure how to explain this. Testosterone, a little bit of which goes a long way toward tweaking women's desire, may be felt more distinctly in that initial surge than at any other time. Or the midcycle peak's influence on the urge to merge may be delayed. Or, women's fluctuating desire may be nature's way of keeping a man guessing—and around. He never knows if he's going to get the lady or the tiger. A more politically sensitive answer may be that the ovulatory surge of hormones has the same effect upon women as it does on men: it makes them assertive and aggressive. Some women have higher levels than others, and are thus likelier to be more career-oriented as well as libidinous. And not all men find that attractive.

But, as a man with impeccable sexual manners, you will. It's the new way.

• • •

A SEXUALLY WELL-MANNERED man also has some enlightened views about how to negotiate domestic conflict. Let's say you've had a fight about sex. You want to try a few new *things,* but she's willing to go along with the plan only if she can get you to modify your technique— namely, to slow down to her pace. Not having practiced fantasizing about being a woman in a while, you have no idea what she's talking about. *So how long is this going to take?* The discussion gets a little heated, regrettable things are said, feelings are hurt, and you head to the basement to drill some holes in boards and cool off. Soon, it's time for bed. You're still pissed but feel a little, well, frisky. Perhaps it's time to apologize. You decide to head upstairs, slip between the sheets beside her, make your move, and see what develops.

In support of your questionable and, in fact, downright idiotic decision is a now outdated but still oft-invoked apothegm: *Never go to bed
mad.* For generations, wise old long-marrieds have offered this advice
to spatting couples—an enjoinder really directed at wives, who, as
gatekeepers of their husband's emotions and overall mental health,
were taught to use sex as a way to calm their raging bunkmate. This
injunction against fleeing to the guest bedroom or drawing a Maginot
Line on the marital couch after a fight has always received a blanket
endorsement from men. Anger is passion, too—and all the better if it
results in some vigorous carnal groping. Not so for most postfeminist
women, as you may know if you've ever tried to brush up against one
whom you've enraged. The one I love and periodically enrage has her
own italicized injunction after a nasty dustup: *Noli me tangere.*

Why do men become sexually aroused when angry? Paul MacLean,
the former chief of the Laboratory of Brain Evolution and Behavior at
the National Institute of Mental Health, suggested some answers years
ago when he identified the neurological links between sex and aggression in the squirrel monkey. Within a one millimeter area of the brain
called the amygdala, MacLean evoked responses (by electrical stimulation) that included salivation, teeth grinding, and chewing; fearful
and angry vocalizations; and penile erection. The proximity of neural
structures governing such seemingly disparate behaviors made perfect sense, for in male primates, fighting is often a preliminary to both
feeding and mating.

The same structures in our brains don't seem to have evolved much
beyond those in the squirrel monkey's. A newborn baby will fight his
mother's breast if no milk is forthcoming while sporting an erection. A
romantic dinner is often a prequel to sex. Teeth grinding accompanies
erection during REM, or dream, sleep and during particularly hot or
prolonged sexual encounters. And a number of men—15 percent
according to one report—admit to being aroused when they get mad.
And they're just the ones willing to admit it.

Women, on the other hand, find anger anything but arousing. Lacking a libidinous motive to kiss and make up, they often nurse a grudge
until it grows a beard instead. Why do women often resist a speedy
reconciliation and spurn their contrite mate when he comes sniffing
around? Again, there are clues lurking in our past, or rather, theirs.
The early human female was under pressure to control her emotional

responses—by stifling her urge to sneak off to the bushes with a snake-hipped playboy she maximized her chances of snagging a high-quality partner who would provide not only good genes to her off-spring but status, protection, and room and board. As a result, women are less impulsive than men and better able to resist temptation and delay gratification—not to mention hold out for an apology that includes some pricey material rewards.

So when is it safe for the sexually well-mannered man to approach his offended spouse? After you've proved yourself—and your love—all over again. Women are incapable of the emotional amnesia men can induce in themselves after a calming half hour or so in the basement. Obviously, it's better, and less expensive, not to get so pissed off in the first place.

■ ■ ■

AT THE FANCY but overpriced restaurant you've taken her to as part of your penance, your wife decides it's a good time to talk about just what happened the other night. However well intentioned, this is a lit-tle unfair and a sign that her sexual manners could use a tune-up. In trying to reestablish intimacy, which in today's female-friendly psychgeist is defined by expressing feelings and disclosing worries, she may have you at a disadvantage. If you're like most men, you're fre-quently oblivious to your internal state—an advantage while search-ing for air-crash victims in 120 feet of water but a serious impediment to intimacy. Men can express their love by talking, but they feel more comfortable showing it—by loading the freezer with strip steaks, catching their wife as she trips off the curb into the path of a taxicab, or having sex. Which is how you wanted to resolve this thing to begin with.

But you, a psychologically astute and sexually well-mannered man, plan to sit calmly, acknowledging, at least intellectually, that what looks like another emotional confrontation is simply the distaff way of reconnecting and not a personal attack. In the past, you might have tried to circumvent this troubling little chat by offering a practical solution or—an even worse choice—a "logical" analysis of the prob-lem. Hoping for a simple acknowledgment of her feelings, your wife would then instead feel diminished and patronized. The bickering, highlighted by the now universal accusation that you "just don't get it" (a catch-all reprimand that sexually well-mannered women should give up), would again escalate into a nasty conflict and suddenly you'd become "flooded"—inundated with feelings you couldn't process, not to mention a bunch of nasty chemicals that are bad for the manly arteries. Flummoxed by this state of hyperarousal, you'd instinctively stonewall—or retreat from the discussion entirely. Almost immediately, your disengagement would bring relief from the disturbing symptoms while causing your wife's distress to soar. Stonewalling, next to physical violence, more accurately predicts perpetual discord—and divorce—than any other single male behavior.

The neurobiology responsible for this ill-mannered response has long served us well in Darwinian competitions, but is not terribly well suited to the touchy-feely requirements of the modern pair bond. Men's nervous systems are organized around dominance or status, which in the old days was challenged by physical threat. Women's nervous systems are organized around loss of connectedness, rifts in the linkages—one reason they're hypersensitive to the sound of a baby's cry. During a marital dispute, men shut down their emotions and focus on winning the battle—preserving their status—while women become more distraught and concentrate on relinking. The two emotional styles couldn't be more poorly suited to each other.

The ability to blunt emotion is partly tied up with serotonin—or rather, the lack of it. A lot of serotonin translates into a superior ability to sense the needs and emotional temperatures of others (and yourself)—a talent that contributes not only to women's linker skills but to those of the best male leaders. As primary nurturers, it seems fitting that women should have more of the hormone in their systems than men. Looked at another way, as the ones responsible for searching for land mines, rescuing babies from collapsed buildings, and rousting cat burglars from the basement, it also seems fitting that men should have less of it.

This ability to clamp a lid on emotions evolved during our knuckle-dragging epoch. When monkeys are young, their serotonin levels are high: dependent on others for survival, they need to be as socially winning as possible. Levels of the hormone diminish as the animals approach puberty and then stabilize. Females end up with more, males with less. The amount of the chemical circulating in the primate noodle seems calibrated to each sex's adult-life agenda. Females remain in the troop in which they were born; if separated from their primate pals, they suffer inconsolably. Males, on the other hand, break from their troop as young adults and can spend a couple of years in kick-ass male gangs before being accepted into another. For them, their one separation is a cakewalk. By depriving them of serotonin and thus dampening their stress response, nature protects them against the pain of striking out on their own. The males, and their species, are better served by their feeling too little than by feeling too much.

The same might be said of you as you resist the urge to interpret your wife's entreaties as an attack. All you need do is listen, maintain eye contact, stay cool, nod empathically—reroute the incoming data through your inner female. Then you can have dessert, go home, and finally let the Warren Beatty in you seal the deal.

■ ■ ■

IT'S SATURDAY MORNING, the kids are parked on Sesame Street, and you're fulfilling your end of the unspoken domestic compact while your wife is at step class. You hose down the bathrooms, shovel out the twins' bedroom, scrape clean all surfaces in the kitchen, even fold a load of wash. Your goal is to be on the golf course before noon. Of course, first you have to pass inspection. Upon returning from the gym, pleasingly fragrant and pumped and spandex-sexy (only nine more hours and you can put the kids to bed, you think), your eagle-eyed spouse immediately nods toward a dust bunny quivering in the corner of the dining room, and is fairly blinded by the greasy sheen radiating from the kitchen countertops. Weird, how you don't notice this stuff until she points it out. She picks up your two-year-old, sniffs his diaper, and throws you a look: *How'd you like to live like this?*

A blistering rejoinder revs at the edge of your forebrain, but the links beckon. You can't help but think that, in your ongoing struggle to contribute equally to home and kid maintenance, your contributions are never properly appreciated. Sure, maybe she changes more diapers, but last weekend you spent an entire Saturday afternoon cleaning gutters. The weekend before it was glazing windows—real scut work. She hassles regularly with the logistics of play dates, day care, doctors, and "enrichment," but you disappear with the kids all day every Sunday in the park. For a whole day. She shops more, but when the car is broken whose job is it to fix it? And how many times has she offered to go into the basement and stick her arm shoulder deep into a backed-up sewer pipe to fish out the toothbrush your three-year-old regularly flushes down the toilet?

For years, researchers have churned out studies showing that, while working dads are performing more household chores than their fathers did, women still do most of them—and often after racing home from the office themselves. The problem with this research is in what it looks at—shopping, cleaning, and diaper-changing, typically. Men could make the same argument: while some women do cut the grass, stack firewood, load the minivan with cases of Similac and 120-packs of Pampers from Costco, and install satellite dishes on the garage roof more than their mothers did, their husbands are still mostly responsible for these chores. Men don't get credit for these contributions because women assume they enjoy doing them.

Which is true, of course. Men like fixing stuff, but they're no longer allowed to admit it to their wives for fear their skills and contributions will be disqualified from inclusion in the weekly tally of domestic duties. Many women feel the same way, many about cleaning. As anyone who's been married more than a week knows, the female brain enjoys folding and sorting, behaviors that seem to emerge during moments of high dudgeon or stress, or—don't repeat this—just prior to menstruation. In the animal world, this is known as "scuttling"—a reference to the behavior of pregnant rodents who furiously organize dirt, fur balls, masticated plant materials, and other detritus to construct a nest for their pups. Few women, though, are willing to acknowledge the pacifying effects of nesting behavior (although an elderly lesbian friend once told me that washing the kitchen floor was kind of like sex with her ex-husband: she didn't look forward to it, but once she got into it, it was kind of enjoyable).

If a perfectly equal domestic partnership is a marital concept that seems awfully difficult to achieve, it's not solely because of manly foot-dragging. Men now put in 75 percent as much time as women taking care of domestic grunt work—up from 30 percent in 1977. Add the time they spend with their arms probing blocked sewers and it might be a draw. But the issue of who will care for the kids is fraught. When the Families and Work Institute published recent data showing that working fathers now spend almost as much time caring for their kids as working mothers do, the figures were roundly attacked by female editorialists as bloated and preposterous. Critics accused fathers in the study of overestimating the time they spent with their kids, never stopping to think that guilt-ridden career mothers might do the same.

But their blanket dismissal of the study's findings may mask a more fundamental and decidedly impolitic truth: many women are unwilling to give up the unique power that arrives when they become mothers. I know men who complain that it's a struggle to be involved with their kids as much as they'd like because, as a young colleague put it, "I feel like I'm leaving one boss at work for another one at home." A variety of studies have documented what my friend has learned firsthand: no matter how much he contributes around the house, his wife is typically far more critical of his performance than he is of hers, particularly regarding his care of the kids. He's damned if he does, and damned if he doesn't.

Sexual manners demand an end to the debate over whether moms or dads make better mothers, or whether responsibility for every household chore can be divided exactly down the middle. Most women are more attuned to the emotional and social needs of their children than most men. It's part of being a linker. Social constructionists will argue that this comparative advantage is due solely to conditioning, that men can learn to be as emotionally intuitive as women. Regarding the latter point, they're right. Women can also learn to box, as a few have. But most women are more capable nurturers than most men, and most men have a more intuitive feel for the Sweet Science than most women. On the other hand, that's not to say men can't be "good enough" caretakers and put in as much hard, if different, time as their wives. But, as every father who has spent a day or a night with a mommy-fixated toddler knows, it may mean that a strictly equal partnership is impossible in most families, particularly when very young kids are involved.

Dual-career marriages can work smoothly for childless couples and those whose kids have left the roost, but in the absence of universal day care and more kid-friendly corporate attitudes, working parents of young children can face years of rancor over how to divvy up childcare duties. Studies show a couple reduces marital discord when a wife ratchets down her career involvements and assumes more domestic responsibilities, but this is obviously not a happy solution for a woman who loves her job—and particularly if she's one of the 25 percent of married women who are primary wage earners. And it's a solution that, to a lot of women, sounds like an attempt to reinstate a fifties-like status quo.

But it is a choice some women are making. They feel unfairly coerced and tricked by the feminist revolutionaries—all of whom, with the exception of Betty Friedan, were childless and some of whom lurched from one lousy relationship to another—who denigrated women for choosing marriage and child rearing over career. Much of the backlash against feminism, in fact, has originated not with men but with women who were told by their iconic leaders that housewives were "mindless," "parasites," and "infantile"—only to learn later that child rearing was often far more rewarding than making big bucks. They now know that the idealistic notions they had while single or childless about maintaining an aggressive career and having a family are almost impossible to realize, that if they choose to go toe-to-toe with men and childless women in the workplace, they sacrifice in some part their attachment to their children. Conversely, if they scale back their time at the office to care for their children, they're no longer considered team players. They understand that the burnished images of the modern woman who "has it all" have little basis in reality—and nothing to do with the mortifying truths of family life.

Still, although a third of married mothers now stay home to care for their kids full-time—including some high-profile CEOs who jumped off the fast track and onto the mommy track—that number is unlikely to grow. For one thing, most moms *must* work—the single-paycheck middle-class family is history. But there's another reason men have to help solve the work/family conundrum: There's plenty of convincing evidence that mothers who work, whether full- or part-time, do confer a variety of advantages upon their family. The moms are happier, their sons more resourceful, their daughters more cheerful and likely to have careers of their own, and their husbands more engaged in family life. The women are healthier, too. Contrary to expectations that cardiac problems in career women would rise to the level found among men, heart disease, depression, and chronic illness are more frequent among homemakers than among working women of all strata. When women go to the office, the level of their stress hormones actually drops and rises again when they return home—the opposite of men's patterns.

One school of logic, then, would suggest that men downsize their career and earning potential—as well as their blood pressure and heart-attack risk—so that they can pick up the kids from school and make macaroni and cheese every night while their wife, who finds the office kind of fun and relaxing, cheerfully assumes responsibility for filling the family coffers. Nice try. The problem is that when a man loses status, either involuntarily or by choice, his wife typically loses respect for him and no longer finds him sexually attractive—a cardinal rule in the old mating paradigm still observed, however unconsciously, by most modern couples, despite their protestations to the contrary.

■ ■ ■

So how does a sexually well-mannered standup guy support his wife's career and her role as chief nurturer? A tenet of sexual manners—and one that reverses the obligations of previous generations—is that one of a man's most important jobs is to keep his wife happy. When positive female energy flows throughout a family and home, everyone benefits. When it doesn't, everyone suffers. The commitments a man must make to help his wife balance her needs and talents will be different for every couple, but he'll vastly improve his chances for success if he observes a simple sexual manner authored by Norman Mailer: Never let your wife get tired.

What can you expect in return from your grateful, well-rested mate? Praise, perhaps, for the things you do for the family that are often overlooked—your willingness to fix the car, repair the furniture, coach the soccer team, and help with the math homework. Good sexual manners enable women to admit that they often enjoy monitoring the domestic front more than men do, and don't have to feel martyred if they decide to devote a few years to it. As a team, the sexually well-mannered couple should divide work up along fair lines and then feel free to praise and enjoy each other's gender advantages, which is a lot more satisfying and sexy than competing or complaining.

And just because she may have a good job and career, don't assume she doesn't need emotional support simply because you don't. You can advise her on how to weather corporate infighting—and keep from getting exhausted by it—by putting a filter on her emotions the way you can on yours. (Remind her of the utility of this talent during your next penitential postfight dinner date.) Becoming her professional booster requires only a slight shift in the domains of your competence. You can now derive manly pride and self-worth not just from your own special occupational talents, but from the admiration and respect you show for your wife's and from your ability to share in her glory in the way women have always shared in their husband's. For her part, your wife has to understand that sexual manners require that she appreciate the mixed feelings you may have when she advances to the corner office before you. In the same way that you can never let her tire, she has to find a way to honor your deeply innate desire to provide for and protect her and the kids, even if it is outside the traditional financial realm.

This is not such a new idea, only one that has yet to find a firm footing in the collective male psyche. Jim and Pat Schroeder know what it takes, as did Julia Child, the cookbook author and star of the television kitchen, and her late husband, Paul. During their forty-eight-year marriage, Paul, an artist, writer, linguist, teacher, polo player, photographer, former lumberjack, furniture maker, and Foreign Service agent, gradually became his wife's road manager, agent, traveling companion, and general factotum, often washing dishes at her demonstrations. If a polo-playing lumberjack spy can devote himself to his wife's career, the average office drudge ought to be able, at the least, to respect and support it.

Put her on a pedestal, worship her, and be grateful she's on your team and not some other jerk's. Her financial contributions are not only liberating you from total fealty to the company store but freeing you up to perform tasks more important than ever to standup masculinity's universal construct: being a father.

DADDY'S BOYS

. . .

ONE DAY NOT LONG AGO, a tall, well-built, middle-aged black man, perspiring and fidgety, entered a restaurant outside Los Angeles, acutely aware that he was about to begin a new chapter in his life. The man surveyed the room and then, after spotting a chiseled, buff, teenage boy sitting alone—a boy whose handsome features resembled his own—walked over to him, introduced himself, and sat down. He had rehearsed his words, but they stumbled from his lips nevertheless. "In one day, I can't explain the whole past," he told the boy. "I want to break the ice right now and build up from this point. I'd like to get more involved in your life. Would you like that?"

And so after sixteen years of refusing to acknowledge the boy's very existence—Lawrence McCutcheon, a star running back for the Los Angeles Rams in the 1970s and now a scout for the relocated Rams of St. Louis, decided to enter the life of his son, Daylon. However ambivalently, he also took the first step toward reversing a multigenerational trend in his own family of paternal absenteeism—a trend widespread in the black community, which is why McCutcheon chose to publicize his own humbling experience in interviews with *The Wall Street Journal.*

Whatever his past failings, McCutcheon's decision took a lot of courage, for even among the best of circumstances, the tie between father and son is thought to be the most critical and dangerous relationship on earth. There is perhaps no obligation of fatherhood more demanding or complex—nor a more crucial predictor of a boy's ability to become a standup guy himself—than his father's commitment to him. Girls present special challenges, too, but in raising them, we rarely feel the specter of our father looming over our shoulders or, worse, sitting astride them. With our boys, another man—whether rivalrous or generously supportive, whether a mentor or a bully—is always present. What we choose to do with that figurehead—how we "process," internalize, and, finally, honor him—goes a long way toward determining our own standup status, and our sons'.

A gifted athlete from Plainview, Texas, McCutcheon, who had burned up state high school rushing records, got football scholarship offers from twenty-three colleges. The young Adonis was a magnet to women, some of whom apparently believed the best way to snag him was to carry his baby. Shortly before he went off to Colorado State University, his high school girlfriend announced she was pregnant. She dropped out of school and gave birth to a girl, Adrian. When it became clear McCutcheon was not going to skip college and a likely professional career and return to Plainview to raise a family, she moved to Dallas to find work. McCutcheon paid child support and stayed in touch with Adrian, though, and as his fortunes rose with the Rams he frequently flew her to Los Angeles to take her to Disneyland. "She was my firstborn, and kind of special to me," he explained.

But he felt no such instinctive tenderness toward Daylon. The boy was conceived during a brief affair McCutcheon had during his fourth season with the Rams with Deborah Sterling, whom he'd first met in college. Although he visited the baby in the hospital, the gridiron star denied paternity. Sterling pressed the issue, a blood test determined that he was indeed the boy's father, and a judge ordered him to pay support, which he did. But by then, his relationship with Daylon's mother had chilled, and he stubbornly decided not to see his son.

McCutcheon admitted that, in retrospect, he had behaved no differently from his own father, an auto mechanic, who left his wife and eleven children to fend for themselves when Lawrence was six. McCutcheon remembered that his mother offered no explanation for his disappearance or for his return four years later. "You go from one relationship to another," McCutcheon learned, "and that's a part of life."

A year after retiring from pro ball—he rushed for more than 6,500 yards in a twelve-year career—McCutcheon married Myrna Emerson, a teacher and basketball coach he had met during a visit home to

Plainview. They moved to a spacious house south of Los Angeles and decided to raise a family. McCutcheon was now working with the Rams as a scout, traveling the country and evaluating college players. He was overjoyed when Myrna became pregnant. "This was the first time I was going to be in an established relationship and be there and see the baby grow up," he said. He accompanied his wife to Lamaze classes and was in the delivery room when his son, Marcus, "the love of my life," was born.

McCutcheon had told his wife about Daylon, the son he still didn't believe was his, and about his firstborn, Adrian. Myrna urged him to get in touch with his son, but McCutcheon resisted. Then, one day in 1986, Lawrence was evaluating players at a Rams camp in Los Angeles, and after the session signed an autograph for a ten-year-old boy. A few minutes later, he spotted Deborah Sterling on the sidelines with the boy—her son, Daylon—who had just gotten his father's autograph. Daylon had grown up about an hour away with his mother and stepfather, whom he called Dad. Deborah had made sure her son knew who his father was—she had given Daylon his father's surname—and showed him pictures from McCutcheon's college yearbook. When friends would ask Daylon if he was the famous running back's son, he'd say yes, but no more. That was as much as he knew about his father.

At the tryout camp that day, Sterling introduced Daylon to McCutcheon who, suspecting that the meeting was an attempt to embarrass him, seethed. He spoke briefly to the boy's mother, then offered a few words of encouragement to Daylon. Later that night, he told Myrna what had happened, and said he still didn't think Daylon was his biological son.

Six years later, though, Myrna again challenged McCutcheon to see Daylon. Like his father, Daylon had been breaking high school rushing records and drawing the interest of scouts and sportswriters who often mentioned his athletic pedigree. Marcus, now eight, was old enough, too, to understand what his friends might say about the local high school star who shared his last name and some of his genes. Even though he felt uneasy about reappearing in Daylon's life just as he was on the edge of stardom, McCutcheon asked a friend to arrange a meeting in a restaurant with the boy.

"I thought he might hate me," McCutcheon remembered thinking, as he nervously approached Daylon in the restaurant. For his part, Daylon was "fine with it. If he would never have called, I would never have called. But if he was going to make the effort, I would make the effort." Yes, Daylon told McCutcheon when he asked whether the boy would like him to have an active presence in his life. He could go for that.

Over the next couple of years, McCutcheon attended Daylon's games when he could, then worked with Sterling to help him narrow down his college choices. He decided to go to USC, where he plays cornerback. The senior and junior McCutcheons talk on the phone frequently, but their occasional meetings are still awkward. Daylon values his father's advice, but says his career decisions will be made by himself and his mother. "I don't see him as a father," Daylon said. "I look upon him as an older friend. There's a big difference. A father is someone who grows up with his child, gives him things, and teaches him things as the child grows up. Other than making me, he hasn't made me the person I am today."

Still, McCutcheon is pleased with the progress he and his son have made. "You don't just compress what should have happened over eighteen years into two or three. When you meet a kid at sixteen and all of a sudden you're in his life as a dad, it's going to take a while."

Meanwhile, though, everyone in McCutcheon's extended family seems to be benefiting from his new involvement with Daylon. Marcus worships his half-brother, who often drops by to play catch. And McCutcheon has renewed his commitment to visit Adrian and his two grandchildren regularly. "Now that I am around for my kids, I would like to be a good role model for them."

Daylon, too, acknowledged a steady improvement in the relationship. "I think he's a good person," he said. "Some people make a mistake and never try to correct it. He did come back. It was brave of him, but it's also what he should have done even earlier.

"That's what a father should do."

■ ■ ■

WHAT A FATHER SHOULD DO . . . What a father should do, of course, is teach, protect, feed, play with, discipline, and care for his children—some of the most essential and defining duties of manhood in virtually every society in the world. They're obligations that are difficult to fulfill if he's not around. Daylon McCutcheon was lucky: he had a devoted stepfather—the real hero of the McCutcheon family drama—and was surrounded by uncles and a doting godfather. Most of the other 24 million American children who are currently living without their biological fathers in the home—about 40 percent of all the kids in the country—quietly suffer in the absence of a strong masculine presence. Particularly boys.

How is it possible to explain the collapse of American fatherhood, in my opinion the greatest social tragedy of the past thirty years? In the most prosperous society in the world, how could so many men reject two of the most fundamental responsibilities of manhood—to protect dependents and provision kith and kin? To become, as one South Pacific island people calls irresponsible shirkers, "rubbish men," unproductive parasites with an appalling lack of family and social commitment? From the evolutionary view, men seem to be reverting to a more primitive reproductive strategy: they're happy to insert their genes into the next generation but loathe to stick around to make sure all of their progeny survive. (The dickfesters, wary of commitment but willing to hook up anonymously, seem to be in perpetual training for this style of paternity.)

Of course, there have always been rubbish men with precarious attachments to their spouse and children. "Family men" who emigrated to America often discovered how flimsy their ties were after struggling with the hardship they met there. Every wave of immigration, in fact, has been marked by high rates of paternal and husbandly abandonment. Humiliated fathers who couldn't adquately provide for their families often just left.

But the timing of the recent explosion of disappearing and deadbeat dads suggests a different, although no more forgiveable, explanation: Contemporary bounders have ignored their responsibilities as part of a very cynical response to feminism. As women have gained economic power and authority, men, unable to come to terms with the power shift, have decided to let them take care of themselves. Their sense of self-worth too narrowly defined by their paycheck, which may be smaller than their wives', many men have jettisoned their families just as their impoverished immigrant forebears did theirs.

Not that men's unwillingness to stick around has discouraged women from having babies. Today, a third of all births are to unmar-

ried women, compared to 5 percent in 1960. As if to boost the morale
of the expanding population of single mothers—some of whom were
professional women for whom having a baby without an involved
father around was a "lifestyle choice"—some social researchers in the
eighties pursued an anti-nuclear-family bias in their studies of the
family. Children need a dad, to paraphrase a famous feminist quip, like
a fish needs a bicycle. (Recently, many of the same researchers, apparently hoping to assuage the guilt of working mothers, have trained
their sights on attachment theory, concluding that how securely an
infant bonds with his mother is incidental to his psychological growth
and maturity.) By the mid-nineties, the message that fathers are superfluous—"redundant" was the preferred descriptive—to what is now
called "parenting" had apparently taken up residence among the sen-
sibilities of even young childless adults. Surveys showed that a third of
men between ages eighteen and twenty-nine and two thirds of women
in the same age group believed that one parent can bring up a child as
well as two.

But the male responses in those surveys also give voice to a cohort
of fathers who get less attention than their support-shirking brothers:
the committed, nurturing, new generation of hands-on fathers—the
new standup dads—who have been far more involved with their children than their own fathers were with them. When a third of young
men say one parent can successfully bring up a child, some are
undoubtedly thinking of themselves.

Whatever their past failings, do the New Dads, along with reformed
fathers like Lawrence McCutcheon, signal an end to this unfortunate
chapter in the history of fatherhood? Many more men appear to be
interested in "going wide"—shifting the domains of their competence
from the exclusive and narrow realms of work, from the drudgery of
simple providing, to the more complex (but often equally drudgelike)
business of raising their kids. A very recent survey, in fact, found that
84 percent of men in their thirties and forties now feel that a primary
definition of success is being a good father.

Certainly, the avowed family commitments from the Promise Keepers and Million Man Marchers suggest a major shift in attitude. A variety of social service organizations have also dedicated themselves to
affirming and bolstering fatherhood. Groups like the National Institute
for Responsible Fatherhood and Family Development in Cleveland are

taking on one of the most intractable problems of all: young unwed fathers. The institute organizes and trains men from the local community to work with the mostly teenage fathers, many of whom have dropped out of school, are unemployed, or have substance problems, and teach them how to reenter the lives of their children and to support their mothers.

Another group, MAD DADS, Inc. (Men Against Destruction Defending Against Drugs and Social Disorder), is demonstrating the power of a strong and renewed masculine presence in the community. The organization geared up a few years ago in Omaha after the twenty-year-old son of John L. Foster staggered home, beaten and bloodied by a gang of teenagers. Foster got a gun and immediately went out searching for the thugs but, fortunately for everyone, didn't find them. He did, however, learn something about himself: "I was literally a mad dad and I knew I wanted to organize strong black men who were willing to stand up and fight this thing." This "thing" was the oppressive and menacing presence of drug dealers, crack addicts, and prostitutes in his neighborhood. He and a friend, Eddie Staton, conscripted a group of about one hundred black men who began "father street patrols" to scare off the lowlifes. Today, MAD DADS has forty-five thousand members in fifty-two chapters around the country, and has expanded its mission to include support for young fathers and the mentoring of fatherless children. They report crime and drug sales to police, paint over gang graffiti, challenge drug dealers and gang members to leave their neighborhood, conduct gun buy-back programs, and provide special assistance to thousands of runaways and other troubled youth. Their tutelage of fatherless boys may be their most important work. In a broad study of troubled youths done by the Carnegie Task Force on Adolescence, not one of the boys who did manage to grow up to be a productive adult did so without the intervention of a caring adult, whether an uncle, teacher, coach, or mentor.

One of MAD DADS' vital missions is to restore an image of masculine power and responsibility to the black family and community, which over the past thirty years has shifted much of traditional male authority to women. But any community might turn to the group of working-class black men who are profiled in *Slim's Table*. The white author, Mitchell Duneier, spent nine years recording the conversations of the men who gathered for lunch every day at the Valois "See Your Food" cafeteria in Chicago. Admiring the sense of moral worth and self-esteem evinced by men who were "reared up," often without fathers, in the ghetto, Duneier writes

> They are consistently inner-directed and firm, and they act with resolve; their images of self-worth are not derived from material possessions or the approval of others; they are disciplined ascetics with respect for wisdom and experience; usually humble, they can be quiet, sincere, and discreet ... sensitive but not "soft" ... They know how to put their foot down, and how to "show their swords." They learn that when it is time to take a risk or when resolve is needed, they cannot afford to "come up short."

■ ■ ■

ANOTHER SIGN THAT THE epidemic of fatherlessness may have peaked comes from one of the kitschier corners of pop culture. Women—those in Harlequin Romance novels, anyway—are again making room for Daddy—and actively pursuing him. Harlequin heroes are no longer fabulously wealthy and handsome sheiks or playboy pirates but nurturing men—albeit men with the requisite six-pack abs and jutting jaws—for whom children and home come first. The billion-dollar romance-novel industry now puts logos on its books characterizing its modern dream lovers as "Family Man," "Fabulous Father," or "Accidental Dad." Not surprisingly, Harlequin plots often demonize the modern career woman. A typical offering is *Jacob's Girls,* whose protagonist is a handsome California radio host whose wife leaves him and their triplets for a big-time job in Washington: "Jacob knew that ultimately the fault for his divorce—for his children's motherless state—lay with him. He'd been too unbending, he expected too much. But where his children were concerned, he wasn't going to change. And he wasn't sorry for that."

The hunky dad is also hero of *Mr. Family,* about a Hawaiian widower's search for the right mother for his daughter: "Erika kept her eyes away from Kal. She should have guessed that he was a man who would lie on the floor and let children and dogs climb all over him. She liked men like that. And she already liked Kal too much."

Like women in the real world, the Harlequin heroines are expressing a preference for qualities in a mate that rank right up there at the top with dominance on the female wish list: kindness and understanding. A man who treats his kids well is likely to treat his wife well, too, providing her with the emotional support that enhances the quality of her own relationships with her children and the kids' overall adjustment. It's a happy picture from every angle.

And it's happiest of all for sons. At his father's funeral, Vice President Al Gore credited his father, a former senator, with being his first political mentor, a man who brought him to the Senate as a toddler, where then Vice President Richard Nixon bounced him on his knee and let him play with the gavel. In eulogizing his father, who was described as a man "willing to walk into the teeth of enemy fire," Gore said, "Children with strong fathers learn to trust early on that their needs will be met, that they're wanted, that they have value. They can afford to be secure and confident."

Boys with strong fathers also learn empathy. The Sears study, which has followed a group of men over several decades, has found that those who were best able to resolve conflicts through personal sacrifice—in other words, sensible capitulation—when they were twenty-three, were raised by fathers who were as hands-on as their mothers. When the same men were assessed for empathy at age thirty-one, and the quality of their social relationships and intimacy were measured at forty-one, the greatest determining factor turned out to be the level of their dad's involvement. Workaholic fathers, take note.

Devoted fathers also directly affect their son's material success as an adult. The Glueck study, a four-decade analysis of 240 working-class fathers from Boston and their sons, all born between 1946 and 1964, has delineated the relationship between paternal involvement and adult achievement. Fathers who supported their son's social and emotional development during the first decade of childhood—a task thought in the recent age of psychology to fall to women—tended to produce boys who excelled in high school and college. When that emotional support continued through adolescence—a tall order for many fathers as their sons seek independence from them—their son's career mobility was exceedingly high.

The Glueck investigators, who measured paternal support in three critical domains—social/emotional, physical/athletic, and intellectual/academic—concluded that it is impossible for fathers to be overinvolved with their boys. In fact, they simply do better and better the more time their fathers spend with them. Almost anything the fathers did with their sons had a positive impact, but those who stayed involved with their boy's intellectual development during both childhood and adolescence, affirming his academic achievements as much as his athletic talents, were even more likely to have successful kids.

This contrasts with the study's findings about girls, who actually do more poorly in school when their fathers are too closely involved with their emotional development during their first decade. The benefits of his attention are, however, keenly apparent during adolescence, when his daughter uses him as a stepping-stone from her mother to the larger society, and he helps her not only establish independence and autonomy but assertive relationships with her male peers. Interestingly, fathers who provided their kids with what researchers called nontraditional support—teaching their daughters how to play golf or wield a Sawzall and accompanying their sons to dance classes—had the most successful kids of all.

The firm hand of paternal guidance, whether from a biological dad or a mentor, shows up repeatedly in analyses of accomplished tyros. A study of more than a hundred jet fighter pilots done in the early eighties revealed that most were firstborns with unusually close relationships with their fathers; the flyers exhibited enormous self-confidence, showed a great desire for challenge and success, and like most heroes, had little use for introspection.

Today's Top Guns fit the same profile, but with a notable exception. The F-15 pilots of yore were legendary womanizers and prided themselves on a lifestyle in which marriage and children were secondary to the needs of the Air Force. Consequently, the divorce rate in the group was high, and almost all of the separations were initiated by wives. Many of today's fliers have reversed the priorities. In fact, the Air Force is having difficulty retaining its pilots, many of whom are resigning to take jobs with airlines that promise more regular hours and the opportunity to spend the kind of time with their kids that their dads did with them. "When I was twenty-two, flying fighters was all I thought I'd ever want to do," says Captain Carl Butts, a thirty-one-year-old pilot stationed in North Carolina. "But then after marriage and kids, family becomes more important than a fighter jet. They're your priority."

■ ■ ■

THE SPORTS WORLD, too, is populated by professional athletes whose fathers' authoritative but loving involvement helped guide them toward superstardom—and toward their own appreciation of family life. Whatever his image as a corporate front man, gambler, and cultural icon during his career, Michael Jordan was consistently devoted to his family, his team, and, until he was murdered, his father, "Daddy," to whom he dedicated his fourth NBA championship. He publicly credits his wife for her support of his career and made sure to include his three children in the celebrations of his many spectacular achievements. His paternal concern extended to minor-role players on the Bulls, too. When Trent Tucker and Darrell Walker were veteran spares on Jordan's first championship-title team, they were amazed at how often Jordan talked about their having a chance to join him on the final stage, how much he wanted that for them—"almost like a father wants to provide for his kids," Tucker says.

Tiger Woods, too, often refers to his father, a twenty-year Army veteran who served two tours as a Green Beret officer in Vietnam, as his hero and only role model, and seeks his counsel now as often as he did as a teenager, when he was playing U.S. Junior Amateur Golf tournaments around the country. Male golfers, including Bob Jones, Arnold Palmer, Jack Nicklaus, and Davis Love III, have always been daddy's boys, forming special bonds with their fathers over countless long afternoons on the links, and Tiger and his father, Earl, are no exception. In addition to valuing his deep friendship, Tiger credits his father with teaching him initiative and instilling in him the drive to achieve, mental toughness, and confidence. As Tiger's fame grew as a handsome, articulate, gifted black professional in a white sport, father and son also developed a unique way of communicating. When the swirling crowds press close, they'll call each other Sam, and the rest of the world, they say, vanishes.

The world received a touching glimpse of their special relationship immediately after Tiger won his first Masters when, following the final putt, he moved immediately into his father's arms for a long embrace. The hug symbolized how much Earl had meant to his son's success. "It's an understanding that he and I have," Earl says. "I want him, when he brings it to closure, I want to have him in my arms. I told him right then, let it go. He knows that all the heartbreak and effort and strain and tension are over, that he's safe in his dad's arms."

Chris Mills, the power forward for the Golden State Warriors with a $33 million contract, also spent a lot of time in his father's arms, though under more austere conditions. Mills's father, Claude, had separated from his mother when the boy was three. Chris, who wouldn't see his mother again until fourteen years later, lived with his father, often in motel rooms in West Los Angeles—all they could afford. "I remember he would give me the bed and he would sleep on the couch or even the floor," Chris says. "He always put me first."

Claude did all the "mother things," Chris says. After sending his son off to elementary school in the morning, he'd prepare a hot meal on an electric burner in the motel room, cover it, and put it on a warming plate before he went to work. Dinner would await his son when he got home from school. Basketball was important, but Chris's education came first. "My dad had rules," Chris says. "I had homework first, then it was vacuum, do the dishes, and dust. My dad was strict, but he had to be."

Like other poor kids in big cities, Mills was tempted by the easy money of the booming crack cocaine trade, which peaked when he was in high school. His classmates had new cars, nice clothes, and beepers, while Mills and his dad continued to struggle. Temptation was everywhere, including within his own family—a cousin was a gang leader. "Hanging with him," Chris says, "I've seen gunfire, fights, people lying there bleeding to death. As I got older, I realized I couldn't be around that." Claude Mills warned his son to keep his distance, and his protégé, his work in progress, did.

Today, Claude Mills continues to watch his son closely, but from a different perspective. "When I look at Chris today, when he's playing basketball . . . well, it's like when you're a painter or an artist and you can step back and look at your work. Sometimes, it's nice just to step back and look at Chris and what he has become, not just as a player but as a person, too."

■ ■ ■

THE MAD DADS, Earl Woods, and Claude Mills know what all fathers who keep a close watch on their sons know. Young boys instinctively invite their fathers or surrogate fathers to roughhouse as a way to explore the boundaries of socially acceptable behavior. It's a remarkably simple but effective tutelage. Without a limit-setting masculine presence, a boy's natural aggression can intensify into a whirlwind of pure destruction. One measure: Two thirds of rapists, three quarters of adolescent murderers, and 75 percent of long-term prison inmates grew up without a father in their home.

Though the anger and aggression of such men is often associated with extreme masculinity, psychologists say they are actually masking a high degreee of uncertainty about their sexual orientation. (The men, of course, see themselves as the alpha males of the street.) Many boys without a father fill the void by creating a caricature of one, usually a hypermasculine stereotype from pop culture—half Terminator, half Mortal Kombatant—identifying with it, and becoming hyper-aggressive, mean, and remote. Some run in a pack, and display a defensive misogyny—they're attracted to the extreme sexual violence in rap music or twisted video games in which boys chase coeds in lingerie and then dispatch them with power tools—to keep women, who threaten their masculinity, at a distance. They're sexually confused, though you wouldn't want to suggest this to an agitated young mugger as he runs a gun upside your head and demands your credit cards.

Understandably, the need to squelch the baser instincts of "demonic males" has been the focus of countless child-rearing books and social tracts. It's beyond dispute that boys demonstrate far more confrontational behavior and rough-and-tumble play than girls and, as adults, are responsible for almost all violent crime. But as experts are quick to point out, violence is not a natural or even common endpoint of aggression. As Jerome Kagan, a developmental psychologist at Harvard, has repeatedly demonstrated in forty years of research on children, aggressiveness in a young child, properly modulated and socialized, is highly correlated with what he calls assertive competence—success—as an adult.

Ironically, the merits of male-style assertiveness were given a boost a few years ago by feminist psychologists who tried to prove the value of a concept called psychological androgyny. In tests given to men and women that measure feminine and masculine characteristics, those who were loaded in both—they could be aggressive and nurturing, sensitive and rigid, dominant and submissive—were shown to have superior psychological health. To antimasculinists, this was proof that a highly evolved man had a strong feminine side. But the androgyny-is-best theory crashed and burned when more sophisticated analyses of data on masculine and feminine traits showed that the former accounted for all of the benefits. Aggression and dominance, not sensitivity and submissiveness, were responsible for the superior self-esteem in both men and women.

. . .

STILL, MOST OF US with sons agonize over just what sort of limits to impose upon our kids' feistiness. I was reminded of how tricky this business is the other day after watching my ten-year-old son's hockey game. Tom was jockeying for position in front of the goal with an opposing defenseman, the two boys started rapping each other's sticks, and the referee signaled them both for slashing penalties. In a professional game, or even a high school contest, their tussle would have been ignored, but the squirt league they play in strictly enforces the rules of the game. As he headed off to serve the first penalty of his young career, Tom found me in the crowd and shrugged impishly. (His casual attitude nonetheless represents an improvement in focus from his beginner years when, in the middle of play, he'd spot me in the stands and wave.) I shrugged back, as if to say, "A rule's a rule." You have to learn how far you can bend it.

After the game, the teams skated off the ice, then mingled near the stands to bask in the customary adulations of their parents. As Tom talked to one of his teammates, his sparring partner approached him, grabbed his helmet's wire-cage face protector, shook it along with Tom's head, then walked away. Tom and I headed off to the locker room. "That kid's a jerk," he said.

"You shouldn't have let him do that to you," I responded. Tom spun around to go look for the boy. I laughed and called him back. "But it's too late to do anything about it now. You should have dealt with it when it happened, done the same thing right back to him. No more, no less."

Was this the right advice? Maybe not for every kid, but for mine it was. He's hardly a loose cannon that requires constant muzzling. He's a boy with a generous and sensitive heart, in fact, which has something to do with his having grown up in the gentle company of his twin sister, Molly, upon whose tummy he rested his head during the last two months in their mother's womb. "Molly's upset," he'll report to my wife and me, his lip quivering empathetically, unable to tolerate it when his sister is distressed. When I tickle Molly, Tom squirms and giggles in delight, his nerve endings buzzing as though he were receiving the stimulation. One night at dinner, we learned that Tom, up until a couple of years ago, thought my wife and I were twins. Like him and his sister, he reckoned, we slept in the same room together, spent much of our free time together, laughed and joked and argued with each other. Tom, my wife is convinced, is going to make a great husband. He's a lover, not a fighter, she says.

I don't see why he can't be both. In an earlier, more gender-friendly era he would have been described as all boy. He's constructed like a coiled spring, with zero body fat, terrific coordination, and a tireless metabolism. He loves speed, physical contact, and playing the kind of pranks on his friends at school that this year alone have earned him and his parents three visits to the principal's office. When he's in the country, he loves to terrify his mom by shinnying up a maple sapling and arcing through the forest or hunting in the dark, murky crawl-space beneath the house for snakes. He'll often sneak out of the house in the middle of the night with his sleeping bag to lie among the forest critters, listening to the woods breathe, he says. He has great confidence in his physical skills and is basically fearless.

That would make him the junior thrill-seeker in the family—and at greater risk of getting into trouble than other boys. Like his dad, he's biologically bored, and as he gets older he'll continue to look for new ways to tweak his sleepy metabolism. There's nothing like the fear of getting caught—at anything he's not supposed to do—to get a thrill-seeker jazzed up. This includes everything from house rules—no climbing on the roof—to the criminal.

My own youthful escapades—more specifically, the ones that got me in trouble—tended toward joyriding (in a "borrowed" car) and hopping trains. Tom's "naughtiness," as his mother calls it, occurs mostly at school. Once, after dropping a ball from the fourth-story playground roof to the street to see how high it would bounce, he was asked to write an apology note to his teacher and then have his mother sign it. Deciding he would spare his mother needless worry, he cleverly asked her to sign a blank piece of paper, claiming he was beginning an art project that centered around her signature. Around the same time he discovered how easy it was to change the grade on the cover of his book report from a B-minus to a B-plus. We discovered the extent of Tom's cleverness when, once again, we were hauled into the principal's office to discuss his rowdy behavior, which included standing up on a roller-coaster ride during a year-end class trip to an amusement park.

Obviously, the moral transgressions demanded a quick and harsh response, while the roller-coaster recklessness required a sensible lecture about safety. Jacking up your thrills on the Scream Machine is one thing, lying and cheating another. Although he has settled down a lot in the past year, Tom still has difficulty sitting quietly in the classroom. He'd much rather be in the playground scripting a good-guys-versus-bad-guys drama or changing the trajectory of a moving object in the air. Ever since he went to preschool he's lagged behind his sister in several academic areas—discrepancies that often show up across the board between young boys and girls. He's a lefty, which has put him at a further disadvantage, but the biggest problems he has in school are due to the fact that he is, simply, male—impulsive, restless, a tester of authority. As I follow the twins' academic progress and marvel at Molly's focus, diligence, and all-round success, I can't help but wonder why much of the emphasis in education research over the past two decades has been on how to redress the "inequities" girls are subjected to in the classroom, despite the fact that boys are far more likely than girls to be emotionally disturbed, suffer from attention deficit disorder, or endure other learning disabilities.

Still, I'm not terribly concerned about Tom. His intense absorption in the natural world is the sign of a good mind, and he'll catch up with Molly. He experimented with lying and cheating—and got busted. He will probably always be a thrill-seeker; if I can have anything to do with it, his risk-taking will serve him well. As personality researcher David Lykken points out, the senator, the corporate takeover artist, the war hero, the roller-coaster fanatic, as well as the psychopath are all twigs on the same genetic branch. The qualities that put a boy at risk for violence are the same ones that, cultivated in a different way, make him into a leader or hero, says Lykken. If a boy is encouraged to take pride in risky accomplishments that have a positive goal—becoming a football player, rock climber, or pilot—he can achieve great things by following that course. If, on the other hand, the only authoritative model in his life is a criminal or dangerous peer group, he will become a victim—and a victimizer.

Meriwether Lewis, the great American explorer, is a good example of a boy who could have gone either way. Lewis lost his father when he was a toddler, and the boy, a born daredevil, passed an adventurous and undisciplined youth in a series of breathtaking experiences that progressively desensitized him to fear. When he was eight, he calmly shot dead a charging bull from a few feet away. Left to his own impulses, Lewis could easily have fallen into a life of crime but for a powerful mentor, Thomas Jefferson, who both encouraged his sense that he was special and pushed him toward productive challenges rather than mere danger. After presiding over his youth, Jefferson commissioned Lewis and William Clark, a wily woodsman and naturalist, to chart the American West in an ultimately futile but grandly heroic attempt to find a water passage from the Atlantic to the Pacific.

Like other fathers and mentors of his generation, Jefferson had no qualms about affirming his charge's natural feistiness. Today, however, standup dads who encourage their sons' aggressive engagement with the world occupy a philosophical outpost on the far side of political correctness. But fathers' affirmations of sons who are "all boy" have never been more important. The passive-aggression the bitch-festers find so troubling among men they know is just a more elaborate version of a weasely, resistant, manipulative behavior that begins in childhood. The boy who "forgets" to do his chores, the young man who retreats from women, the father who never sets limits for his son, the boss who says "maybe" when he knows he means "no"—there is no behavior quite so unattractive in a man as passive-aggression. Passive-aggressives are never angry, disappointed, or frustrated, but everyone around them is. It's a perfectly misguided but understandable response by men to exhortations from the gender police that they be gentler, less concerned about dominance and status, less energetic and impulsive, and more in touch with their "feminine" side. Passive-aggression is the child-rearing, romance, and management style of the day.

So as Tom ventures out into the world, I'm right behind him, alternately nudging him forward and reining him in, knowing that simple paternal proximity has a profound effect upon his development and that validation of his essential maleness will help him become a standup boy. I coach his hockey team, accompany him on drums as he learns the electric guitar (he's already drawn, of course, to metal), monitor his schoolwork, and crawl with him belly-by-belly through the woods to view with binoculars the coyotes he believes inhabit the shallow caves at the rear of our country property. I pay particularly close attention to how he resolves conflict with other boys, making sure he learns the difference between assertiveness and authority— sticking up for himself—and mere bullying. I want to preserve both his gentle heart and his warrior soul. Modern fatherhood is a delicate business.

• • •

FORTUNATELY IT'S A business that pays off, not just for Tom but for me. Perhaps the most important and surprising finding of the Glueck study—two thirds of whose participants were either highly involved (24 percent) or significantly involved (40 percent) fathers—is that men who have an active and influential role in raising their children reap long-lasting benefits themselves. According to psychologist John Snarey, who analyzed the findings, being on the parent track is not incompatible with being on a career track, as it so often is for women. Rather than stifling a career as so many men fear, a commitment to child rearing actually enhances it. Active fathers are much more likely to advance in their occupations, particularly in middle age, than fast-track workaholics.

"The fathers in the Glueck study experienced a sequence of healthy generativity," says psychologist John Snarey, the Glueck survey analyst. "They experienced biological generativity when they fathered a son, parental generativity when they cared for and raised him, and then went on to experience societal generativity, in which they mentored the next generation. The fact that they advanced in their careers is almost an evolutionary reward for their work as a parent. Having raised their sons, they're better managers, shop stewards, mentors to apprentices—more concerned with the generation coming up than with themselves. This contributes to the life of society and to the survival value of their own particular family."

The Glueck study fathers who were particularly well rewarded were the ones who hung in during their son's adolescence, when boys are doing all they can to put some distance between themselves and their dads. These fathers, having taken the time to negotiate this difficult passage when teenage boys are often unconsciously running up against their dad simply to feel the force of his authority, later went on to enjoy better promotions in the workplace and to be involved in other important care-giving activities, like being a mentor, coach, union officer, or civic leader. Clearly, a man who can learn the skills necessary to guide a son through the teen years is ready for anything.

Marital stability and happiness in middle age are two other big rewards for fathers who put in the necessary hard time with their kids.

Family harmony is a three-way street: the amount of praise a dad lavishes upon his preschool children directly correlates with how highly esteemed he is by his wife. The father and son bond, potentially explosive as it may be, can also be wonderfully symbiotic: not only does a father have a powerful influence on his son's chances for success and happiness, his son is also highly significant to the father's psychosocial development.

Like standup dad, like standup son.

■ ■ ■

GOOD DADS LAUNCH productive sons, enjoy a stable and loving marriage, and are catapulted up the corporate ladder. Having learned how to work and to love, they can, as Tolstoy once said, live "magnificently" in the world. But some of us, myself included, have to ask: What's wrong with this picture? We've managed to find some measure of love and success despite having fathers who were physically and emotionally distant—except when they were being abusive. Proud to have escaped our father's shadow, we're nonetheless plagued by a troubling fear: Will we one day turn into the kind of father to our children that our own father was to us?

Is there a father anywhere who doesn't dread repeating his own father's mistakes? Not in my house. At least a small part of my desire to stay close to Tom, I know, is to show my father how properly to deal with a kid with a wired mind and body and a mischievous streak. But I wonder if my father is still too much with me, whether in trying so hard to differentiate myself I'm creating a new set of problems for Tom. When I find my anger rising upon hearing of his latest troublesome escapade, and when I feel the desire to be left alone rather than try to help my son through his difficulty, I wonder how different I really am. Much of what we all know about loving and raising a child, we learned by having been somebody's kid. For a lot of us—and our children—the model of fatherhood we carry around inside is a scary one.

But from the clinical perspective, the reality is much more cheering. Perhaps the best news to emerge from the ongoing flood of research on psychosocial development comes again from the Glueck study of fathers and sons. The take-home: Yes, the things that go right in our lives, including having had a good father, do predict future success. But the events that go wrong, like having had a lousy one, do not necessarily forever damn us. In fact, foremost in the mind of many of us who may still be resentful about our distant, unloving, or harsh father is a powerful commitment not to pass on the same experience to our own sons.

Among the 240 "very normal" Glueck participants, two thirds were hands-on fathers whose care and attention made a significant difference in their son's life. That means that the other third of these very normal men were lousy fathers, and their son's happiness and success—his ability to work and to love—was impaired, at least by the researchers' standards. How did the poor model of fatherhood they were subjected to in childhood affect their own style and behavior as parents?

One truly unexpected finding of the study was that, just as their nurturing abilities might have been fortified by pleasant memories of their father's care, the men's capacity to be effective fathers could also in many cases be strengthened by an awareness of their father's shortcomings. The Glueck study provides the first long-term documentation of men's ability to rework negative aspects of their experience with their own fathers, and not repeat their fathers' mistakes. We are not always, as we so often imagine, straitjacketed by our upbringing and experience.

Typically, men in the study whose fathers did a poor job realized in midlife that their fathers may have had hard times, difficult circumstances to deal with, that many had done their best, and that, at any rate, no father is perfect. The men didn't deny the hardships of their boyhood experience, but they also didn't grant them the power to determine their lives. Many had transformed the anger they felt into sadness, and committed themselves to being the kind of fathers to their sons that they wished their own fathers had been to them. As Jay Belsky, a Penn State psychologist who arrived at similar conclusions from a study done in the early nineties, says, "Adults who acknowledge and seem to have worked through the difficulties of their childhood are apparently protected against inflicting them on their own children."

For those of us with less than ideal dads, our own sons offer us a way of mastering our painful past. We can pass on the good we received and rework the bad and as we do so, slowly come to terms with our own father—a process that, as I belatedly learned in middle age, can be accelerated by his impending death.

DAD

. . .

ONE SUMMER MORNING, when I was about six or seven, my father loaded our '56 Ford station wagon with a tent, sleeping bags, portable stove, tarpaulin, and a mess of other gear and set out with his wife and four kids for the northern Minnesota woods. Six hours later, after stopping in Duluth at the Paul Bunyan Diner for lunch, we pitched our tent on the pine-needle beds alongside Sea Gull Lake in the Boundary Waters Canoe Area. While foil dinners sizzled on a campfire, my brother and I swam in the deep, cold, granite-black glacial lake, picked blueberries, and explored the surrounding woods, hoping to find a bear. After dinner, Dean and I ventured onto a huge tree limb hanging out over the lake and fished for walleyes as a pair of loons broadcast their shimmering, otherworldly cries across the water. Finally, Dad, in his great, thunderous voice—a voice that terrified neighborhood kids when he summoned us home and, I imagine, anyone unfortunate enough to be grilled by him in the courtroom—called us back. We returned immediately.

Now, as I sat eating a bowl of cereal at the campsite picnic table before going to bed, I watched my father fiddle with a Coleman lantern. He removed the chimney, tied a new filament to the burner, poured white gas through a small funnel into the reservoir, then pressurized the tank with the hand pump. From the long view of middle age, I know that he must have found all this puttering and tinkering, and all the planning and prep work required to pull off our annual camping trip, wonderfully diverting and relaxing, a happy respite from hammering hapless criminals in court. I too am transported after spending an afternoon beneath the hood of my pickup truck tuning up the engine or taking apart a chain saw. He and I are good with motors, electricity, and plumbing, although our carpenter skills are equal to those of a six-year-old—the curse of the Ashkenazis, I figure. This is just one of the similarities between us that, after years of stubborn resistance, I've finally allowed myself to acknowledge.

Finally, Dad pulled a pack of Camels from his shirt pocket, lit a cigarette, and with the same match torched the lantern filament. He replaced the chimney and adjusted the gas valve until the lantern threw off a stark white light. He had strung a tarpaulin above the table to protect us from the rain that would inevitably come, and for a brief moment, I felt comfortably cocooned with my father, who seemed transfixed by lantern light and oblivious of my presence in the way that he so often was—except when he felt compelled to adjust my attitude or behavior with some form of punishment. Amid the dancing shadows and tracery of cigarette smoke, I dared to study his face. His straight jet-black hair, already thinning and beating a rapid retreat from his high forehead, was tamed by Brylcreem and neatly parted and furrowed by the wide tines of a comb. He was tall, about six-two, and then, at thirty-five, still lean, with dark eyes, a broad nose, and full lips.

I remember thinking, *I guess he's really not so bad, maybe not as dangerous as I thought.* It was the only time I can recall thinking of my father as handsome.

■ ■ ■

WHAT COULD POSSIBLY have been wrong with me? Some forty years later, the question continues to nag. With Dad and me, all rivalries and jealousies were writ large—it was as though we were trapped in an amateur educational video on Oedipal theory. For reasons I'm still sorting out, my father antagonistically drew himself up before me early in my childhood, and I wasn't able to see my way clear around him until well into my adult years. In some ways, my experience was an exaggerated, pathological variation on what goes on between all fathers and sons. Standing between every boy and responsible, productive—at best, "magnificent"—manhood is his immediate male primogenitor. Wise, confident standup dads, aware of their frightful power, lay themselves down before their sons and offer themselves as a bridge to independence and achievement. Others, like mine, for reasons only they know, present themselves as a formidable roadblock. Even when I felt I'd eluded my father he would appear again at some remote crossroads, without even intending to, and inhibit my way. Superseding one's father, with or without his help, and then, sometimes almost paradoxically, learning to stand as a respectful memorial to him, is a critical test of standup manhood, and essential to developing the capacity—the bigness—to nurture not only one's own family but the larger society. In my case, it took a while.

As a kid, I mostly thought of my father as scary, mean, snarly—at least around me. I could see that he and my mother had a romantic, although sometimes volatile, love, and that he was comfortable showing physical affection to my older sister and to my little brother. And he clearly worshipped Dean. But Dad had troubling feelings about me, feelings that very early on hardened into an obvious physical aversion toward me—an aversion I learned to reciprocate. If memory serves primarily to help invent a personal story, true or not, from which one can take some measure of comfort, my childhood recollections tell the following tale: Dean, a doomed little boy with a big heart, could see that our father didn't much like me, and when he could, he beckoned me to safety beneath his scrawny little angel's wing.

Dean's death just further calcified Dad's and my feelings about each other. I always thought my father couldn't adjust to the new reality: the boy who was often in trouble, at least by his keenly judicial standards, was now his oldest son. I was the un-Dean. There was always something about me that needed straightening out, either by a grounding, a spanking, or other harsh discipline. He could be terrifying: when he thought I was lying, he threatened to haul me down to the police station or have one of his FBI buddies interrogate me. His meanness was often petty: when I was thirteen and wanted to grow my hair longer, I returned home from the barbershop one time with a light trim and he flew into a rage. The Beatles had just conquered America; I had just conquered my first girlfriend, and I was as vain as any other lovestruck teen. He hauled me back and had the barber scrape the sides and back clean, military style. I felt small, humiliated, and refused to speak to him for weeks.

Perhaps to blunt his grief after Dean died, he threw himself into his work, taking on high-profile cases that got him on the local nightly news and in the newspapers. Working for the Justice Department, he successfully prosecuted Chicago hoodlums who controlled liquor syndicates in Minneapolis. A law-and-order Nixonian Republican, he mounted a failed campaign for a seat in the state legislature, was actively involved in the local and national bar associations, and secured the necessary papers to argue cases in front of the U.S. Supreme Court. I was often asked by teachers and the parents of friends whether I was going to be an attorney like my father—"a great guy." "Sure," I'd say, and leave it at that. But I felt that secretly, like a traitorous ingrate, I worked the other side of the law.

My mother assumed most of the duties the dads of my friends considered their province—hauling me around to my various sporting contests or Boy Scout events, even having "the talk" with me about sex because he simply couldn't bring himself to do it. I didn't want to have "the talk" with anyone, but still felt short-changed by my father's refusal and mystified by his squeamishness around the topic. Instead of participating in a manly initiation ceremony, over several sessions I listened to my mother, who had fled a nightmarish upbringing in northern England, share with me her Victorian views on masturbation ("All boys want to do it but you should try not to") and homosexuals ("There are some men . . ."). I never actually heard anything about sexual intercourse between two consenting heterosexual adults—and didn't ask. She never hid the fact that I was her favorite—my "wildness" reminded her of her father, a rakish captain in the British Army—and the disparity in my parents' feelings about me made for endless Oedipal drama. When they argued, I could hear from the second-floor landing outside my bedroom, it was always about me. I was "bad," Dad would say after a policeman came round looking for the kid who was stealing golf balls from the twelfth-hole fairway after each foursome teed off. (He had come to the right house.) I was just "adventurous and high-spirited," my mother would offer in defense, having retrieved me after I hopped a train and, because it got going too fast, couldn't get off until it stopped in the downtown switching yards. The three of us formed a love triangle, with my father and I both competing for her attention.

Sadness also deepened his dependence on alcohol, although he drank only at night. Like so many men, my father kept such a fierce clamp on his emotions that when he allowed one to surface, he had no idea how to handle it. It was big, noisy, and scary, and when it was cut loose, it pressed up against and threatened to suffocate anyone nearby. By late in the evening he was often either sloppy and sentimental or ornery like a pit bull, sometimes swinging scarily between both states. If he had no work to occupy or distract him, his mood, fueled by Early Times, would often darken steadily over the course of an evening, and I could hear him arguing in a low, nasty tone with my mother. Sometimes she would leave, drive around in her car, but return some time before morning, there to make sure breakfast was on the table. Icy silence would prevail at the dinner table for a day or two, then, mysteriously, they'd be connected again, laughing, gossiping, talking about his latest case. His drinking would moderate for a while, but inevitably the black mood would descend again.

Most people had a very different impression of my father. By all outward appearances he was a "family man." He organized a neighborhood improvement association to provide better playground facilities. He paved over our backyard so we could flood it in winter and make a skating rink. He bought hundreds of dollars worth of equipment for our annual camping trip, which we took every year until Dean died. We visited his parents every Sunday in the tiny, oppressive little starter home he grew up in. And he wanted me, his son whom I have to believe he loved in some complicated way but didn't really like, to get the best education available. At a time when he really couldn't afford it, he decided to send me to an expensive private high school. He wasn't entirely bereft of standup qualities.

Having reformed me, he figured, he encouraged me to apply only to elite colleges. I chose one fifteen hundred miles away to minimize my visits to St. Paul. During the summers I lived at home and worked as a construction laborer—I was expected to make money to cover my transportation and incidental college expenses. At night I played hockey in an Olympic training league. I was up in the morning and gone before my parents arose, ate dinner while they were still having their cocktails and headed to the hockey rink an hour later. When I'd get home at ten or eleven, my father would be up, usually reading, nursing a whiskey, and he'd ask me how it was going. "Got a hat trick tonight," I'd say from the kitchen, grabbing a snack. Or, "The car's making a funny noise." I could sense him reaching for a connection, trying to put those empty, violent years behind us—sensed that he felt that, despite being "bad" or "high-spirited" or "wild" in adolescence, I'd turned out okay, in no small part thanks to him. He was right: he had sent me to good schools where I made good friends and adopted myself into their families. I was responsible, industrious—I was his "best hope," he said, for following him to law school and joining his firm. But I just couldn't, wouldn't cut him a break. I'd say good night, and slip upstairs with my food, sensing relief on his part, too. Neither of us had any experience feeling comfortable in the other's company, and it seemed way too late to learn how to now.

As graduation approached, I got married, perhaps not surprisingly to a woman who shared some of my father's good qualities—his outrage at social injustice, his love of hard work—but had none of his meanness. It occurred to me later that it was him that I married, him that I was trying to get close to. They got along well, and she was an effective buffer between the two of us. My dad had mellowed some, I'd seen. His relationship with my younger brother was warm and supportive; my mother told me he'd regretted the mistakes he'd made with me and was trying to atone for them by easing up on my brother. Health problems had taken some of the fire out of him, too, and he'd quit his law practice to take a slower-paced position on the bench. I visited St. Paul from the East Coast on holidays in an effort to maintain a connection to the family, particularly to my brother and sister, but every time I was within a half hour of the city I'd sink into gloom.

An uneasy truce prevailed, but a few years later, when I flew home to tell my parents I was getting a divorce—by then I had a one-year-old daughter—all the primitive hostilities were unleashed, the more poisonous for having been pent up for so long. My father attacked me viciously for an hour, then refused to speak to me for the remainder of my visit. By now our twisted psychodynamics were beyond comprehension: were *we* the ones who were divorcing? Before leaving the next day, I told him what a neighbor had said to me about him many years before after he had handled her divorce: that he was so wonderfully compassionate and understanding during this difficult time in her life and that she would be eternally grateful to him. I was sorry to learn those same feelings didn't extend to me, I told him. But really, I had learned this long before.

When I arrived back in New York, I was still so angry that I called him at the courthouse, pulled him away from a trial, and told him how foolish I felt having assumed I could find some consolation and counsel from my own father. A couple of hours later, my mother called to tell me he was in the hospital with a collapsed lung. Predictably, she asked, "Are you satisfied now?"

In time, I settled into a new family, a happily blended family to which I had contributed one child and my wife two. A couple of years later, the twins came along, giving the stepkids common siblings. As my own happiness grew, my relations with my father deteriorated further, if that was possible, alternating between total estrangement and bare cordiality. But it wasn't until Tom was about five or six and I noticed him studying me with a shy smile as we puttered with some project in the basement that I thought of that night in northern Minnesota, watching my own father as he lit the campsite lantern. *Really not so bad.* My son's love for me seemed so obvious and strong and unconditional, almost a biological given. Yet at his age I had decided that I really didn't like my dad and that he didn't like me.

This time, however, as I looked through Tom and saw myself at his age, I no longer felt that it must have been my fault.

■ ■ ■

EARLY IN MY first marriage, when the first signs of trouble began to emerge, I was working as a mover and left home for three days to drive a van down the Eastern Seaboard with my boss. John Connor, the former mayor of the college town I kicked around in for a year after graduating, was a short, voluble Irishman with six grown children. Connor could haul an overstuffed chair half his weight up five flights of stairs without pausing to catch his breath and, on a good day, he could lecture you about proper lifting technique while doing it. I looked forward to our trips, for John was funny, quick, and never shy about dispensing advice. Good men—a fifth-grade teacher who took me on a canoe trip, my high school hockey coach, two fathers of high school friends, a college English professor, more recently an elderly magazine editor— have entered my life at crucial times, and I've been quick to enlist them as mentors. John was one of them. As we headed to South Carolina to deliver and set up a grand piano, I alluded to the problems my wife and I were having. After pouring coffee from a thermos and handing me a cup, John said, "There's a simple solution. If she got pregnant and had a baby, you'd be amazed at how quickly your problems would clear up."

I recall thinking how John was probably right, although his advice smacked of the kind of patriarchal attitudes toward "the little woman" under attack at the time. Unfortunately, I didn't have the insight then to grasp that our difficulties had everything to do with my slow but inexorable retreat from our union, a withdrawal that had begun even before the wedding. I decided that this is what marriage must be like: companionable but cool to the touch. Romantic heat was for high school, I thought, although I would soon find out otherwise. I was naïve and didn't have the guts to admit my mistake and end the marriage. One reason I hung in, I'm ashamed to say, was to avoid another blowout with my father. A few years later when she suggested that we try to have a baby, I agreed. Maybe, as my old moving buddy predicted, the problems would just clear up.

When Eliza was born, I was a ga-ga father, attentive to her minute-by-minute needs, obsessed with every developmental milestone, over the top in my affections. As genuine as my love for her was, much of it was misplaced, proferred at the expense of the baby's mother. As time went on, she too would have occupied a too-powerful spot on a family love triangle. Instead, we all became divorce statistics. During discussions about custody, I was aware of all the reasons Eliza should spend a majority of her time with her mother, or at least in one household. I had read all the research on divorced kids and knew that, as a girl, she was better off with her mom. But I feared that, in giving up a regular involvement with my child, I would become exactly the kind of parent my father was to me: uninvolved, unknown, remote.

Maybe even dangerous.

■ ■ ■

MY FATHER HAS TALKED to me about dying for thirty years, during those times that he was talking to me at all. After he had a heart attack at forty-two—the trait of cynical hostility in the Type A personality formula will do that to a man—he accepted a judgeship primarily, he said, for the benefits the job would provide to my mother after he died. He became borderline obese in his fifties, lost half a lung to cancer in his sixties, and by his seventies was on home oxygen because of emphysema. A couple of years ago when, in one of my infrequent bids for affirmation, I flew out to surprise my parents on their fiftieth wedding anniversary, he told me that he was shocked to have made it this far. But I never took his complaints seriously, despite his medical history. To me, he was a formidable man with a hardy constitution who had survived heart disease and cancer and the agony of watching a young son slowly wither away and die. I've always assumed he would live as long as his mother, who is now one hundred and three.

So when he called recently to give me his latest pessimistic health bulletin, I was prepared not to take it too seriously. He had complained of a discomfort that sounded like heartburn for months, but was unable to get any relief. He became jaundiced, and during a procedure to unblock his bile duct, a tumor was discovered. He had been getting a lot of conflicting information from his doctors about the cancer and what should be done. But when I talked to them, they were pretty clear and unequivocal: as an emphysema patient, he was a very poor candidate for surgery. If he survived it, surgery might buy him another six months to a year of life. Without it, he had one or two months.

Over the next week, I spoke to my father every day. Given our history, our conversations were devoid of much sentiment and hand-wringing. He laughed when I told him that, whatever happened, it looked like he'd be checking out soon and he'd better start calling in his favors. I asked him if he really wanted to stay alive just so he could be ornery and pissed off for another year. He chuckled again, his laugh collapsing into a gurgling cough, and admitted that I had a point. "I've never fooled myself into thinking there's anyone other than me, with the possible exception of your mother, who wants to keep this miserable old bastard alive," he said.

As the week went on, though, he decided he wanted to talk about his future. He had been mulling over his choices, knowing there wasn't much time. "If I don't wake up from the surgery, that's really not such a bad way to go," he said. "I'm just not ready to leave your mother right now." He paused a moment, collecting himself. "I want to know what you think," he said. "I value your opinion, you know. You're my number-one son."

A number of flip rejoinders danced in my forebrain. Before his latest illness, we had been in one of our cordially distant phases, chatting every few weeks about politics, the stock market, weather. Two years before, he had suddenly stopped drinking and without warning called to apologize for a few decades of bad behavior. At the end of each conversation he'd ask about my family and hint that he'd like to see us. But it was the considered opinion from our end that he was still most safely appreciated from afar. I made vague promises about a future visit, or rebuffed him with humor. Sometimes he made it easy for me to keep him at a distance. "I never worry about you," he told me recently. I laughed and told him I'd gotten over that a long time ago, but I knew he was sending me praise, however backhandedly. Recently, before his latest illness surfaced, he concluded a conversation by saying, "I love you." Shocked, I muttered, "Thanks," and hung up.

I told him I thought he should check into the hospital and begin the tests that would determine whether he'd even be a candidate for surgery. He should get all the prepping out of the way, knowing it would take a few days to schedule an operation, anyway. Meanwhile, I'd get on a plane.

"When can you be here?" he asked.

■ ■ ■

I'VE HAD A LOT of help getting around my father. I periodically test my latest insights on a very knowledgeable psychiatrist who, I realize, had probably planted the seeds of those insights during our previous session, which, given my "allergy" to psychotherapy, could have been years before. My first revelation was a crucial one. After a fast professional start, I slumped badly in my late twenties. My success had scared me. It took some time to figure out, but I realized that I was afraid of surpassing my stern, demanding, judgmental—and accomplished—father, that I was more comfortable feeling small and insignificant. The image of paternal power I'd internalized was simply too dangerous to go up against. I had the classic underachiever's profile.

I also suffered from another father problem. Although I had embraced mentors as a boy and young man, I was now often creating hostile and competitive situations with authority figures—in the same way, I realized, that I had flirted with extreme behaviors as a teenager to enrage my father and test the limits of his authority. Like other defiant men, I provoked fights subconsciously, hoping to submit to greater male power, because I still felt like a little kid with none of my own. Despite all the ways I felt I had outwardly spurned and distanced myself from him, I had yet to give up my father and become my own man. This is the irony of the rebellious, estranged son who vows never again to have anything to do with his difficult father: until he's psycho-

logically independent, the primal authority figure will always be cling-
ing to his back.

I learned about another syndrome—one I managed to dodge—that
often afflicts a man whose father was absent or emotionally unavail-
able: philandering. Without a loving male to usher him into the world
of men, the future philanderer can't fully break away from his mother
and winds up a soft-core Don Juan—a little boy women love to savor,
like Raven, the New Warrior initiate whose mother dragged him into
her bed until he was twelve. A man who likes to roam a lot fears he'll
lose his sense of masculinity in a real relationship, which requires
sustained intimacy and erotic passion. In his repeated dalliances, the
emphasis is usually on foreplay, on looking and being seen, which
helps him define and reinforce his shaky male image.

But now, as I headed out to see my father for what could be the last
time, my earlier achievement and authority problems were behind
me. I don't know whether my life qualified as "magnificent," as Tolstoy
promised, but I had learned to work and to love, and had no complaints. I had few doubts about my ability as a father—in fact, I was an
eager Glueck-study acolyte, consciously reworking and correcting my
father's flaws and deficiencies, although I'm sure I've been inflicting
some new ones of my own design upon my children.

But I did have doubts about my ability to come to peace with my
dad. It was impossible to predict what kind of state he'd be in.

■ ■ ■

"YOU LOOK LIKE shit, Dad."

His hospital gown had climbed above his knees, exposing withered,
hairless legs. A catheter snaked from his side, draining bile from his
blocked duct, an IV sprouted from a vein in his hand, oxygen hissed
through a tube beneath his nose. A wispy gray coxcomb topped his
head, his lips and cheeks were tight, drawn. He had lost a lot of weight
since I'd seen him a couple of years before—his eyes were wide, like a
frightened animal's. He looked totally exhausted. "I feel like shit, too,"
he said.

I leaned over, hugged him delicately, that frisson of aversion prick-
ling my spine, and sat down.

He wasted no time. "I can't see having the operation," he said.
"What's the point?"

"I thought you wanted my opinion."

"I'm asking for it."

"What does the doctor say?"

"First I have to have a pulmonary test to see whether I can get off the respirator after the operation and breathe on my own. If I don't have enough lung, it's like they're committing suicide for me. And no doctor will do that."

"I think you should have the test. If you don't pass, your decision is made for you."

He shifted on the bed and winced. "I don't want to go out as a pussy. I think I should make up my own mind. He wants to pump up my lungs with steroids for a couple of days and then have me take the test."

"So do it. It's a no-brainer. Go for life. You don't want to be a bad example to your grandchildren. With your own children, you're already too late."

"Listen," he said, ignoring my joust, his anxious, jaundiced eyes like two yellow beacons. "I don't want to die with a bunch of tubes hanging out of me. I don't want my life prolonged by extreme measures. It's major surgery. It'll take me two months to recover from it. And for what? So I can live another week?"

"Maybe a year."

"My ass. On the outside. If I were twenty years younger and had two lungs. They just want to use me as a guinea pig."

His cynicism, which had always coursed through him like a negatively charged life force, was still powerful. I guessed it was a good sign, since it had got him this far. "No one wants to use you for anything, Dad," I said. "We don't have to decide this minute, right? Let me talk to the doctor."

"Would you? Because I'm not tracking well. I don't understand half the things he says." He winced again, and pushed a button on a console attached to his bedrail. A pump dispatched morphine through a tube jutting from his collarbone and he sunk back into his pillows, his eyes rolling back and then closing, tension melting from his furrowed brow, jaw slackening, mouth agape, his face smoothing into a death mask.

He was a lot further along than I'd thought.

• • •

THAT NIGHT, AFTER DINING with my mother, I went back to my hotel room and sat on the balcony, smoking cigarettes, which I hadn't touched in twenty-five years. In some crazed commemoration of my father's bad habits and his passive attempts to kill himself for the past forty years, I had bought a pack of Camels. What was I doing? Trying to postpone his death sentence? Take his cancer into me? The smoke made me dizzy, intensifying my panic and fear. I had arrived with all my defenses on hyperalert, prepared to fend off his attacks as always, but found him weak, shrunken, powerless. Our mutual hostility had always defined a protocol both of us understood; now I was flying solo, at a loss on how to be around him, still a little wary that if I got too close he'd revive just long enough to take a bite out of me. I had talked for years about burying the hatchet with him, about trying to learn more about him, even acknowledging the good he'd done for me. My older sister had told me about his own difficult and joyless childhood, his no-account father with whom he shared a bed and bedroom while his sister and mother shared the other. What does that do to you? What did it do to him? Make him afraid to express tenderness toward his son? Sleeping in the same bed, he must have felt the same physical aversion toward his father that I felt toward him. Did he dislike his father, who died when I was ten? Did he in fact dislike me when I was a kid? Was there some transgenerational pattern I should know about, a defective father gene? I had long wanted to ask him that simple question—*Do you like me?*—and to hear his answer. I had long planned a conciliatory heart-to-heart, but could never bring myself to pull it off. This was my last opportunity—if it wasn't already too late.

I wanted to do all the right things for both my sake and his. I needed his blessing, which I'd never really gotten, and I know he must have needed mine. I wanted to honor him, forgive him, assuage the guilt and regret he had.

Assuming he had any, the miserable old bastard.

■ ■ ■

"WHERE'S YOUR MOTHER?" he asked, a little panicked, when I entered his hospital room the next morning. He had just awakened from a nap.

"I told her to go home and rest awhile," I said. "I told her I'd sit with you. I thought we should talk a bit."

"Yes." He slowly adjusted himself in bed.

I spooned some crushed ice into his mouth. His stomach had shut down, and he now couldn't drink liquids. "We have some really old *tsuris* between us, Dad."

He sucked on the ice and looked away, nodding. "I've thought long and hard about what I did wrong."

"And what did you conclude?"

He looked at me and smiled wanly. "That I let you get away from me, for whatever reason, and that it was just the biggest mistake of my life. I don't know how it happened, it just did. And I should have done something about it a long time ago."

"I always felt that after Dean died you couldn't look at me, like it was my fault or something."

He tried to raise himself in the bed but settled back, grimacing in pain. "That was such a rough patch. You really don't know what to do, you're sick with grief, you have to make all these decisions, you're wracked with guilt, wondering if there was something you did that brought on his cancer . . ."

"Oh, come on. Like what?" As if I hadn't had the same thoughts.

"Like the neighborhood. Was it toxic? It was directly west of the Waldorf paper plant. Remember how the snow used to turn black? We let him have an early-morning paper route, too. Did it make him too tired, too vulnerable to leukemia? You just don't know."

"Childhood cancer is so rare," I tried to reassure him. "He almost certainly had a genetic hit that predisposed him to it." I neglected to mention that he probably also needed an environmental insult to get the disease.

"So you think about that . . . but God, no, of course I never felt it was your fault. I was proud of you when you were a little boy. You always had a job. You were always making money."

"Money is freedom," I said. "If I had my own, I never had to ask you for any. And I could do what I wanted."

He scowled. "That's where you went wrong. You just damn well did what you pleased." A hint of his old growl returned. "You were wild and reckless. Nothing I could do would stop you. You were a bright kid, and you thought you could get over on everybody. You had charm and you knew how to use it. But you were devious and immune to punishment. You used to spring up after I spanked you, and I'd sit there, my hand throbbing, wondering who was really being punished here."

"It hurt, but I decided no one would ever see me cry." I could too clearly recall the smack of his hand, my butt red-hot and stinging, blinking back tears, seething but relieved it was over, the naughtiness slate wiped clean. Even now, I was reluctant to admit that I had once been close to crying. And I could feel my anger gathering.

"My father used to take his belt to me. Bad as you were, I vowed I would never do that to my kids."

However harsh he was with me, I guess, it represented an improvement over his father's style of discipline. A Glueck-study father. "Did you get along with your dad?" I asked.

"I suppose so. I didn't have any choice. We slept in the same bed, and he was often drunk. Our Romanian genes, I guess." He laid his head back, his breathing quick and shallow. "He was weak, could never hold down a job. His prospects weren't good before the Depression, and afterward he just fell apart. It didn't prevent him from fooling around with women, though." He grimaced. "One night I woke up and smelled gas. I went in the kitchen and he was sitting there with the oven and all the burners turned on."

"What was he planning to do?"

"What do you think? I'll never forget the look on his face, just totally defeated. I pulled him back to bed. I don't think he remembered it in the morning. I never told my mother."

"Jesus. I never heard that before."

"It's not the kind of historical family material you want to share with your kids." He motioned for more ice and I fed him some. "He was a very troubled man. I promised myself my kids would never see anything like that."

"Well, thanks for restraining yourself and not blowing us up, Dad."

He shook his head slowly. "Always the smartass. I'm in a compromised position, I'm trying to tell you something, and you can't resist attacking."

"You taught me well." I flashed on watching him in court once when I was a young boy. My mother had brought me to the trial as if to show me that the grilling I got at home was just amateur stuff compared to this. His voice boomed throughout the courtroom as he questioned a witness, who squirmed and shrunk in terror. I remember thinking, *I know how that man feels.* "Actually, I learned a lot because of you, Dad, and I want to thank you for it." I sensed my time was short.

"I always believed you should get a good education. I wanted the best for you."

"That was important, and I'm very grateful. It made a big difference in my life."

"I guess I always hoped you'd join me in the law business."

I almost did, but I didn't remind him of why I passed up the opportunity. A couple of years out of college, I applied and was accepted at a second-tier law school. I called up my father to give him news I thought he'd be pleased to hear. Instead of congratulating me, he said he'd never heard of the school and would get back to me. The next day he did. "No better than night school," was his judgment. If I was planning to feel good about myself, I may as well just forget about it. I realized that, again, I'd applied primarily to get his approval and that, in fact, the last thing I was interested in was the law, particularly if it brought me into my father's orbit. Law school was like my first marriage—all about him.

Every time I tried to say something nice to him, a nasty memory would intrude. I tried to focus. "The thing I'd really like to thank you for, Dad, is that you modeled for me what a relationship with a woman could be like. You showed me what was possible."

It was true. Despite his choleric temperament, his bouts of drinking, the fights they used to have about me, my parents have always been deeply connected. When I was a boy, my father used to greet my mother every evening with a sweeping, backbreaking kiss, the kind you see in old movies. He called her every day at lunchtime—except when they weren't speaking, of course—just to say hello. As they got older and their kids peeled off, they would sit for hours after dinner talking quietly, usually about the case he was currently hearing. They had a lot in common: they'd both survived rough childhoods and were, in many respects, loners. They didn't like anybody's company as much as they enjoyed each other's. They were a good match.

For a fifties dad, my father also modeled for me some very enlightened views about women. He made it clear that he admired my mother's intelligence, often relied upon her to help construct his closing arguments when he was practicing law, and was proud to acknowledge her contributions to his friends. He was adamant about my sister getting a good education and helped launch her on a business career—before the great feminist wave. He was often invited by local women lawyers' groups to address their conclaves, and accepted proudly. I suspect my romantic history was also modeled after his. He married my mother during the war, before he went to law school, uncertain about his prospects. I met my wife at a time when I was beginning to think I'd be settling for much less in life—from work and from love—than I'd expected. We were both turned around, energized, and became focused and ambitious when we found the right woman. After love, work and family fell naturally into place. I was always mystified by the fact that, as a man who so highly valued the connubial partnership, he was never willing to acknowledge mine.

"Your mother's a great, great woman," he said. "We've had a good time together." He misted over a little. "You want to credit me for your good fortune in marriage, I'll take it, although I'm not sure I deserve it." Then, suddenly realizing he missed his wife, he demanded that I call her. "Tell her I think it's time she got over here." He fiddled with the tubes in his arm, again a little agitated and nervous. He reached for the cup of ice on the console, apparently no longer aware that I was there.

My time was up.

■ ■ ■

MY FATHER WAS PERKY the next morning. He asked about my kids and wife, whom he refused to see for the first few years after we married. I told him everyone was fine. "I want to get to know everyone better," he said, "so I've decided to go for it, try for the surgery, and let the chips fall where they may." His doctors had scheduled a pulmonary test for that afternoon, which was to be followed by a procedure to open up his bile duct. "Maybe they'll say I don't qualify for the operation, but if I don't have it, it won't be because I gave up."

"I think that's the right choice, Dad," I said. "You've never backed down from a fight."

"Well, there have been times I should have. Like with you. When you and I fought, neither of us won." He looked away. I sensed one of his Big Emotions and braced myself. "But I guess you'll have the last word."

"What do you mean?"

"One of you kids will probably say something at my funeral. My guess is it'll be you."

"Well, I will if you want . . ."

"You'll do a good job. And . . ?" He looked away again.

"And what?"

"It'll be good for you." He held out his palsied hand, the one free of tubes, and I grasped it. Tears pooled in the corners of his eyes. The only other time I'd seen him cry was the morning Dean died. He had sat at the breakfast table, holding the newspaper before him, tears streaming down his face, trying to pretend it was like any other day. A constellation of memories spread themselves before me: walking to the playground after breakfast and telling my friends that my brother had died, running into the neighborhood hockey coach and telling him. Everyone had known he was going to die but me.

We held hands for a minute, both smearing away tears. Finally I gave him a tissue. "What I say may not be so good for you, though."

He laughed and blew his nose. "That's okay. I won't be around to hear it. You could try to include some good stuff."

"Are you afraid to die, Dad?"

"Nooo," he said in a strong voice that, for a moment, boomed like it did when he was a young lion. "I've had a really good life, a really successful life. I'm proud of you kids, proud of my career. You know what I really got a kick out of?"

"What?"

"I was the only judge from the state to be elected as a delegate to the National Bar Association. You know why they did that? They wanted to honor me for having the guts to keep the goddamned cameras out of the courtroom. And when we went to London for the annual convention, I got to take your mom to a reception to have tea with the queen. I was really proud of that, that I could do that for her. Not bad for a poor Jewish boy from the corner of Snelling and Palace."

"You showed me the pictures."

Though tethered to the hospital bed, he almost swaggered for a moment. "Nah, I'm not afraid of dying. What's to be afraid of?"

"So what do you think is going to happen after you take your last breath?"

"I don't really know," he said, though he was clearly intrigued by the prospect of finding out. He was pensive a moment, then sadness darkened his face. "Do you know what Dean said the night before he died?"

My heart flipped. "What?"

"Your mother was sitting with him in the bedroom. I don't know whether it did any good, he'd been pretty much unconscious for a few days. But for a moment he woke up, looked her in the eye and said, 'I can't go yet because the others aren't ready.' "

What could he have meant? Was he one of a group of kids scheduled to depart from the world on the same ether train? *Don't need no ticket, you just get on board* . . .

He exhaled noisily. "In answer to your question, I believe what Plato said in his dialogues with Socrates: Either we go to a place where we're with all the people who have been good and important to us during this life, or there is nothing. I'm sure I'll be happy if I'm in the first place, but if there's nothing, I won't know the difference."

His voice guttered out, he was now clearly exhausted. He winced, but offered a weak smile. "So you can't lose."

■ ■ ■

WITHIN AN HOUR of returning to his room following a presurgical procedure, Dad's blood pressure dropped precipitously, his heart beat madly, and he began hallucinating. He had sepsis, a serious, often fatal, blood infection. "It's hopeless," he managed to say to me before an oxygen mask was placed over his face and he was wheeled off to intensive care. Two days later, the crisis had passed, but his doctors felt he needed to get stronger before they could consider surgery. I returned home to New York. Awaiting me was a message from his doctor saying he had now ruled out surgery and recommending that Dad return home to receive hospice care. The next day, as I was making the arrangements, I received another call from his doctor. He was too sick to leave the hospital, he said. The cancer was apparently racing through him, and he already had "the look." A week later he was dead.

Over the next two days, I sat at my keyboard, composing his eulogy. I now understood why he had subtly hinted that I write one. Layer by layer, the veils I had drawn over our troubled history were lifted and a more complex picture of him—and of my love for him—resolved. I was startled by an early memory, way before Not So Bad: waiting for his car to turn the corner onto our block each night, hopping in, and riding a few yards to the house with him. Carrying my little schoolbag-briefcase like my role model, I would walk alongside him into the kitchen and proudly announce that the men of the house had returned home from work—just as my own son has so many times done with me.

Other memories, anchored so long in the murk of resentment and envy, broke free and skittered to the surface: milk shakes and popcorn for my neighborhood gang on balmy Sunday summer evenings. Four straight nights together at the smoky St. Paul Arena watching the state high school hockey tournament each February. The Winter Carnival treasure hunt. His incessant bumbling with still and super-eight movie cameras. My eavesdropping on his conversations with FBI agents who came by the house to report progress on their latest investigations. A spring business trip to Phoenix when I was thirteen, just the two of us. For two guys who had a lot of trouble getting along–and really could never stop feuding—we had had a few good times.

As I sifted through the memory bank, I discovered that I had lumped together his meanness with what was stern and disciplined about his paternal style. When I was eleven, he had said I could go to Boy Scout camp if I contributed thirty dollars to the cost. I remember working hard at odd jobs to earn the money, a little irritated that the big-time lawyer wasn't willing to just cough up the necessary dough and let me go. When I gave him the money, he handed it back, told me he had already paid the camp, that he just wanted to see whether I could earn thirty dollars in a month, and suddenly I had a wad of bills to blow on what I wanted. There were other tests. If I learned how to rewire an electrical socket, he'd get me my own department store credit card so I could choose and pay for my own clothes. I couldn't get my driver's permit until I learned how to sweat-solder a copper pipe. He was one kind of man Robert Bly talks about—a mean man who can become beneficent when teaching. He was a self-starter, and wanted me to be one, too. He had escaped his own oppressive upbringing, put himself through law school, married a romantic war bride, and tried to rework and correct his own father's mistakes. His mission was unexpectedly complicated by having a son whose temperament was so wildly in conflict with his own.

Although I had spent much of my youth pretending to ignore him, I recalled every important and controversial detail of his career—from his start as the city's only public defender to his career-building prosecution of Chicago gangsters to his defense of a wife-murderer in the state's most notorious criminal trial. While composing my eulogy, I was interrupted often by colleagues of his whom I'd never met who called to offer their condolences and express their respect for a man they described as a mentor, the conscience of the bench, a model of fairness and probity, a tough-minded independent magistrate who knew what he thought and didn't mind telling anyone who asked. Unlike the other judges, one lawyer told me, Dad wasn't the kind of guy you'd try to schmooze in the elevator on the way to your client's sentencing. He was immune to social stroking in the legal environment. Also no surprise to me, he threw the book at those who deserved it and, as I knew only too well, some who didn't. A newspaper reporter who was working on his obituary told me the local press referred to him as "the hanging judge."

We had come to some sort of understanding before he died and now, from beyond the otherworldly realm that Plato had described, he was asking me to see him in his fullness. He knew I had a very clear picture of his dark side, that I'd become expert at cataloging and analyzing all his flaws and all the ways he had failed me. But he also knew that my resentment had taken on a life of its own, and he wasn't going to leave me with that legacy. He apparently was confident that, at the least, he had imparted to his son a sense of duty and honor, and that I would dignify his memory before his family, friends, and colleagues. In the process, maybe he hoped that my own memory would speak to me about things I had forgotten, things I didn't want to remember because they didn't fit with my neat solipsistic theories, and I would be liberated from the thrall of that harsh überfather I'd internalized as a child and dreaded ever since—and the rage that had consumed me for so long would subside.

He was right. Something had shifted, resentment nudged aside by grudging respect, regret giving way to sorrow. A couple of months after his funeral, I traveled again to St. Paul to attend a memorial service for Dad in the county courthouse. At a reception following the ceremony, which took place during an actual session of court, a recently appointed judge who was about my own age described at length my father's tireless efforts as his mentor, how when he was a young lawyer he regularly received notes from my dad on how to sharpen his presentations or control the tempo of his cross-examinations and how later, not long before he died, Dad had written to the governor recommending his appointment. "He just took me in, almost adopted me as his son," the judge said. "He had a huge impact on my career. He must have been a terrific father to you."

The son of another colleague, again about my age, told me how Dad would sometimes call his father at night to discuss a legal matter and end up talking to the son at length about how things were going in his life. Others told me how my father had repeatedly showed them magazine articles I'd written, how he always talked about how proud he was of me. His former court clerk recognized me from the hockey pictures in his chambers.

I've never thought of my father as a mentor, I can't remember having any conversation about "life" with him when I was a boy or an adult that even approached fifteen minutes, and he never once told me he was proud of me or my work, or even that he had read it. But, rather than feeling angry after listening to the glowing testimonials from his colleagues and his "adopted son," I felt sad—and sorry for him. We had both missed out on a lot.

He never understood that boys are needy creatures, that the business of raising them never ends—from the exclamations of adoration of the toddler, to encouragement of a young boy's enterprise and industry (no matter how "wild" or "high-spirited" he may be), to praise for the adolescent's budding skills, to admiration of the young adult's victories and achievements. He never knew that, with any luck, such praises later would be returned.

Something had shifted, but not the truth: I didn't like him, and he didn't like me. He was mean, stubborn, insular, judgmental, demanding, and way too harsh with me. But he was also tough, principled, independent, smart, and honorable toward women. Despite my denial of him for much of my life, I had allowed more of him inside me than I thought, internalized enough of the good parts of his character to have the strength to be a man in the world. Psychoanalysts say that to reach full maturity we must be able to take others inside us—incorporate, introject, internalize them. The metaphor is not confined just to psychoanalysis: students absorb a guru along with his teachings, Christians subsume Christ through the eucharist, primitive warriors honor an enemy's spirit and courage by eating his heart, ancestors live on through descendants, a lover lives on in one's heart. Our fathers live on through us, too, whether we like it or not, and before we can become fully productive and whole—standup guys deserving, as Tolstoy said, of the "magnificent" life—we must first rediscover them as a source of fresh strength.

That discovery, I've learned, doesn't fully dawn until we accept the responsibility of vindicating our fathers, regardless of their sins. My job, I now know, is to acquit my father of all the misdeeds of which I've accused him and let all the good in my life stand as testament to the value and success of his. I am his living memorial, evidence of much of what he did right when he was in the world.

Some of us, the fortunate ones, reach this milestone earlier than others. Men with "good" fathers arrive at this understanding, happily, while their fathers are still alive. The important thing is to get there, though, for if we forever reject the people who have been so important to our development, we have nothing inside to "give back." We're bereft of the inner strength necessary for mentoring, nurturing, and protecting the society we belong to—a final, fundamental obligation of the standup guy.

BIG MAN

...

LAST SUMMER, on the kind of sweltering evening in which the inevitablity of random violence hangs thick in the air, a man I'll call Owen Sanders, a fabulously successful former investment banker, drove his twenty-year-old Mercedes-Benz through the pocked and littered streets of Newark's Central Ward, the epicenter of the 1967 riots and a neighborhood whose residents have since survived mainly by pushing drugs or peddling sex. Sanders, fifty-five, dressed in the sporty apparel of the white suburbanite that he is, eased his car to the curb in front of a grimy brick tenement and sat for a few moments with his hand on the shoulder of his passenger, a black teenaged boy who anxiously scanned the gritty streetscape. The two shook hands, then the boy bounded from the car and raced into the building as if through an imaginary gauntlet. Sanders proceeded down the deserted block to a stop sign, where his car was instantly surrounded by a group of jittery young men wearing tank tops and slouchy outsized shorts, their heads wrapped in do-rags. One of the young men hoisted himself onto the car's hood and sat with his feet planted on the front bumper as he lit a cigarette. Calmly, Sanders honked his horn, motioned the man away from his car, then lowered his window and peered up at one of his other visitors. The man's eyes flickered in recognition—this white man was no chickenhawk or suburban crank fiend—and, after shooing his accomplice away from the car, shuffled back into the shadows of a nearby overgrown vacant lot. The other men followed, griping in low tones. As he rolled up his window and drove away, Sanders heard one of them say his name.

Sanders had been through the drill dozens of times before over the past decade—ever since he had gotten involved with the Boys Clubs and Girls Clubs of Newark in the mid-eighties. On Saturday mornings, he would sit in a Central Ward church basement listening to a boy describe how his brother died after being shot, from out of nowhere, it seemed, on a playground while they were playing basketball. He would wonder how his own daughters would fare if, like some of those in the Girls Club, their mother suddenly disappeared for a week on a crack-cocaine jag, leaving them and their baby brother with no food. He remembers being so moved by hearing some of the kids' wrenching stories on those weekend mornings that he found himself thinking about them at his office on Monday instead of the next big-ticket leveraged buyout he was negotiating. He decided to get involved with at-risk kids, not simply by funding programs—and he's funded plenty of them—but by being a regular, reliable presence in their lives and, for virtually all of them, their only positive male role model. Some of Sanders's boys have died, gone to prison, or been sucked into the ravening maw of the ghetto's insatiable drug machine. But many others have graduated from high school and gone on to college, which he's paid for—escaped the 'hood for good. Every new initiate into Central's turf battles, even the most skittish crack-running homey eager to pop just anybody to secure his props, learns to leave Owen Sanders alone. "As bad as they are," Sanders says, "they're willing to protect a force for good."

And by every measure, Sanders is that and more. Having successfully competed in the world and raised a family, he has decided to focus his considerable talents, energy, and compassion on improving the commonweal—the final and noblest obligation of the standup guy.

Sanders's most notable success has been Juwan, who, a year after they first met, when Juwan was nine, asked if he could call him Daddy. Sanders met the boy one Saturday morning when he and other directors of the Rigorous Educational Assistance to Deserving Youth (READY) foundation, which promised to pay the college tuitions of one thousand at-risk kids from Newark, dropped in on the program's first class. After the directors addressed the kids, the teacher asked the boys if there was anything they'd like to say to their visitors. Juwan raised his hand. "I'd like to compliment the board on how nice they look today," he said. Sanders laughed and called the boy over. "You're either going to be president of the United States some day," he said, "or the head of a crime syndicate."

Over the next few years, Juwan, whose father died in prison, was a frequent visitor at Sanders's house and office, and was regularly invited to family beach vacations and holiday gatherings. The boy and his mentor spent afternoons talking—often at Yankees games—about life, racial differences, and how to express machismo without dealing drugs or dissing women.

Sanders also had many meetings with his mother, who has three other children, and school principals to discuss the boy's behavioral problems, like the time he was found with a joint in the schoolyard. Whatever privileges he was exposed to during the day—Sanders has paid for Juwan to attend private high school the past three years—he still had to go home to the 'hood at night. None of Juwan's boyhood friends, says Sanders, has managed to escape jail, drug-dealing, or death.

One of the more interesting challenges, Sanders says, has been teaching the boy how to maneuver nonviolently but confidently in the male world and how to be less cowed by the female. Sanders recalls that when Juwan was about ten and staying at his house one weekend, he and his son tried to throw the boy in the swimming pool. "He ended up almost throwing us in," says Sanders. "That's how strong and scrappy and fierce he was." The same weekend, though, a little girl from the READY program was also staying with the family and at one point became angry with Juwan. "She grabbed his ear, pulled him through the house looking for an adult, and he went meekly. He would fight fiercely with me or any other male—and, in fact, was getting into a lot of fights at school—but if he was in trouble with a woman or girl, he recognized that he was part of a matriarchy, and capitulated immediately."

Much of his mentoring involves providing the same tough love any devoted father would give a troubled son. "It's been a chore," says Sanders. "But I feel just about as close to him as I do to my biological children. When he was eleven he was playing football in Newark one afternoon, I was the only white person at the game, and he kicked the winning field goal. I felt such a surge of joy and pride. It wouldn't have been any greater if it had been my own son."

Juwan was the "project" that turned Sanders into a full-time philanthropist. In 1986, the last year he made the *Forbes* magazine list of the four hundred wealthiest Americans, he was worth an estimated $200 million. A year later, the leveraged-buyout expert, then forty-five and the father of three teenaged children, put up $10 million to jump-start the READY foundation. He's gone on to set up several other foundations—including Ten Thousand Mentors in New Jersey, a program adopted by three state colleges, and the national One to One organization—that are focused on mentoring the fifteen million kids living beneath the poverty line. Sanders, the son of a steel warehouse manager who grew up in the West Ward of Newark, has also given away tens of millions of dollars to a variety of schools and nonprofit groups in New Jersey. He was the driving force behind the effort to build a $180 million Performing Arts Center in Newark, putting up the first $12 million and rallying other wealthy businessmen to the cause. The second phase of his almost single-handed effort to rehabilitate the ailing city involves heading up the group that recently bought the New Jersey Nets and then formed a partnership with the New York Yankees and moving the basketball team's arena next door to the Performing Arts Center.

That project, too, was inspired by noble intentions. Sanders and a friend, Lewis Katz, each invested $25 million in the Nets and then donated their 38 percent stake to a newly formed nonprofit trust called the Community Youth Organization. Whatever profits the two realize will go to CYO, which will provide scholarships to needy kids, along with tutorial and nutritional programs and, they hope, housing and health care in New Jersey's poorest inner-city neighborhoods. For Katz in particular, purchase of the franchise represents the culmination of a lifelong dream. Growing up poor in Camden—his father died when he was an infant—he adopted athletes as his role models, particularly the basketball Warriors of Philadelphia, who played across the river. In bringing the Nets to Newark, he hopes not only to revive the inner city economically but to inspire the neighborhood's children, many of whom are also growing up without fathers. A lawyer who recently sold a parking business worth $225 million, Katz has entered what he calls "the third chapter" of his life—"the giving-back chapter."

Aside from his unavoidably high-profile philanthropy, Sanders chooses to do his gift-giving anonymously. He agreed to talk to me in his foundation office in New Jersey only if I didn't use his real name, not because he fears for his or his family's safety or to avoid being deluged with requests for money, but because recognition would only dilute the joy he receives from helping others. "I'm absolutely convinced that the more we show unconditional love and the more we expect nothing in return, the more satisfaction we receive," he says. "I recognize that there are certain offsetting arguments—that by getting rid of the cloak of anonymity, you might encourage others to emulate you. I also know that people need to thank you. But that's the decision I've made. I've learned that the greatest satisfaction comes from asking for nothing in return."

By any standard, Sanders, who is tall and sandy-haired—a handsome hybrid of Robert Redford's and Ted Turner's best features—seemed to have it all during the eighties. He had a good marriage, solid kids, vast wealth, many friends—he still plays piano in a jazz band that's been together for twenty-five years—but was quietly suffering from a vague sense of unease. "My partner said to me when we were having great successes in the early eighties, 'You don't look happy, you should be on top of the world.' I said I guess I'd be happy if we lost it all and could start again. But that didn't seem practical. There was a void there. I couldn't put my finger on it, but I knew I had to do something else. I had no idea what it would be."

After meeting Juwan at the Boys Club of Newark, he began to get one. Despite the frequent heartbreak—some have killed, some have been killed—he finds the hands-on experience of working with needy kids far more gratifying than simply writing a check. "At a certain point in your life, it becomes more important to get away from focusing on the self or specific outcomes and thinking about how you can make a difference in someone else's life. I'm incredibly grateful to these kids for enabling me to step back and look at my own life. I've learned so much from them. I've found that the more of them I've helped the more satisfied I feel about my own life—much more satisfied than I ever felt hitting the ball out of the park in the business world."

■ ■ ■

ACCORDING TO THE LATE psychologist Erik Erikson, Sanders is experiencing a surge of midlife generativity, the seventh of eight stages in Erikson's lifespan model of successful psychosocial development, and the one central to achieving a sense of manly fulfillment. Like each of the other stages, this one, which occurs between the ages of

202 · STANDUP GUY

thirty-five and fifty-five, follows a "crisis" or turning point—what Erikson called "a period of increased vulnerability and heightened potential." Successful negotiation of this midlife passage results in an active concern for the life and spirit of the next generation, particularly for young adults and children who are not one's own. Failure results in stagnation and self-absorption. Erikson put it this way: "The ethical rule of adulthood is to do to others what will help them, even as it helps you to grow." Erikson's ethical rule is also a vital component of the deep structure of manhood ideology: good men feel a natural responsibility to protect and nurture their communities, however retro and "patriarchal" that may sound.

Sanders, of course, is in an enviable position to help those less fortunate. But mere wealth is incidental to a man's generative potential. Anyone can help mentor the generation nipping at his heels by serving as a labor-union leader, founding a neighborhood improvement association, volunteering at a local social service center, or sitting on the school board. Many men, like me, discover coaching. While our efforts may not seem as grand as those of Sanders, we often can make as large an impact on a kid's life. A friend of mine, a Boston ophthalmologist who, like me, sees sports as a training ground for life, says his most gratifying seasons often have nothing to do with winning. Last year, for instance, one of his players, a not particularly gifted third-line forward, was diagnosed with cancer and had to have an operation. His parents called the coach and told him their son would be unable to play anymore, but he convinced them to let the boy play out the season before having his surgery. In the last game, in the third period no less, the boy scored the only goal of the game, his first of the season, and was mobbed by his teammates. In the stands, my friend told me, all the parents were crying.

Erikson's theory of generativity complements an observation made by Carl Jung: As they get older, men become more like women, and women more like men. This "convergence" can be traced in each gender's shift in attitude toward work and family. As they mature, Jung noted, rankers become more involved in intimate relationships; they seek gratification not just from work but from being with their wives, kids, and friends. Linkers begin to show greater interest in independence and achievement—even a first career.

At one time, researchers conjectured that these shifts were due to endocrine changes. Diminishing levels of estrogen in women do allow for greater expression of testosterone, the go-getter hormone. But the decline in testosterone in men is so gradual over decades that it couldn't possibly cause dramatic behavioral shifts. The massive flow of women into the workplace in the 1970s made the question moot, anyway. They no longer get jobs and focus on achievement after their kids are launched; most have had them all along.

But that doesn't change the fact that men do become more interested in nurturing in midlife. (And even if they've had jobs all along, many women often adopt a more serious attitude toward their career after their kids are out of the way.) Many of us marvel at how our own fathers, so tough and distant when we were kids, morph into old softies around their grandkids. We often quietly shift into the early stages of this epoch after doing some serious reckoning about our careers. We may discover, shockingly, that we've topped out, professionally, by midlife, and feel a need to direct our energies into other areas. This feeling intensifies over the next decade: while half of forty-year-olds still aspire to advance, only about a fifth of fifty-year-olds are interested in further ascendancy. We lay down our swords, temper our fierce competitiveness, cede our power to the up and coming, and become mentors instead.

Mentoring is not uniquely human. Wizened chimps bond with youthful males after the females leave to find their way into a new troop. They share food with their protégés and instruct them in the nuances of chimp politics. Mature baboons also teach their apprentices what to worry about in the forest. The senior simians work tirelessly to convey to their callow troopmates the difference between the alarm call that signals the presence of a snake and the one used to announce a nearby hawk. For their own sake, they've got to be sure that the younger guys don't mix them up.

Just as the occasional renegade chimp is banished because he's not a team player, not all men become generative. At some point in our careers, most of us have been exposed to a power-mad, perhaps even downwardly mobile, superior who jealously guards his own skills and refuses to take on a protégé or name a successor. This man is an archetype—a King Laius, the mythic antigenerative parent who tries to kill his son, Oedipus. He's angry, envious, selfish, narcissistic, and doesn't have much in the way of libido or feeling to invest in other people, including the next generation. When he does mentor, he wants his protégé to submit to him as if he were a clone.

Erikson theorized that having a child is a necessary precursor to generativity, but a study of infertile men suggests it's not an absolute requirement. Psychologist John Snarey found that about three quarters of men who, though childless, showed an interest in other people's kids were likely, by age forty-seven, to have become guides, coaches, or mentors to young people outside their own family. Only about a quarter of those whose coping strategy involved substituting a non-human object—a pet, car, hobby, or fixer-upper home—became generative. And none of the infertile men who focused on themselves demonstrated a later interest in shepherding young people. They became preoccupied with bodybuilding, personal health, or macho sexuality.

The same study also found a direct correlation between generativity and marital happiness. More than three quarters of the childless men who got involved with the children of others remained happily married, while more than half of those who substituted nonhuman objects or themselves ended up in loveless marriages or divorced. Snarey also discovered that childless men who are involved with important caregiving activities, just like those with kids, tend to enjoy better promotions in the workplace.

■ ■ ■

IF SANDERS LIVED HALFWAY around the world—in New Guinea, say—he would have earned the honorific of "Big Man." This tribal standup guy, whose relatives can be found in virtually all of the world's cultures, transcends the universal requirements of manhood: he not only competes fiercely to attract and impregnate a desirable female and provide for his family but feels a distinct sense of obligation to "give back" to his community. Tapping his charisma, political leadership, and economic power—he possess a special knack for bartering and trading on behalf of his fellow tribespeople—the Big Man of New Guinea achieves a coveted position in the social hierarchy by personifying masculine power at its most forceful and robust.

Big Men typically ascend to their vaunted position by performing dramatic acts of derring-do that benefit their village, tribe, or country. The Big Man of New Guinea has proven himself a fearless warrior, often by blithely wading into battle amid a thicket of arrows and spears, and like the glorious American war heroes who later became president, commands widespread loyalty, admiration, and respect as a result.

The New Guinea Big Man is also much like the Western capitalist who figures out how to make hundreds of millions of dollars for himself by creating jobs for hundreds of workers—by serving his fellow man. He is an economic power unto himself, an engine of production who motivates and enriches his followers. As a farmer or herder, he is the unofficial manager of the village, exhorting his people to produce, work hard, and to save. The defining mark of the Big Man is that he accumulates food and goods so that he can bestow them upon his followers at feasts and ceremonies. Like Sanders, he enriches himself to gain the larger satisfaction and honor of helping others.

Loyalty to followers is a universal hallmark of Big Manhood. For that quality alone, Aaron Feuerstein, the owner of Malden Mills, a 130-year-old textile company in Massachusetts, deserves to join Sanders as an American Big Man. After fire destroyed three of the company's factories, Feuerstein decided to rebuild and keep on payroll the 3,200 employees left jobless by the disaster. Within three months, 80 percent of his employees were working at a borrowed factory, and the remaining workers were brought back when the new plant was completed. Feuerstein could have pocketed a big chunk of the $300 million in insurance money and used the rest to build a plant in Mexico or South America, as other textile manufacturers have done. But his obligations as a community Big Man and a religious Jew convinced him otherwise. "What kind of ethic is it that a CEO would be prepared to hurt three thousand people who are his employees and an entire city of many more thousands in order for him to have a short-term gain?" he asks. "There's some kind of crazy belief that if you discard your responsibility to your country, your city, your community, your workers, and think only of immediate profit, that somehow not only your company but the entire economy will prosper as a result. And I think that's dead wrong."

One measure of the Big Man is that he relishes life on the public stage—which often means the battlefield. In ancient Greece, Big Man potential was measured by the risks a man was willing to take on behalf of the commonweal, hence Achilles' willingness to trade a long and undistinguished life for a brief one filled with honor and glory (and, not incidentally, the Trojan mother's humiliation if her son returned home after surviving his army's defeat). Among latter day Big Men, Ted Turner, as flamboyant as any who has strutted across the boards of the civic theater, happily fulfills his public role. Turner has led his crew to victory in the America's Cup, bought and sold professional baseball and basketball teams, revolutionized the television and communications industries, and won the heart of one of America's legendary actresses. Not surprisingly, his generosity is also expressed with flair. It's not enough for Turner to help out his neighborhood, city, state, or even his country. At a black-tie fundraiser, Turner shocked everyone by impulsively pledging a billion dollars to the United Nations.

Some Big Men choose to leverage their power by trying to change public policy. Financier George Soros, who amassed most of his multi-billion-dollar fortune by taking huge risks—in his case, in the currency markets—has personally subsidized action committees to change American drug policy. He has given the bulk of his billions to build free societies in former Communist countries, pledging $500 million to Russia alone. His charitable ventures finance fifty offices and employ more than a thousand people worldwide. A felt obligation to give back seems to run in the family: recently, Soros's older brother Paul created a $50 million trust to help underwrite American graduate education for immigrants and their children.

But just as many Big Men, like Sanders, prefer to wield their influence and divest themselves of their fortunes more quietly. In 1984, to avoid disclosure, Charles Feeney, the founder of Duty Free Shoppes, secretly turned over the business, worth billions of dollars, to two charitable foundations he set up in Bermuda. Over the past fifteen years, the foundations have quietly funneled $600 million to universities, medical research centers, Irish charities, and other organizations. A substantial gift to Cornell University helps students of modest means pay down their student loans if they earn good grades, work, and volunteer—in other words, become Big Men in training. Feeney lives modestly and, although he has set up trusts for his five grown children, has kept only a tiny fraction of his amassed fortune for himself.

"Money has an attraction for some people," he says, "but nobody can wear two pairs of shoes at one time."

Some men manage to have a Big Man–like impact by performing small acts of generosity. Thomas Cannon, a retired postal employee from Richmond, Virginia, whose wife is paralyzed, has indulged a habit of giving away money. Although his salary was never greater than $30,000, Cannon has moonlighted as an anonymous philanthropist for twenty-five years, sending $1,000 checks to needy strangers—a total of $98,000 in all. "There's this illusion that I'm a multimillionaire," says the seventy-two-year-old local Big Man. "But I've spent most of my life living on the brink of financial disaster."

· · ·

FEENEY, SOROS, SANDERS, AND TURNER are all self-made men, which distinguishes them from old-money philanthropists in one important way: They take an active interest in seeing that they get a robust return on their donations and manage their philanthropic efforts as aggressively as they do their businesses. They have a hands-on, participatory approach to giving, which means that they often show up unannounced at project sites they've financed to make sure their contributions are being put to the best use.

Paul Tudor Jones II exemplifies this style. Jones arrived in New York from Memphis with a bachelor's degree and $1,700 twenty years ago, hoping to get rich as a commodities trader. In 1987 he anticipated the stock market crash and made a "tremendous amount" of money. "I was thirty-three, and had a huge appetite for trying to give back what I had enjoyed since moving to New York, which was great good fortune," he says. He joined the "I Have a Dream" Foundation program and adopted an entire New York City high school freshman class from an impoverished neighborhood, promising to pay for every kid's college education if they hung in and graduated. But, as Sanders had, Jones quickly learned that unless poor kids can improve their life away from school and be protected against the corrosive effects of poverty, they often don't even make it through junior high school. "I was spending about four thousand dollars per child per year," Jones says, "and not making any difference at all. Unless you can equip the kids to deal with the problems they face at that age—to deal with pregnancy at fourteen or a parent's drug addiction—you're doing nothing but spitting in the wind."

So in 1988, Jones founded the Robin Hood Foundation, which deploys what he calls "guerilla philanthropy" to try to break poverty's stranglehold in New York. He put up $3 million of his own money and lured two fellow Wall Street players into putting up equally substantial gifts. In its first year, the foundation gave away $52,000 in cash, goods, and services; this year it will give away $15 million.

Jones's idea was to apply the same aggressive, rigorous principles of investment banking—"a no-nonsense businesslike approach"—to helping people, ensuring donors that they will get the highest return possible on their gifts. He and the other board members pay all the foundation costs, including the salaries of its twelve employees, so that every penny given to the Robin Hood Foundation goes directly to helping the poor. Essentially a "mutual fund" for those interested in relieving suffering but who don't have the time to research the organizations they pledge money to, Robin Hood does thorough analyses of city nonprofit agencies before issuing grants, and provides them with managerial, legal, and accounting assistance. "If we find an organization with a big heart that wants to renovate ten city buildings but is intimidated by the legal work, we know how to blitzkrieg that," says Jones.

Most of the Robin Hood Foundation's focus, aside from taking from the rich and giving to the poor, is on preventing poverty rather than curing it. "Fighting the symptoms is far more costly," Jones says. "You're always late. By the time someone hits a soup kitchen, you're dealing with late-stage symptoms." Accordingly, the foundation's next project is to pull together the best researchers on parenthood and develop a multilevel curriculum that can be taught in junior high and high school. "You have to get a license to drive a car, but anyone can have a child."

The lessons of responsible parenthood, says Jones, are particularly directed to men. "A man's role is first and foremost to be there as a father to his children. If you're talking about fixing most of what's wrong in the world, that's the end of the story. I realize that I never could have gotten where I am if I hadn't had devoted parents and most importantly a real friend as a father. The most important thing we can do is to create as many two-parent families as possible. That's the whole game."

From his perspective, the world is teeming with Big Men. "In New York, where you have some of the most powerful and successful people in the world, there are twenty thousand nonprofit agencies trying to do good. I see professional people of every age busting their ass to give a helping hand to people in need. If you've had any kind of financial success at all, it's clear what you have to do."

■ ■ ■

DESPITE THE SO-CALLED death of patriarchy in America, the Big Man is alive and well. And psychologically healthy. One of the few long-term studies of men confirms the dynamic link between the aggressiveness and self-assertion of the Big Man and the more modestly effective generative man—and a prosperous, virtuous life. Since 1937, researchers from the Grant Study of Adult Development have tracked the psychological and physical health of several classes of Harvard graduates, many of whom are still alive. Among this elite group, which includes college presidents, politicians, partners of Wall Street law firms, foundation presidents, and society surgeons, psychiatrist George Vaillant, the study's director for the past thirty years, identified a special group of "Best Outcomes"—men who enjoyed not only material success but stable relationships and mental tranquillity and sought fulfillment by helping others.

Vaillant was particularly interested in the differences between the men who willingly and faithfully observed Erikson's "ethical rule of adulthood" and those who didn't. Those who were unwilling to assume responsibility for other adults—the ungenerative—were far more likely to be pessimistic, filled with self-doubt, passive, and fearful of sex at age fifty than the Best Outcomes. At age thirty, a third of the Worst Outcomes were unmarried, as opposed to 3 percent of the Best. They were less likely to have internalized their fathers as role models and tended to be dominated by their mothers as adults. As fathers they were, in turn, apparently not much of a role model for their own kids, for their children could neither achieve their academic success nor adjust socially and emotionally to the world as easily as the offspring of Best Outcomes. Interestingly, Vaillant found that the urgent need of Best Outcomes to be in charge was directly linked to their concern for and involvement with the commonweal: the Best gave six times as much money to charity as the Worst, yet as a group exhibited six times as many displays of aggressive behavior as their less exalted and stingier classmates. As they grew older, they became even more active in competitive sports than they'd been in college, whereas the less successful participants avoided competition altogether.

Perhaps the most significant finding of the Grant Study's Harvard grads was that the most accomplished men typically enjoyed long and satisfying relationships with their spouses; great success had not been won at the expense of poor marriages, neglected children, and a rudderless neighborhood improvement association. Embracing challenge, seeking out risk, and channeling their natural aggression into business, sports, and community affairs, they proved lucky at work and in love—and got to enjoy Tolstoy's "magnificent" life.

In other words, the Best Outcomes were masters of their environment: they were able to work, love, play, and efficiently solve problems. Unlike the Spanish *gamberro,* the New Guinea "rubbish man," the clueless withholder of sex, and the deadbeat dad, they were inspirational models of righteous action, "other-directed," disciplined at directing their focus away from themselves toward worldly concerns. They resisted indolence, squeamishness, self-doubt, and the impulse to withdraw or surrender, even when they were threatened with extinction, as Owen Sanders discovered so often on his nightly excursions into Newark's violent Central Ward.

Do the Best Outcomes represent, finally, the model of standup guy I've been looking for? Instead of working on psychological autonomy at New Warrior retreats, probing the mysteries of male sexuality in nude encounter groups, scrapping with hyper-rankers in locker rooms, separating dicks from assholes, and stalking guilt-ridden evangelical Christians, should I have been paging through old Harvard yearbooks? Well, no, but the Grant study does illuminate a crucial point. Thirty years into the feminist era, as men strive to formulate their "defense" in the coevolutionary arms race, it's important to remember that one essential standup quality—the desire to compete—will never go out of style. Most of the men on the previous pages are working hard to change in ways that women want them to, and together form a characterological composite of the new standup guy: emotionally independent, sexually sophisticated, committed to fatherhood, enlightened by sexual manners, and possessed of an ego unthreatened by accomplished women. Most important, they also share a willingness to jump in and mix it up in the ranking contests and mating pools—an underpinning of the timeless construct of masculinity and sadly missing among men in retreat.

For all the ways men have changed, despite their new "strategy" in the never-ending arms race, women still want a man who is competitive enough to prove his love to be greater than that of a rival, strong and tough enough to protect his children, and aggressive enough to amass the goods he will later give back to those who need them more than he or his family. Among the best men, it has ever thus been so, and ever will be.

· · ·

WITH A COUPLE OF NOTABLE differences, however. While aspiring modern standup guys would do well to reacquaint themselves with the good parts of the old manly code the Best Outcomes lived by, they also need to retrofit that code for the newly egalitarian world. The new standup guys need to know that their potency will be enhanced by their mate's personal power in the world and by the skill and devotion they show in helping get their kids launched. And they need to realize that while the happy, successful Best Outcomes undoubtedly relied upon women to manage their emotions, their modern successors are required to be psychologically self-sufficient, endowed with the fresh emotional insight that enables them to form a deep, lasting, and mutually supportive bond with an alpha female, who has redefined the concept of trophy wife. The reward for acquiring these new skills: the richness of an erotic life with a sexually frisky and assertive mate.

The final, true measure of a standup guy: a willingness to live up to his personal potential, no matter how modest and within whatever socioeconomic niche. This fact should not be lost on those men, beaten down by political correctness, who have embraced an unthreatening and watery brand of androgyny; nor by the beta males who have cynically responded to women's demands for equality by letting them, and their children, fend for themselves; nor by the generation of young men that seems to be evincing a historic aversion to intimacy. For hundreds of thousands of years, men have measured themselves by their willingness to compete with and rise above those around them; by their ability to, in the Darwinian sense, "win" a mate and through their children project their DNA into the next generation; and by their desire to act as caretakers and protectors of their communities. This definition of righteous masculinity is timeless and universal, prevailing in virtually every culture in the world.

As it will, again, in ours.

EPILOGUE

■ ■ ■

SHORTLY BEFORE THIS BOOK was typeset, I checked in with some of the men and women who appear in the previous pages to see what they were up to.

Of the "bitchfesters," Kate has moved to Chico, California, where she teaches creative writing at the state university. During a Christmas break I received a postcard from her saying she was traveling in London with her new "beau" and would be dropping in soon to introduce him to us. We'll see . . .

Sarah met an Italian businessman at a magazine party and, after ditching her surfer boy, moved with him to Rome. Feminism has yet to hit Europe, she says, so the men aren't wary and withdrawn like American men her age. She plans to stay awhile.

Two of the "dickfesters" I interviewed have pulled themselves together somewhat. Adam, the investment banking trainee whose idea of perfect payback was to withdraw from a sexual encounter at the last moment, says he now realizes that until he can ditch his resentment, he'll never find a woman he can be happy with. "After our talk, I decided I'd just aggressively pursue women I was interested in. The worst that can happen is that they say no." That's not to say he's no longer resentful, he adds, but he's trying.

Jeff, the ad agency account executive whose payback fantasy was to be forty-five, fat, and balding with a twenty-eight-year-old aerobics instructor sitting next to him in his Porsche, has met a young real estate lawyer who could be "a real possibility. We've only had one date, but I happen to know that she hates aerobics. So maybe I'm reforming."

Jonathan, who accompanied me to the New Warrior weekend, broke up with the woman who motivated him to attend. "It may be too late for me to change," he says. "I'm calcified in my ways." Manuel, my other traveling companion, has moved out of the city to parts unknown.

The Police and Fire Hockey League broke up, and I haven't seen my FBI rival, Fred, since the season ended. Three months after moving to North Carolina, Don, my PC-wracked former squash partner, sent a postcard with his new address, but I haven't heard from him since.

When I reached David, my Promise Keeper rally roommate, at three o'clock on a Friday afternoon, he was frantically making last-minute arrangements for a weekend visit to Cape Cod he was springing on his wife as a surprise anniversary present. He hadn't attended a rally since Washington, but didn't really feel the need to, either. "I took Coach McCartney at his word when he said, 'Treat your wife like a goddess.' So that's what she gets, particularly this weekend."

Owen Sanders continues to mentor troubled young boys and rehabilitate Newark singlehandedly, while Paul Tudor Jones's Robin Hood Foundation gave away more money last year than it ever has.

My son Tom recently shot a chipmunk with a bow and arrow, which caused him great remorse but provided me with a good opportunity to instruct the avid young hunter about his responsibility to the natural world. Last year, we had to make only two trips to the principal's office to hear about his impulsive escapades.

Last summer, I erected a screened tent in a little fern patch not far from where we held Dean's ceremony, where I did much of the revising of this book. It gave me great comfort to know he was wandering around among us.

And I miss my father.

SOURCES

∎ ∎ ∎

As a journalist over the past several years, I've interviewed many smart and articulate psychiatrists, evolutionary psychologists, brain researchers, anthropologists, sex experts, and other scientists who have generously shared with me their knowledge, much of which has found its way into this book. Among the most helpful: John Munder Ross, Ethel Person, John Bancroft, David Buss, David Lykken, Robert Cairns, John Snarey, Paul MacLean, Jerome Kagan, Drew Westen, and John McKinlay. I've also read much of what they've written, some of which is listed below. But in composing a decidedly unscientific book, I decided not to sprinkle footnotes throughout the text or send the reader scurrying to the back pages for obscure references. For the same reason, I decided that lengthy identification of sources in the text was of interest only to those who were being identified, and decided to spare the reader these intrusions. In some parts of the book I have acknowledged them, but more often I have not. I've tried to do so here.

Books that proved particularly relevant and useful to my topic include:

Adaptation to Life, by George E. Vaillant (Harvard University Press, 1995).

The Adapted Mind: Evolutionary Psychology and the Generation of Culture, edited by Jerome H. Barkow, Leda Cosmides, and John Tooby (Oxford University Press, 1992).

Ambition: How We Manage Success and Failure Throughout Our Lives, by Gilbert W. Brim (Basic Books, 1992).

By Force of Fantasy: How We Make Our Lives, by Ethel S. Person, M.D. (Basic Books, 1995).

Dreams of Love and Fateful Encounters: The Power of Romantic Passion, by Ethel S. Person, M.D. (W. W. Norton & Company, 1988).

The Evolution of Desire: Strategies of Human Mating, by David M. Buss (Basic Books, 1994).

Fatherless America: Confronting Our Most Urgent Social Problem, by David Blankenhorn (Harper Perennial Library, 1996).

How Fathers Care for the Next Generation: A Four-Decade Study, by John Snarey (Harvard University Press, 1993).

Human Sexuality and Its Problems, second edition, by John Bancroft (Churchill Livingstone, 1989).

Manhood in the Making: Cultural Concepts of Masculinity, by David D. Gilmore (Yale University Press, 1990).

Observing the Erotic Imagination, by Robert J. Stoller, M.D. (Yale University Press, 1985).

Primitive Passions: Men, Women, and the Quest for Ecstasy, by Marianna Torgovnick (Alfred A. Knopf, 1997).

Sex, Power, Conflict: Evolutionary and Feminist Perspectives, edited by David M. Buss and Neil M. Malamuth (Oxford University Press, 1996).

Sexual Nature/Sexual Culture, edited by Paul R. Abramson and Steven D. Pinkerton (University of Chicago Press, 1995).

Slim's Table: Race, Respectability, and Masculinity, by Mitchell Duneier (University of Chicago Press, 1992).

Undaunted Courage: Meriwether Lewis, Thomas Jefferson, and the Opening of the American West, by Stephen E. Ambrose (Simon and Schuster, 1996).

Violent Land: Single Men and Social Disorder from the Frontier to the Inner City, by David T. Courtwright (Harvard University Press, 1996).

THE BITCHFEST

The names and identities of the young men and women I interviewed have been changed.

Much of the information about mating strategies—such as women's historically effective withholding technique—is eloquently stated in David Buss's book *The Evolution of Desire.*

Statistics on singles, single-parent families, divorce, age of marriage, etc., come from U.S. Census data analyzed in 1997 and is summarized in the Commerce Department's "Current Population Reports."

The ubiquity of campus e-mail systems—at Dartmouth it's known as Blitzmail—has been documented by Kenneth C. Green, director of the Campus Computing Survey, which collects data annually from 650 colleges and universities.

The historical link between single men and violence is well articulated in David Courtwright's *Violent Land.*

The national attitudes about infidelity are culled from National Opinion Research Center polls and from a Princeton Survey Research Associates polling of 751 adults in 1996.

The statistic on the number of women's and men's studies courses comes from Aaron Kipnis of the Gender Relations Institute in Santa Barbara, California.

For a sampling of profeminist thinking in the academic world, consult *A New Psychology of Men,* edited by Ronald F. Levant and William S. Pollack (Basic Books, 1995).

SIFTING THE ASHES

Inherent in "carpet work" is the idea that grief opens a door to men's hearts, an idea that has been well articulated by Robert Bly, who, by the way, has never attended a New Warrior gathering.

COCKTALK

For more on primate communication and diddling, consult the work of primatologist Barbara Smuts of the University of Michigan and anthropologist J. M. Watanabe of Dartmouth College, who have written about the phenomenon in the *International Journal of Primatology.* Also see *Good Natured: The Origins of Right and Wrong in Humans and Other Animals,* by Frans de Waal (Harvard University Press, 1997).

The symptoms of *koro* are detailed in David Gilmore's *Manhood in the Making.*

William Eberhard's essay "Animal Genitalia and Female Choice" appeared in the March-April 1990 issue of *American Scientist.*

The "Adam" fantasy is explored in Ethel Person's *By Force of Fantasy.* She also elaborated on the thesis during an interview.

The consoling pleasures of masturbation, in both infants and adults, were articulated to me by John Munder Ross, a Manhattan psychiatrist who has written several books on men. Ross also weighed in on men's compulsive desire to sexually gratify their mates.

For more on the latest in fetishes, see the magazines *Fetish* and *Hustler's Taboo,* or consult the Web site titled "Exclusively Crushing." For theories on the origins of fetishes see "Paraphilias: Phenomenology and Classification" by John Money in the April 1984 *American Journal of Psychotherapy* and *Fetish: Fashion, Sex and Power,* by Valerie Steele (Oxford University Press, 1996).

The study of homophobia was done by Henry Adams, a research professor of clinical psychology at the University of Georgia, who reported his findings in the *Journal of Abnormal Psychology* in 1997.

The hypersexual activity of superachievers, and the "narcissistic injury" theory, are examined by psychiatrist Steven Berglas in *The Success Syndrome: Hitting Bottom When You Reach the Top* (Plenum, 1986).

Alan Booth, a psychologist at Penn State and a leading authority on the behavioral effects of high and low testosterone levels, has also done longitudinal studies on the relationship between testosterone and happy or unhappy marriages.

The REM-sleep theory of hypersexuality is mine. It's based on several unrelated studies cited in *Principles and Practice of Sleep Medicine* (W. B. Saunders, 1994).

For a highly readable and intelligent disquisition on the pursuit of the "oceanic," see *Primitive Passions: Men, Women, and the Quest for Ecstasy* by Marianna Torgovnick. I have borrowed liberally from her thesis.

I'M A WHAT?

For more on the connection between sex and anger see primatologist Frans de Waal's essay "Sex as an Alternative to Aggression" in *Sexual Nature/Sexual Culture;* Sigmund Freud's *Three Contributions to the Theory of Sex;* and Paul MacLean's 1962 monograph, "New Findings Relevant to the Evolution of Psychosexual Functions of the Brain."

To my knowledge, there have been no surveys on whether women think there are more dicks in the world, but my anecdotal evidence suggests they do.

David Buss and Todd Shackelford report on their investigation of nineteen mate-retention tactics in couples in "From Vigilance to Violence: Mate Retention Tactics in Married Couples" in the *Journal of Personality and Social Psychology,* 1997, Vol. 72, No. 2.

Men's unfortunate reaction to the rape of their spouse is detailed in "The Man Who Mistook His Wife for a Chattel," by Margo Wilson and Martin Daly in *The Adapted Mind.*

Women's response to mate-value disparities is also documented in Buss and Shackelford's study on mate-retention tactics cited above.

Relate, the U.K. marriage-guidance council, released its report on the increased impotence of men in April 1996.

Picasso's sordid treatment of women is documented in John Richardson's *A Life of Picasso* (Random House, two volumes, 1991 and 1996).

The decline in frequency of sex has been documented in a variety of studies, including one done by the National Opinion Research Center and reported in the February 1998 issue of *American Demographics.*

John McKinlay, director of the Massachusetts Male Aging Study, provided me with the information on the friskiness regained by older men when they marry a younger woman.

Women's tendency to end a marriage after committing adultery is documented in "Sexual Strategies Theory: An Evolutionary Perspective On Human Mating," by Buss et al. in *Psychological Review,* 100.

PROMISES, PROMISES

The names of my traveling companions on the pilgrimage to Washington, D.C., have been changed.

WHAT WOMEN REALLY WANT

Alas, the Police and Fire League, thanks largely to the mean-spirited play of the FBI, has since disbanded.

Felicia Pratto shared her thoughts with me in an interview. She also articulates her thesis in "Sexual Politics: The Gender Gap in the Bedroom, the Cupboard, and the Cabinet," which can be found in *Sex, Power, Conflict.*

More information about Moulay Ismail and his kind can be found in *The Adapted Mind.*

For more on the lively antics of Goldsmith, see *The Life and Times of Sir James Goldsmith,* by Ivan Fallon (Little, Brown, 1992).

Gender differences in dreaming were explained to me by psychologist Rosalind Cartwright, who has studied dreams for three decades, and by psychiatrist Milton Kramer, who has done a meta-analysis of dream studies. Both researchers detailed their findings to me in interviews.

The best work on Type T people has been done by David Lykken, who shared his findings with me in interviews.

If you're thinking of nominating yourself or a friend for a Carnegie Award, contact the Carnegie Hero Fund Commission in Pittsburgh, Pennsylvania.

The study of kids' games and the gender differences in the settling of disputes was related to me by psychologist and aggression expert Robert Cairns.

Theories about the connection between single men and violence are nicely advanced in David Courtwright's *Violent Land.*

The science of physical attraction has been advanced in recent years by the work of Randy Thornhill, a University of New Mexico ecologist.

The schmoozing talents of high-serotonin primates have been studied by J. Dee Higley, a researcher at the Laboratory of Clinical Studies in Poolesville, Maryland, who detailed his findings to me in an interview.

Cross-cultural preferences for certain physical characteristics in men are well documented in David Gilmore's *Manhood in the Making.*

Powerful women's preferences for powerful men have been documented in David Buss's surveys (see *Evolution of Desire*).

Wage-gap figures are documented in the Bureau of Labor Statistics "Facts on Working Women" and the federal government's "National Longitudinal Survey of Youth."

Sexual Manners

Jim Schroeder was kind enough to detail for me the genesis of the Dennis Thatcher Society during an interview.

I owe the theory about men's and women's conflicting ideas about relationships to Drew Westen, a Harvard psychologist, who articulated this thesis to me during an interview.

The dinner-party query was suggested to me by the quirky and entertaining anthology of feminist writings, *Dick for a Day,* edited by Fiona Giles (Villard, 1997).

Couvade was explained to me by author and psychiatrist John Munder Ross.

The vaginal orgasm is still a hotly disputed phenomenon. Women who have had one know it when they feel it, however, as do their lucky partners.

The modern version of the pill is less likely to flatten out the desire curve. The information on women's sexually active times comes from John Bancroft's *Human Sexuality and Its Problems.*

In his book *The Erotic Mind: Unlocking the Inner Sources of Sexual Passion and Fulfillment* (HarperPerennial Library, 1996), psychologist Jack Morin explores in detail the erotic underpinnings of anger.

Evidence for women's greater ability to control emotional responses is advanced in "Parental Investment Theory and Gender Differences in the Evolution of Inhibition Mechanisms," by David F. Bjorklund and Katherine Kipp, *Psychological Bulletin,* 1996, Vol. 120, No. 2.

The "flooding" men experience during moments of emotional distress is well documented in Daniel Goleman's *Emotional Intelligence* (Bantam, 1995).

The gender differences in serotonin levels in monkeys have been documented by Stephen Suomi, a researcher at the National Institute of Health's Laboratory of Comparative Ethology.

In addition to doing more housework, men are spending more time with their children, according to the Families and Work Institute's 1998 "National Study of the Changing Workforce."

DADDY'S BOYS

The story of Lawrence McCutcheon's reconciliation with his son Daylon was reported in a lengthy piece by Jonathan Kaufman titled "A Football Star, Long Silent and in Denial, Reaches Out to His Son" in *The Wall Street Journal* on December 11, 1996.

Figures on fatherless kids and unmarried mothers come from the latest "Current Population Reports."

"Rubbish men" can be found in David Gilmore's *Manhood in the Making.*

The Sears and Glueck studies are well analyzed in John Snarey's *How Fathers Care for the Next Generation.*

The fighter pilot studies are part of Minnesota personality expert David Lykken's inquiries into the bold temperament.

New York Times reporter Selena Roberts explored Chris Mills's relationship with his father at some length in a March 1, 1998, profile titled "His Father's Handiwork."

The defensive misogyny and confused sexuality of violent inner-city kids were articulated by John Munder Ross in an interview.

David Buss described for me the follow-up studies of Sandra Bem's work on androgyny.

The emotional and learning difficulties suffered by boys are well summarized by Spokane, Washington, psychotherapist Michael Gurian in *The Wonder of Boys* (Putnam, 1997).

Anecdotes about Meriwether Lewis come from Stephen Ambrose's *Undaunted Courage*.

Wade F. Horn, president of the National Fatherhood Initiative, also articulates just how thoroughly the forces of ideology have negatively influenced the importance of the father to children in the July-August 1997 issue of *Policy Review.*

MAD DADS national headquarters are at 3030 Sprague Street, Omaha, Nebraska 68111.

BIG MAN

As I mention in the text, Owen Sanders is a pseudonym. All other details about him are factual.

A good Erik Erikson text to begin with is *Adulthood* (Norton, 1978).

For data on the life cycle and professional ambition, see Gilbert Brim's *Ambition.*

The information on chimp mentoring was conveyed to me by Tom Insel, director of the Yerkes Primate Research Center in Atlanta, Georgia.

For more on the Big Man of New Guinea, see David Gilmore's *Manhood in the Making.*

Details on the Robin Hood Foundation were received from Paul Tudor Jones in an interview.

The data on the various philanthropists' divestments come from various news reports and from issues of *American Benefactor* magazine.

The Grant study findings are explicated in George E. Vaillant's *Adaptation to Life.*

INDEX

. . .

A

Abdur-Rahman III, 123
abuse:
   of children, 172–73, 175–76
   of women, 86–87, 110
academic careers, 78–81
accountability groups, 105–6,
   111–12, 116–17
Achilles, 205
achromatic dreaming, 124
acrotomophilia, 67
"Adam" fantasy, 62
addiction, sexual, 71–73
adolescence, 165–72, 178–79
adoption, 45
adultery, 110, 123
   gender differences in, 17, 24,
      83–84, 92
   politicians and, 90–91
   sexual addiction and, 71–73, 184
Africa, masculine beauty in, 132
Agent Orange, xv
aggression:
   in father-son relationships,
      165–71
   marriage and, 130–31
   mating and, 121–36, 145
   passive-, 44, 129, 170
   philanthropy and, 209–10
   in sports, 118–21
   success and, 72–73, 82
   testosterone levels and, 72, 91,
      121, 130, 144, 202–3
alcoholism, 177–78, 188

Alda, Alan, 139
Aldrin, Buzz, 126
alienation, 129
Ally McBeal, 56–57
American Medical Association
   (AMA), 56, 64
androgen, 131–32
androgyny, x, 166–67, 170
anger, 36, 44–45, 80–81, 82, 145,
   194
anhedonia, 75
anorgasm, 89
anti-Semitism, 97
anxiety, 53, 62–63, 68, 90
aphrodisiacs, 89–90
apologies, 144, 146
appetite, 72
arousal, sexual, 66, 68, 70–71,
   89–90, 141–44, 145
attachment theory, 159
attention deficit disorder, 169
Auerbach, Red, 106
authority, parental, 98, 154–57, 169,
   170–71, 183–84, 188, 209
autonomy, 143, 162

B

baboons, 54, 203
baby boomers:
   divorces of, 16–18, 19, 26
   as parents, 3, 16–18, 26
back-scratching, 134
baptism, 116

Baptists, 104–5, 107, 110
Beatles, 176
Beatty, Warren, 141, 142, 148
Beethoven, Ludwig van, 9, 129
Berle, Milton, 56
Best Outcomes, 209–10
Bible, 53–54, 88, 96, 104, 106
Big Men, ix, 197–210
biologists, evolutionary, 20, 121, 136
birth control, 144
bitchfests, 3–9, 14, 17, 24, 78, 87,
    122, 135, 139, 211
blacks, 160–61
Blair, Tony, 133
Bly, Robert, 30, 193
Bobbitt, Lorena, 59
body language, 53
bondage, 67
boomers, *see* baby boomers
born-again experience, 104–5, 107,
    113–14
Boston Strangler, 126
boundaries, 124
boys, 128–30, 166
Boys Clubs and Girls Clubs of
    Newark, 198, 201
Boy Scouts, 177, 193
boy toys, 9, 15, 16, 24
brain, 121, 122, 124–25, 126,
    134–35, 145, 147
Braque, Georges, 68–69
breasts, 57, 59, 145
breeding-experiment metaphor,
    121, 130, 131, 136
Brown University, 19
bullying, 170
Butts, Carl, 163

C
Cairns, Robert, 129
Calvary Baptist Church, 94, 96,
    104–5

cancer, 174–96
Cannon, Thomas, 206–7
Carnegie Hero Fund Commission,
    127
Carnegie Task Force on
    Adolescence, 160
case studies, xi–xii
    Adam, xi–xiii, 211
    Alison, 3–9, 14
    Ben, 69–70, 71
    Billy, 96, 101–2, 103, 105, 107,
        110, 111, 112, 114, 115
    Bonnie, 77
    Chandler, 12–16
    Christina, 100
    Dave, 12–16
    David, 96, 101, 102–5, 107, 110,
        111–12, 114, 115, 116, 117, 212
    Don, 77, 78–82, 212
    "Eagle" (John), 46–47, 48
    Frank (Man Week participant),
        56, 60
    Frank (Promise Keeper), 110
    Fred, 128, 133, 212
    George, 96, 98–99
    Gretchen, 77
    Griff, 52–56, 60, 61, 65, 69,
        71, 75
    Hughes, 34–35, 38, 40–41, 48
    Ivan, 108
    Jack (Man Week participant),
        65–66
    Jack (Promise Keeper),
        99–100
    Jayson, 71–73, 75
    Jeff, 12–16, 211–12
    Jeremy, 69–70, 71
    Joe, 77, 78, 80, 82
    John ("Eagle"), 46–47, 48
    Jonathan, 32, 33, 48, 212
    Julie, 77, 78–81
    Juwan, 198–200, 201

Kate, 3–9, 11, 76, 93, 119, 135, 139, 211
Kim, 108
Manuel, 32, 33, 48, 212
McCoy, 31–32, 34, 41, 46
Marcy, 103–5
Mark, 98–100
Nate, 60–63
Pat, 77
Paul, 12–16, 20
"Raven," 42–43, 184
Sarah, 3–9, 135, 211
Steve, 63–65
Walter, 101, 110
Cassidy, David, 56
catharsis, 28–31
cats, 58
cellulite, 57
Chasing Amy, 123
cheating, 169–70
Cheney, Dick, 137, 138
Child, Julia, 153
Child, Paul, 153
child care, 149–50, 151
child custody, 181
children:
  abuse of, 172–73, 175–76
  female vs. male, 128–30, 166
  illegitimate, 130–31
  preschool, 172
child support, 155
chores, 170
Christian right, 107, 117
Christians, evangelical, 96–97, 103–5, 106, 107, 113–14, 117, 210
Clark, William, 170
Cleveland, Grover, 91
Clinton, Bill, 67, 88, 90, 91, 123, 133
clitoris, 59–60, 143
cocktalk, 52–76, 117

commitment:
  dating and, xi, 3–4, 24, 158
  in marriage, 16–18, 26, 138
Community Youth Organization (CYO), 200
compassion, 42, 162
competition, x, xvi, 19, 72–73, 83–84, 118–21, 123
compulsion, sexual, 71–73
computer dating, 18–19
concubines, 123
conflict avoidance, 129–30
confrontation, 129
Connor, John, 180–81
consensus, 133–35
control, male preference for, 74
convergence, 202
Cornell University, 6, 206
cornflakes, 64
courtship, 18, 24–25, 57–58, 89, 127, 141
  see also dating
couvade, 142
Crawford, Cindy, 55–56, 61
crime, 24, 85, 128–29, 166, 169
crush fetishists, 67
cryptic female choice, 58–59, 73
Cunningham, Walt, 136
cynicism, 181, 185

D

danger, desire for, 125
Dartmouth University, 18
dating:
  in colleges, 5–6, 18–19
  commitment and, xi, 3–4, 24, 158
  communal, 22, 23–24
  computer, 18–19
  double standards in, 12
  early experiences in, 21–25
  marriage and, 6–7

dating (*cont.*)
  mate value in, 85, 86, 117,
    121–36, 152
  postfeminism and, xii–xiii
  rejection in, 4, 7–8, 13–14
  role reversals in, 10–11
  rules for, 24–25
  short-term goals in, 17–18, 25
  standards in, 82–83
day care, 150
death penalty, 122
debt, 99–100
defense mechanisms, 93, 136
defense spending, 122
Dennis Thatcher Society, 137–38
dependence, mutual, 136
depersonalization, 32–33
depression, 38, 80
diabetes, 88–89
dickfests, 11–16, 24, 89, 121, 139,
    158, 211–12
diddling, 54, 65
disengagement, 146–47
dissociation, paraphiliac's levels of,
    68
divorce, 85, 161, 179–80, 181
  of baby boomers, 16–18, 19, 26
  causes of, 87, 92–93, 138, 163, 204
  predictors of, 147
Dole, Bob, 138
Dole, Elizabeth, 138
dominance, 121–22, 124, 128,
    131, 133–35, 139, 147, 166–67,
    170
Donne, John, 9, 135
dreams, 72, 124–25, 145
drug abuse, 160, 165, 198, 207
Duneier, Mitchell, 160–61
Duty Free Shoppes, 206
Dyak tribe, 59
Dylan, Bob, 114

E
Eberhard, William, 58
ecstasy, 73–75
education, 21, 25, 168, 169, 177, 178,
    179, 189
Eisenhower, Dwight D., 131
ejaculations, 84
Emerson, Myrna, 155–56
emotions:
  acknowledgment of, 146–48
  camouflage of, 53
  catharsis in, 28–51
  disconnection of, 75
  expression of, xiii–xv, 35, 48,
    91–93, 146
  management of, x, 145–46,
    152–53
  in men vs. women, 144–48
  projection of, 80–81
  suppression of, 35–38, 53,
    126–27, 146–47
empathy, 42, 162
endocrine, 202–3
endometriosis, 61
endorphins, 42
erections, 56, 57, 67–68, 71, 76, 89,
    145
Erikson, Erik, 201–2, 204, 209
Esalen Institute, 34
Esquire, x
estrangement, 183–84
estrogen, 202–3
evangelical Christians, 96–97, 103–5,
    106, 107, 113–14, 117, 210
evolution, 20, 57–59, 84, 121, 127,
    136, 158
extroversion, 133

F
facilitators, 33–34, 39, 54
fallopian tubes, 59

families:
  decline of, 17, 130–31
  generational patterns in, 186, 188
  nuclear, 159
  responsibilities of, 95–117
  stability of, 171–72
  see also fathers; mothers; parents
Families and Work Institute,
    149–50
fantasies, sexual, 61–63, 64,
    141–44
fathers, 154–96
  absentee, 154–57
  abusive, 172–73, 175–76
  authority of, 154–57, 188
  biological, 158
  black, 160
  death of, 174–96
  organizations for, 159–61
  power of, 175–76, 183–84
  as redundant, 159
  responsibilities of, 20, 24, 33,
    116–17, 153, 154–73, 208
  as role models, 172–73
  single, 158–60
  sons and, 42, 44, 107, 113–14,
    154–96
  step-, 158
  see also parents
father street patrols, 160
fear, 126–27, 169–70
Federal Bureau of Investigation
    (FBI), 119–21, 122, 125–28,
    131, 133, 176, 193
Feeney, Charles, 206, 207
feminine identification, 63
feminism, feminists:
  backlash against, 151
  in colleges, 12, 20–21
  female orgasm and, 59–60
  male insecurity and, 53

male oppression as viewed by,
    121–22, 128–29, 135
  men's groups criticized by, 30,
    95–96, 107
  men's resentment against, ix,
    xii–xiii, 10–11, 24, 136, 158, 210
  post-, ix, xii–xiii
fertilization, 58
fetishes, sexual, 66–69
feudal lords, 54
Feuerstein, Aaron, 205
fights, 130–31, 134, 144–48
foot binding, 84, 122–23
Forbes, 200
foreplay, 89, 184
forgiveness, 195–96
Foster, John L., 160
Fox, Fanne, 91
Freud, Sigmund, 59, 142
Friedan, Betty, 151
Friends, 23–24
friendships:
  intergender, xi, xii, 15, 23–24
  male, ix, xv, 99–100, 111, 130
frigidity, 86
frotteurism, 67

G
gamberro, 210
gametes, 58
Gardner, Ava, 59
gauntlets, human, 42–43, 45
gender bias, crimes motivated by,
    24
gender differences, x–xi
  adultery and, 17, 24, 83–84, 92
  in children, 128–30, 166
  emotions and, 144–48
  politically correct view of, 20–21
  see also males; men; women
gender ratios, violence and, 130–31

gender war, 4, 25, 77, 139
Generation X, 16–18, 19
generativity, 171, 201–4
genes, x, 58, 75, 91–92, 122, 131–32, 146, 158
genital mutilation, 84
genome, 75
gerewol ceremony, 132
gibbons, 58
Gide, André, 74
Gingrich, Newt, 88
Ginsburg, Ruth Bader, 137
girls, 128–30, 166
Glueck study, 162–63, 171, 172, 173, 184, 188
God, 105, 106, 107, 108, 113
Goldsmith, James, 123
Gore, Al, 162
gossip, xiii, 129
Grant Study of Adult Development, 209, 210
Greece, ancient, 205–6
grief, 35–42, 194
grudges, 129, 145–46
G-spot, 60
"guerilla philanthropy," 207
guilt, 38–39, 40, 41, 187, 210
guts work, 28–51

H
harems, 62, 123
Harlequin Romance novels, 161–62
harm avoidance, 126
Hart, Gary, 91
Harvard University, 21, 209
Hays, Wayne, 91
heart attacks, 37
Helping Undergraduates Socialize (HUGS), 19
hermoso man, 132
heroes, 126, 127, 163, 204–5

heteronormativity, 21
heterosexuality, 59–60, 73
hierarchies, men in, 122, 130, 133
   see also rankers
Higley, J. Dee, 134
Hill, Anita, 88
Hockert, Christopher, 127
hockey, 118–21, 125–28, 133, 167, 170, 178, 193, 212
homicides, spousal, 85
homophobia, 69–71
homosexuality, xiii, 3, 20–21, 32, 59–60, 63, 63, 69–71, 73, 177
   see also lesbianism
hooking up, 5–6, 17, 158
hormones, 72, 91, 121, 130, 131–32, 134–35, 144, 147, 148, 202–3
Horner, Charles, 137
Horner, Constance, 137
husbands, 95–96, 106, 107, 109, 116–17
   see also marriage
Hussein, Saddam, 133
Hustler, 76
Hybels, Bill, 111, 112
hypersexuality, 72
hyperthymic temperament, 72

I
"I Have a Dream" Foundation, 207
illegitimacy, 130–31
immigration, 158, 206
immune system, 132
impotence, xi, 10, 56, 62–63, 86, 88–90, 91, 138
impulsiveness, 126, 134, 146
incest, 63
infantilists, 67
infants, 67–68, 145, 159
infibulation, 122–23

inhibitions, 62–63
intellectual development, 162–63
intercourse, painful, 61
internalization, 195, 209
intimacy, x, 17–18, 92–93, 140, 146–48
intuition, 43–44
isolation, 106

J

Jacob's Girls, 161
Jefferson, Thomas, 123, 170
Jesus Christ, 97–98, 108, 116, 117, 195
Jews, 97, 111
Jews for Jesus, 111
Johnson, Lyndon B., 56
Johnson, Magic, 123
Johnson, Virginia, 59
Johnson, Walter, 106
Jones, Bob, 164
Jones, Jenny, 70
Jones, Paula, 90
Jones, Paul Tudor, II, 207–8, 212
Jordan, Michael, 164
Jung, Carl, 74, 202

K

Kagan, Jerome, 166
Katz, Lewis, 200
Keener, Earl, 94, 96, 98
Keener, Jimmy, 94–95
Kellogg, John Harvey, 64
Kennedy, John F., 90–91
Kinsey Heterosexual-Homosexual Rating Scale, 70–71
kissing, 22–23
Koedt, Anne, 59
koro, 57
Kramer, Milton, 124

L

Larson, Kit, 22, 23
Lawrence, D. H., 74
leadership, 133–35
Leadville, Colo., 130
learning disabilities, 169
lesbianism, 61–63, 65, 149
Levine, Arthur, 17–18, 21, 23, 24
Lewinsky, Monica, 88
Lewis, Meriwether, 169–70
Lewis and Clark College, 20
liberationist theology, xii
libido, 72, 89, 144, 145–46
  see also sex, sexuality
linkers, 122, 124, 134, 136, 140, 141, 147, 148, 150
Lombardi, Vince, 106
Love, Davis, III, 164
low-desire syndrome, 90
loyalty, 205
Lydon, Susan, 59
lying, 169–70
Lykken, David, 126, 169

M

McCartney, Bill, 108–9, 111, 117, 212
McCartney, Kristyn, 109
McCartney, Lyndi, 109
McCutcheon, Adrian, 155, 156
McCutcheon, Daylon, 154–57, 158
McCutcheon, Lawrence, 154–57, 159
McCutcheon, Marcus, 156, 157
MacLean, Paul, 145
magical thinking, 40
"magnificent" life, 172, 175, 184, 195–96, 209
Mailer, Norman, 64, 152
male beauty belt, 132
males:
  alpha, ix–x, xv–xvi, 22, 89, 95, 139, 166

males (*cont.*)
  beta, x
  biological imperatives of, 53,
    57–60
  "demonic," 166
  hypermasculine, 4, 9, 14–15, 166
  Type A personality, 181
  Type T personality, 126, 168–70
  see also men
"Male Mind, The" (Segell), x
manners, sexual, 136, 137–53
Man Week, 52–76
Maples, Marla, 67
marbles, penile, 59
marriage:
  adultery in, *see* adultery
  age gap in, 85
  aggression and, 130–31
  avoidance of, 25–26
  careers vs., 6, 16, 78–81, 83, 103,
    137–38, 150–53
  commitment in, 16–18, 26, 138
  counseling for, 103–4
  critical period for, 18
  dating and, 6–7
  dual-career, 137–38, 150–53
  fighting in, 144–48
  generativity and, 204
  intimacy in, 17, 92–93, 140,
    146–48
  as long-term goal, 17–18
  men's movement and, 30, 47–48
  necessity of, xvi, 59
  oppression and, 122–23
  postponement of, xi, 18, 19–20,
    26, 83, 85, 130, 158–59
  power in, 85–87, 137–38, 153
  rate of, xi
  reproduction and, 59
  rivalry in, 78–81, 136
  stability of, 171–72
  violence in, 86–87
  see also divorce
masochism, 142
Masters, William, 59
masturbation, 60, 62, 63–65, 67–68,
  144, 177
"maternal mystery," 74
mate value, 85, 86, 117, 121–36, 152
matriarchy, 199
Matthews, Dave, 14, 111
Mayer, Louis B., 123
Mazur, Allan, 131
Mead, Margaret, 129
men:
  ambition of, 72–73, 82, 87, 91,
    118–36, 144, 165–71, 202–3,
    209–10
  Asian, 57
  as assholes vs. dicks, 76, 77–93,
    139
  Big, ix, 197–210
  black, 160–61
  as breeding experiment, 121, 130,
    131, 136
  code of conduct of, 78–79
  facial types of, 131–32
  as fathers, *see* fathers
  feminism resented by, ix, xii–xiii,
    10–11, 24, 136, 158, 210
  height of, 132–33
  household chores done by,
    148–49
  as husbands, 95–96, 106, 107,
    109, 116–17
  insecurity of, 16, 25, 53
  insensitivity of, 127
  physical appearance of, 131–33
  as providers, 140, 153, 158
  as rankers, 122, 124, 125, 128,
    129, 130, 136, 147, 202, 210
  "résumé," 4–8, 12, 24, 25, 122, 139

"rubbish," ix, 158, 210
self-esteem of, 12–13, 26, 53, 57,
   140, 162–63, 166–67
self-image of, 183–84
single, xi, 19, 26, 130
standup, *see* standup guys
status of, 76, 82–87, 122, 135–36,
   139, 141, 146, 147, 152, 170
see also males
Men Against Destruction Defending
   Against Drugs and Social
   Disorder (MAD DADS, Inc.),
   160–61, 165
ménage à trois, 61–63
men's movement, 28–76, 94–117
   assertiveness in, 29, 30
   author's participation in, 28–76,
     94–117
   energy released in, 44–45
   feminist critique of, 30, 95–96, 107
   marriages helped by, 30, 47–48
   psychological impact of, 29–32,
     38–39, 41–42, 48–49
   retreats for, 28–76
   role-playing in, 28–51
   self-affirmation in, 31, 32, 38–39,
     41
   self-deception in, 31, 41–42
   standup guys and, 30, 35, 48, 97,
     116–17
   see also individual organizations
menstruation, 149
mental health, 145, 209
mentors, 180–81, 183, 194–95, 203
Messier, Mark, 132
metabolism, 168
microphiliacs, 67
midlife crisis, 201–2, 203
military, 131
Million Man March, 95, 159
Mills, Chris, 164–65

Mills, Claude, 164–65
Mills, Wilbur, 91
misogyny, 67, 77–78, 140–41, 166,
   170
"mission" statements, 29
Mr. Family, 161
mistresses, 123
monitoring mechanisms, 84–85
monkeys, 54, 58, 145, 147–48, 203
mothers, 20, 42–43, 46–47, 68,
   158–59
   see also parents
mothers-in-law, 63
motivation, 99, 111–12
Moulay Ismail the Bloodthirsty, 123
Mozart, Wolfgang Amadeus, 9
Mutawakkil, al-, 123
"Myth of the Vaginal Orgasm, The"
   (Koedt), 59

N
Nabokov, Vladimir, 123
narcissistic injury, 72–73
Narcissus band, 132
National Bar Association, 191
National Institute for Responsible
   Fatherhood and Family
   Development, 159–60
National Opinion Research Center,
   17
National Organization for Women
   (NOW), 95–96, 107
National Organization of Men
   Against Sexism (NOMAS), 20
National Relate, 86
natural selection, 58
nervous system, 121, 122, 124–25,
   126, 134–35, 145, 147
nesting, 149
New Age movement, 128
Newark, N.J., 197–202, 212

New Guinea, 205–6, 210
New Jersey Nets, 200
New Warriors, 28–51, 95, 97, 99,
    117, 184, 210, 212
New Wave fetishes, 67
New York Times, 18
Nicholson, Jack, 123
Nicklaus, Jack, 164
nit-picking, by monkeys, 134
Nixon, Richard M., 162

O
oaths, 53–54
O'Connor, Sandra Day, 137
Oedipus complex, 63, 66, 175, 177,
    203
old age, 124
Old Testament, 53
onah, 75
Onania, or a Treatise upon the
    Disorders Produced by
    Masturbation (Tissot), 64
One to One, 200
oral sex, 62, 82, 87–88, 89
orgasms:
  faked, 75
  female, 59–60, 65, 68, 73–75, 89,
      131, 141–44
  lack of, 75, 89
  male, 68
  multiple, 143
ostracization, 129
overachievement, 72–73, 123
oxytocin, 68

P
Packwood, Bob, 88
palang, 59
Palmer, Arnold, 164
paraphilias, 67–69
parents:
  authority of, 98, 154–57, 169,
      170–71, 183–84, 188, 209

baby-boomer, 3, 16–18, 26
  complementary roles of,
      140–41
  guidance by, xi, 9, 17, 19, 163,
      172–73
  as role models, 16–19, 26, 172–73,
      209
  see also fathers; mothers
passive-aggression, 44, 129, 170
passivity, 74, 88, 142
patriarchy, 121–22, 128–29, 135,
    202, 208–9
payback, xii–xiii, 4, 7–8, 10–11,
    13–14, 16, 53, 76, 86, 210,
    211–12
peer groups, 129, 169
penetration, 143
penile marbles, 59
penis:
  enlargement of, 57, 59
  envy of, 142
  erection of, 56, 57, 67–68, 71, 76,
      89, 145
  evolution and, 57–59
  female attitudes toward, 52,
      56–60, 142
  male attitudes toward, 52, 57,
      75–76
  nicknames for, 54–55, 60, 63
  shriveling of, 57
  size of, 56–60, 64, 76
  symbolic, 54–55, 56, 60, 63, 65,
      69, 71, 88
Pennsylvania, University of, 25
phallomania, 57
phallus, 54–55, 56, 60, 63, 65, 69,
    71, 88
philanthropy, 197–210
phone calls, 5–6, 25, 81
Phung, Tran Hai, xiv
Picasso, Pablo, 68–69, 87, 123
pill, birth control, 144

plateau, preorgasmic, 143
Plato, 192, 194
play, 128–30, 166
plethysmograph, 68
Police and Fire Hockey League, 118–21, 125–28, 133, 212
political correctness, x, xi, 12, 20–21, 26, 88, 119, 123–24, 170, 210
"Politics of Orgasm, The" (Lydon), 59
pornography, 101
potency, 62–63, 64, 66
poverty, 160–61, 165, 197–202, 207–8, 212
Powell, Colin, 131
Pratto, Felicia, 121–22
prayer, 112–13
predators, sexual, 87–88
primates, 58, 84, 89, 133–35, 145, 147–48
primitive cultures, 58–59, 74, 132
procreation, xvi, 57–59
projection, 80–81
promiscuity, 72
Promise Keepers, xiii, 93, 94–117, 159, 212
prostitutes, 61–62, 65
psychopaths, 126, 169
psychosomatic illness, 37
psychoticism, 126, 129
pubic hair, 57
pulse rate, 126
puppy love, 23

Q
queer theory, 20–21, 59–60

R
rankers, 122, 124, 125, 128, 129, 130, 136, 147, 202, 210
rape, 84–85, 142, 165–66

rapid-eye movement (REM), 72, 124, 145
Ray, Elizabeth, 91
"Reclaiming Your Manhood," 96
rejection, 4, 7–8, 13–14
relationships:
    commitment in, xi, 3–4, 16–18, 24, 26, 138, 158
    dependability of, 17–18
    importance of, 93
    intimacy in, x, 17–18, 92–93, 140, 146–48
    see also dating; marriage
reptilian nervous system, 126
"résumé" men, 4–8, 12, 24, 25, 122, 139
rhesus monkeys, 58
Rice, Donna, 91
Rigorous Educational Assistance to Deserving Youth (READY), 198–99, 200
risk-taking, 121, 126–27, 136, 169, 209
ritual space, 28–29, 31, 42, 44–45, 47, 49–51
Robin Hood Foundation, 207–8, 212
rodents, scuttling by, 149
Rodman, Dennis, 64
"rubbish men," ix, 158, 210
Rules, The, 24–25
RuPaul, 66
Rush, Benjamin, 64
Ruth, Babe, 123
Ryle, James, 113–14

S
"sacred" carpet, 28–29, 31, 42, 44–45, 47
Sanders, Owen (pseud.), 197–202, 205, 207, 210, 212
Schmitz, Jonathan, 70
Schroeder, Jim, 137–38, 153

Schroeder, Pat, 137, 153
screw-your-buddy pass, 79–80, 120
scuttling, 149
Sears Study, 162
seduction, 10–11, 89
Seinfeld, 23–24
self-affirmation, 31, 32, 38–39, 41
self-deception, 31, 41–42
self-esteem, 8, 12–13, 14, 26, 53, 57,
    86–87, 140, 162–63, 166–67
"self-pollution," 64
self-preservation, 74
self-starters, 193
separations, 41–42, 46, 148
serotonin, 134–35, 147, 148
"Serve Somebody" (Dylan), 114
Seven Promises of a Promise Keeper,
    95–96
sex, sexuality:
    aggression and, 121–36, 145
    casual, 5–6, 17, 24, 158
    conservatism in, 17
    consideration in, 141–44
    definition of, 88
    desire for, 10–11, 64, 72–73, 90
    education on, 177
    ejaculations in, 84
    erections in, 56, 57, 67–68, 71, 76,
        89, 145
    foreplay in, 89, 184
    impotence in, xi, 10, 56, 62–63,
        86, 88–90, 91, 138
    love vs., 5, 13–14
    masturbation and, 60, 62, 63–65,
        67–68, 144, 177
    meaning of, 53
    ménage à trois in, 61–63
    money and, 123
    oral, 62, 82, 87–88, 89
    orgasms in, *see* orgasms
    painful intercourse in, 61
    performance in, 13, 52, 60, 89
    power and, 75, 139
    tantric, 60
    trusting state in, 142–43
    withholding of, xii–xiii, 4, 7–8,
        10–11, 13–14, 16, 53, 76, 86,
        210, 211–12
        of women, 73–75, 84, 89–90, 136,
        137–53
sex drive, 10–11, 64, 72–73
sexual arousal, 66, 68, 70–71,
    89–90, 141–44, 145
sexual compulsion, 71–73
sexual fantasies, 61–63, 64, 141–44
sexual fetishes, 66–69
sexual harassment, 12, 90
sexually transmitted diseases, 13
sexual manners, 136, 137–53
sexual orientation, 21, 70–71, 166
    see also heterosexuality;
        homosexuality
Shackley, Dennis, 33–34, 38, 39,
    40–44, 46, 47, 48
"shadow" work, 28, 34
shoes, women's, 66–67
shyness, 68
silicone, 57
sin, 98–99, 101, 109, 110, 111
Sinatra, Frank, 59
sleep, 72, 124, 142, 143, 145
Slim's Table (Duneier), 160–61
Smith, Harlan, 111, 112–13
Smith, Walter, 96, 111, 112–13
smoking, 88–89
snails, 58
Snarey, John, 171, 204
social constructionists, 20, 150
social dominance orientation, 122
socialization, 126
Socrates, 192
Soros, George, 206, 207

Soros, Paul, 206

spatial skills, 68, 124

sperm, 58, 60, 84, 86

Spike, 67

Spock, Benjamin, 64

sports, 53, 72, 106, 113, 118–21,
162–65, 202, 209

squirrel monkeys, 145

standup guys:
alpha males vs., ix–x, xv–xvi, 95
characteristics of, 26–27, 76, 78,
117, 135, 178, 210
emotions expressed by, 35, 48,
91–93
men's movement and, 30, 35, 48,
97, 116–17
sexual manners of, 136, 137–53
social contributions by, 197–210
tests for, 176, 195–96

Staton, Eddie, 160

Sterling, Deborah, 155, 156, 157

Stoller, Robert, 68

stonewalling, 147

subincisions, 59

subjugation, as paraphilia, 67

success:
drive for, 72–73, 82, 123
father-son relationship and,
162–63, 171–73
status and, 135–36

Sutter's Mill, 130

Sweden, 136

symmetry, physical, 131

Symphony No. 9 (Beethoven),
129

T

taboos, 63

tantric sex, 60

teeth grinding, 145

temptation, 98–99, 101, 110, 146

Ten Thousand Mentors, 200

"testament," 53–54

"testifying," 53–54

testosterone, 72, 91, 121, 130, 144,
202–3

"testosterone poisoning," 121, 130

Thatcher, Dennis, 137–38

therapy, 86, 183

Thomas, Clarence, 88

thrill-chasers, 126, 168–70

Tiresias, 73

Tissot, S. A., 64

Tolstoy, Leo, 172, 184, 195–96, 209

Top Gun, 126, 163

To Saloe-maoge tribe, 59

transference, 48

transvestites, 66

trophy wives, x

trust, 54

trusting state, in sex, 142–43

Tucker, Trent, 164

Turner, Ted, 201, 206, 207

Type A personality, 181

Type T personality, 126, 168–70

U

unconscious, 74

underwear, women's, 65–69

Unitarians, 97–98

United Nations, 206

Unity Church, 97–98

University of Pennsylvania, 25

urban violence, 130–31

V

vacuum pumps, 57

vagina, 59–60, 65, 74, 142, 144

Vaillant, George, 209

vandalism, 24

Vassar College, 18–19

veiling, 84, 122–23

Viagra, 10, 56, 88, 91, 138

vibrators, 60

Vietnam War, xiii–xv

vigilante techniques, in mate guarding, 84

violence, 24, 85, 86–87, 128–31, 166, 169

voyeurism, 68, 75

W

"waiting it out," 61

Walker, Darrell, 164

Wall Street Journal, 154

Washington Post, 97

wealth, 122, 197–210

West Point, 131

Willey, Kathleen, 90

wives, x, 95–96, 106

  see also marriage

Wodaabe tribe, 132

womanizing, 43

women:

  abuse of, 86–87, 110

  ambition of, xi–xiii, 3–4, 6, 12–13, 24, 25, 86–87, 90, 129, 135–36, 141, 144

  career, 6, 16, 26, 78–83, 103, 135–38, 150–53, 171

  childless, 26

  competition for, x, xvi, 83–84

  education of, 21, 25

  energy of, 152

  equality of, ix–x, 8, 122, 141

  fear of, 67, 77–78, 140–41, 166, 170

  gossip by, xiii, 129

  in government service, 137–38

  harassment of, 12, 90

  independence of, 135, 158

  as lawyers, 189–90

  as linkers, 122, 124, 134, 136, 140, 141, 147, 148, 150

  magazines for, 56

  mate selection by, 85, 86, 117, 121–36, 152

  as mothers, 20, 42–43, 46–47, 68, 158–59

  nurturing by, 147

  oppression of, 84, 121–23, 128–29, 135

  passivity of, 74, 88, 142

  physical attractiveness of, 76, 82–87

  postfeminist restrictions on, ix, xii–xiii

  salaries of, 26

  self-esteem of, 8, 14, 86–87, 166–67

  sexual fulfillment of, 74–75, 84, 89–90

  sexuality of, 73–75, 84, 89–90, 136, 137–53

  single, xi, 19–20, 26, 83, 85, 158–59

  as victims, 124

  as wives, x, 95–96, 106; *see also* marriage

  in workforce, 25, 26, 203

Woods, Earl, 164, 165

Woods, Tiger, 164

Woodstock, 114

Woolsey, James, 137, 138

workaholics, 162

Y

Yankelovich survey, 19

Yippies, 120

yoni, 60

Z

Zumwalt, Elmo, III, xv

Zumwalt, Elmo "Bud," II, xiv

Zumwalt, Jim, xiii–xv

About the Author

Twice nominated for National Magazine Awards, MICHAEL SEGELL has written for a wide variety of publications, including *Rolling Stone, Esquire, Cosmopolitan, The New York Times, Sports Illustrated,* and *People.* He is currently a columnist for MSNBC, an editor at the Sunday *Daily News* in New York, and editor of the anthology *Simple Abundance: A Man's Journey.* He lives in New York City with his wife and children.